A New Dictionary of Eponyms

A New Dictionary of
Eponyms

Morton S. Freeman

Oxford University Press
New York   Oxford

Oxford University Press

Oxford   New York
Athens   Auckland   Bangkok   Bogotá   Bombay
Calcutta   Cape Town   Dar es Salaam   Delhi
Florence   Hong Kong   Istanbul   Karachi
Kuala Lumpur   Madras   Madrid   Melbourne
Mexico City   Nairobi   Paris   Singapore
Taipei   Tokyo   Toronto   Warsaw

and associated companies in
Berlin   Ibadan

First published in 1997 by Oxford University Press,
198 Madison Avenue, New York, NY 10016

First issued as an Oxford University Press paperback, 1997

Oxford is a registered trademark of Oxford University Press, Inc.

Library of Congress Cataloging-in-Publication Data

Freeman, Morton S.
    A new dictionary of eponyms / Morton S. Freeman.
        p.   cm.
    Includes bibliographical references (p.).
    ISBN 0-19-509354-2 (alk. paper)
        1. English language—Eponyms—Dictionaries.   2. Names, Personal-
    Dictionaries.   3. Biography—Dictionaries.   I. Title.
PE1596.F73   1997
423'.1—dc20   96-32608

ISBN 0-19-509354-2 (Pbk.)
9 8 7 6 5 4 3 2 1

Printed in the United States of America

To Mildred, my wife—the best

Foreword by Edwin Newman

Writing the foreword to someone else's book is not the same as testifying in court, or appearing before a Congressional committee. Nonetheless, one should declare one's interest. Mine is that Morton Freeman and I are friends, from which it follows that I have a friendly interest in the success of this book.

Still, permit me to say how Mort and I came to be friends. It was through a mutual interest in English, in preserving and protecting the language. Not only, however, in preserving and protecting it. There was more: a view both of us had that when it came to English, too many Americans were leading sadly and unnecessarily deprived lives. That was because they had never been led to understand the satisfaction that can come from using the language well. It was also because they had never been led to understand the delight that English imaginatively used, precisely used, humorously used, appropriately used, can offer.

In his books, Mort has sought to drive that lesson home, not in an academic way, but by example, by showing how using the language well can be profitable, can be fascinating, and can be fun.

Here, then, is his latest undertaking in that line. Because this is a foreword, however, I get to go first: An eponym is a proper name that comes to stand for a place, or a thing, or an institution. Let's see now—freeman? Forget the dictionary definitions: a person not in slavery or serfdom, or one who loves English and appreciates its value, and helps the rest of us—to our great benefit—to do so, too.

Preface

The term *eponym* was created about a century ago. Samuel Johnson's *Dictionary of the English Language,* published in 1775, did not include it. The word was a coined from two Greek words, *epi,* "on" or "upon," and *onama,* "a name." But its broadened meaning, as dictionaries set it out, refers to the person for whom something is named. For example, a *derrick* is a hoisting crane. This is an eponymous term for Godfrey Derrick, the notorious hangman. It is the thing named for him. And the same may be said about the word *guillotine,* the instrument for decapitation, named for Dr. Joseph Ignace Guillotin.

In these two examples the eponymous words are nouns, but many such words are adjectives—Shakespeare, Shakespearean; Victoria; Victorian; Rebelais, Rabelaisian. Some are verbs—Macadam, macadamize; Paseur, pasteurize; Bowdler, bowdlerize. But a trend among some writers is to consider the eponym the word that stems from the proper noun rather than the root word itself. With them, *Shakespearean* and *macadamize* would be regarded as eponyms. In this book, however, the eponyms will honor their original meaning, a name-giver, the person or thing from which the eponymous words were derived.

The number of eponyms to select from is astronomical, for any proper noun can be a candidate. The size and purpose of a book on eponymy must therefore be considered in the selection process. Many excellent possibilities may have to be discarded and some fields—such as medicine—satisfied with a smattering of entries.

In the text that names of prominent writers, from whose works citations have been borrowed, are given by their surname only if their full name and accreditation is given in the bibliography. For example, Morris is named for William and Mary Morris; Brewer for E. Cobham Brewer.

The compiling of these many, and unrelated, entries has been a real but pleasureable challenge. Delving into the lives of so many historical figures—scientists, inventors, and writers, all long gone—has brought new life to me, as I hope it will to those who read this book.

A word of thanks to my wife, Mildred, for her assistance and encouragement and for her understanding of my need to spend long hours by myself in research and writing. Any my gratitude to James T. McDonough, Jr., Ph.D, for volunteering to review the manuscript and for offering helpful suggestions. And thanks to Jean Toll, editor par excellence.

A New Dictionary of Eponyms

A-1, LLOYD'S OF LONDON

Lloyd's Register of British and Foreign Shipping, which deals with the design and construction of ships, was first published in the mid-1700s. Lloyd's of London, as the world-famous association came to be popularly known, insured vessels based on information contained in the *Register*, which classified and graded the condition of ships with a system of letters and numbers. The state of a ship's hull was designated by letters and that of its equipment (anchor, cables, etc.) by numbers. This meant, for example, that a ship classified A-1 was first-rate. If classified A-2, the hull was considered first-rate, but its equipment second-rate. This classification of A-1 to mean excellent, perfect, the very best in ships, has come to apply to almost anything else after Charles Dickens used the designation A-1 to describe people and things.

Lloyd's, an insurance society, is an association of more than 8,000 individual underwriters grouped into about 400 syndicates (or committees), varying in size from a few persons to several hundred people. Each individual underwriter must deposit a sum of $45,000 or more to guarantee claim payments. Under reinsurance contracts, insurers spread their risks among many companies. This method has enabled Lloyd's to pay off enormous claims for which they have issued policies—the San Francisco earthquake and fire in 1906, the sinking of the *Titanic* in 1912, the airship *Hindenburg*, which burned in 1937, and many later disasters, including hurricanes in the United States.

Lloyd's today is known for its insuring of almost any risks, many of them unusual, from a dancer's feet (Zorina's toes), to an actor's nose (Jimmy Durante's), to a starlet's hips against gaining four inches over a seven-year period (Julie Bishop's), and a policy of happiness that insured against worry lines appearing on a model's face.

And all this had its genesis in 1668 in Edward Lloyd's coffee shop, a favorite meeting place for shipping and insurance men. Edward Lloyd had no financial connection with the insurance enterprises that developed, which at the beginning accepted marine insurance, and which is still its main form of insurance.

ACCORDING TO HOYLE

Although card-playing was a favorite among the wealthy for many generations, it was not until the seventeenth century that the manufacture of inexpensive decks of cards enabled the masses to enjoy this game. Cards soon became the rage throughout Europe. The game that held an irresistible attraction for the English was whist, the forerunner of bridge.

Whist could be played according to dozens of systems, which led Edmund Hoyle, an English writer (1672–1769), to write a book of rules called *A Short Treatise on the Game of Whist* (1742); the book eventually became the accepted authority on the playing of the game. Hoyle soon wrote on other popular card games and was quickly regarded as the authority on them, too.

As Hoyle's expertise on the correct play of a game gained exposure, many people would frequently consult his books to see whether the procedure being followed met approval. If the play followed the rules set forth by Hoyle, its correctness was beyond dispute. Because of the frequent and widespread reference to Hoyle, whenever someone wished to indicate that everything was in order, that it was being handled properly—whether or not card-playing was involved—the saying "It is according to Hoyle," came to refer to the final authority in any field.

Incidentally, Hoyle must have lived his life according to the rules because he laid down his last trump at the age of ninety-seven.

ACHILLES' HEEL

The story concerning the legendary hero Achilles has been told many times. Achilles was the central figure and tragic protagonist in Homer's *Iliad*. He possessed athletic strength, warlike prowess, and handsomeness. His mother, Thetis, had a premonition that her son would die in battle. She therefore, when he was still an infant, held him by the heel and dipped him into the river Styx to make him invulnerable. The water touched every part of his body except the heel that Thetis held, leaving it the weak link in his magic armor. During the siege of Troy, a poisoned arrow from the bow of the Trojan prince Paris pierced Achilles' heel, fatally wounding him. W. S. Merwin in *The Judgment of Paris* described the lethal arrow in these words: "In the quiver on Paris' back the head of the arrow for Achilles' heel smiled in its sleep." The elopement of Paris with Helen, the wife of Menelaus, King of Sparta, you may recall, started the Trojan War.

This story gave birth to the saying that the weak part of anything, no matter how small or how large, is that person's Achilles heel. The name *Achilles tendon* (alternative scientific name of *tendo Achilles*) has been given to the strong muscle that connects the calf of the leg with the heel.

Homer had hinted at, but didn't describe, the death of Achilles. His reference to Achilles' death was simply that he died "before the Scaean gates" during the Trojan War.

ALICE IN WONDERLAND

A girl who has recently come to a strange, exotic, fantastic surrounding is sometimes called an "Alice." Ideas, schemes, plans, and projects that are wholly impractical, those daytime dreams that can exist only in the realm of fantasy, may be alluded to as an idea from "Alice in Wonderland."

Lewis Carroll's children's books, *Alice's Adventures in Wonderland* (1865) and its sequel *Through the Looking Glass* (1871), illustrated by Sir John Tenniel, the *Punch* artist, have enjoyed great longevity. Known for their whimsical humor and "nonsense" verse, the *Alice* books continue to attract readers and are arguably the most famous children's books in the world.

The name Carroll was a pseudonym of Charles Lutwidge Dodgson (1832–1892), an Oxford mathematician. *Alice* originated in 1862 on a boat trip with Lorina, Alice, and Edith, the daughters of Dean Henry George Liddell, who also was at Oxford and was best known as a compiler, together with Robert Scott, of the *Oxford Greek-English Lexicon*. Carroll fantasized an impromptu story for the amusement of the children but particularly for Alice, of whom he was very fond. Later the story in book form evolved into a worldwide bestseller.

ALZHEIMER'S DISEASE

Alzheimer's disease is a progressive deterioration of the brain, first described in 1907 by the German neurologist Alois Alzheimer (1864–1915). It is the most common form of dementing, or mind-depriving, illness, affecting cells in an area of the brain important to memory.

Alzheimer's disease or *Alzheimer's syndrome* most commonly strikes elderly adults, but it has also been known to afflict people in their late twenties. Formerly, this disease was known as *pre-senile dementia* or just plain *senility*. It was erroneously attributed to "hardening of the arteries." The disease involves degeneration of nerve cells rather than blockage of blood vessels.

The cause of *Alzheimer's disease* is unknown, and there is no known cure for it. Investigators are studying the role of such possible factors as viruses, genetic influences, abnormal immunological responses, and environmental or toxic agents.

AMAZON, AMAZON RIVER

According to the Greek historian Herodotus, the Amazons were a fierce nation of Scythian women who lived by themselves. They dealt with men only in battle or for procreation, and either killed their sons or sent them to their fathers. Their daughters were raised to become warriors. When grown, each woman hacked off her right breast so that it wouldn't hinder her range with the bow. *Amazon* in Greek is a composite of *a-*(without) and *mazos* (breast).

The Amazons frequently appear in Greek mythology. One of the tasks of Hercules was to obtain the girdle of Hippolyta, queen of the Amazons. He slew her and took her girdle (sash). Another queen of the Amazons, Penthesileia, whose army came to aid the besieged Trojans, was killed in battle by the redoubtable Achilles.

Legend says that one Vincente Yanez Pinzon, the discoverer of the Amazon River in 1500, named it Rio Santa Maria. But in 1541 Francisco de Orellana, an explorer, after descending from the Andes on this river to the sea, was attacked by a savage tribe. Believing women fought alongside men, he then renamed the river *Amazonas*; its name in English, of course, is *Amazon*. This is an intriguing story; the explorer may have assumed that skirted Indians were women.

A strong, aggressive woman, especially if she looks masculine, may be called an *amazon*.

AMERICA, AMERICAN

The injustice of naming two continents after Amerigo Vespucci (1451–1512) can no longer be rectified. And we cannot justify excluding Canada, the second-largest country in area in the world, from the appellation *America*. By the same token, *America, the gem of the ocean* is equally faulty. It should have been *Columbia*.

Controversy concerning the naming of America may never be resolved because who did what and when is not subject to historic proof. Amerigo Vespucci, originally a Florentine navigator, claimed he made four trips—in 1497, 1499, 1501, and 1503—to the New World, then known as the Mundus Novus (a term that first appeared in Vespucci's letters published in 1504). However, only two of these trips were actually documented. A former manager of the Seville office of the notorious Medici family of Italy, Vespucci reported to his patrons an account of his voyages along the coasts of what are now Brazil, Uruguay, and Argentina.

In 1507 Martin Waldseemüller, a German geographer, published an appendix to a work called *Cosmographiae Introductio*, which included a map labeled *America* that corresponded roughly to South America. The name stuck, not only for South America but for North America as well, when mapmakers filled in that continent.

Vespucci took two trips under the aegis of Spain and two under that of Portugal, and became Spain's "pilot major." Nevertheless, some historians say he never did take the voyages he reported, but merely heard stories from sailors and put himself in the picture.

The Spanish refused to accept the name *America*; they called the land, in Spanish, *Colombia*. This remains a distinguished name; many towns, rivers, and other places have been named *Columbia*, including the seat of our government: the District of Columbia. And let us not forget *Columbia, the gem of the ocean*.

AMPÈRE, AMP, AMPÈRE'S LAW

Would you believe that a person so traumatized that he could not speak or read for more than a year went on to become a distinguished scientist, so distinguished that he gave his name to the English language? In every dictionary can be found the word *ampere*: a unit of electric current equal to the steady current produced by one volt acting through a resistance of one ohm.

André Marie Ampère (1775–1836), a French scientist, lived so tragic a life as to make one wonder how his mind could have retained its brilliance. The tragedy that rendered him incapable of speaking at age eighteen was the execution of his father by guillotine during the Reign of Terror. With time, Ampère recovered his voice and at age twenty-four he married. A few years later, his wife died and Ampère became despondent once again.

Ampère poured himself into his work. While a professor of physics at the College de France in Paris, he made important discoveries relating to the nature of electricity and magnetism. He was the first to expound the theory that the earth's magnetism is the product of terrestrial electric currents that circle the globe from east to west. Through mathematics he made his greatest discovery, which formulated the law of mechanical action between electric currents and came to be known as *Ampère's law*. His discovery was instrumental in the development of the science of electrodynamics.

Ampère invented the astatic needle, which made it possible to detect and measure electric currents, and contributed to the invention of the electric telegraph. The International Electric Congress, in 1881, lifted his name forty-five years after his death to designate the unit of intensity of electric current, abbreviated *amp*.

Ampère did his best thinking while walking. He paced his room for long periods and became, possibly, the world's best-known peripatetic scientist after Aristotle.

ANNIE OAKLEY

An *Annie Oakley* is a complimentary ticket to a theater. The ticket has holes punched in it to prevent its exchange for cash at the box office. This oddity came about in an unusual way.

Annie Oakley (1860–1926), born in Darke County, Ohio, was the stage name for Phoebe Anne Oakley Mozee. Annie was probably the greatest female sharpshooter ever. She got her professional start when, at the urging of friends, she entered a shooting match in Cincinnati pitting Frank E. Butler, a vaudeville marksman, against all comers. Butler gave no thought to this fifteen-year-old girl who dared compete with him. But upon seeing Annie's first shot, he paid strict attention. She won the contest, and a husband to boot, for Butler and Annie fell in love and were married. They then began a vaudeville tour as a trick-shooting team.

The Butlers joined Buffalo Bill Cody's Wild West Show in 1885, but it was Annie who became the star attraction. She remained as the rifle sharpshooter for forty years. She thrilled audiences with her expert marksmanship and dazzled them with her trick shooting. In one of her outstanding feats, she would flip a playing card into the air, usually a five of hearts, and shoot the pips out of it.

But what, you might ask, has that to do with a free ticket? Circus performers were reminded of their meal tickets by the riddled playing

6

cards, because their meal tickets were punched every time they bought a meal. Hence they came to call their tickets "Annie Oakleys." The idea of a punched card caught on, so that today a complimentary ticket to a show, a meal, or a pass on a railway has Annie Oakley holes.

Annie Oakley needed no encomiums during her forty years with the Wild West Show, but she was given one, nevertheless, by Sitting Bull, who labeled her "Little Sure Shot." In more recent times Ethel Merman, the star of *Annie Get Your Gun*, popularized Annie Oakley once again, making her for today's generation a "big shot."

ARCHIMEDES' PRINCIPLE

Archimedes (287–212 B.C.) was a legend during his lifetime. He was a brilliant mathematician and an inventor of the *Archimedes' screw*, a machine for raising water. Although the lever had been in use long before Archimedes, he worked out the theoretical mathematical principles of its use. He designed the pulley and the windlass, but is best remembered for his work with hydrostatics. His unforgettable cry "Eureka" has made him famous ever since. But it wasn't the cry, it was what he deduced: the *Archimedes' principle* of specific gravity. His remarkable discovery arose because Hieron, King of Syracuse in Sicily, wished to determine whether a crown was of pure gold or whether the goldsmith had fraudulently alloyed it with some silver. While mulling over this problem, Archimedes came to a place of bathing, and there, as he sat in the tub, realized that the amount of water he had displaced must be equal to the bulk of his immersed body. It is said that he did run nude through the streets and did excitedly shout "Eureka" ("I've found it" in Greek). Ever since, the word *eureka* has been an interjection to express surprise.

Archimedes was born in Syracuse, Sicily, and died there while pursuing a problem. The Romans took the town of Syracuse in 212 B.C. However, orders had been issued by the Roman consul Marcellus that Archimedes was not to be harmed, but brought to him alive. The story has it that a Roman soldier informed Archimedes of Marcellus's order, to which Archimedes replied that he was working on a geometrical problem in the sand. "I'll come when I'm finished," he said. Unfortunately the Roman warrior was impatient and with his sword slew Archimedes.

ARGYLE

In western Scotland in a county named Argyllshire lived a duke of Argyle, the head of the Campbell clan. According to Brewer's *Dictionary of Phrase and Fable*, the duke had a series of posts erected around the treeless part of his estate so that his cattle might rub against them to ease themselves of the torment of flies. The herdsmen saw the value of this practice, and as they rubbed their own itching backs against the posts, they thankfully uttered the phrase *God bless the Duke of Argyle*.

The phrase spread among the Scottish Highlanders and became a generally accepted humorous remark. The clan received additional publicity when it was mentioned in novels by Sir Walter Scott.

Fabric manufacturers found that the Campbell clan tartan, in green and white, would make an attractive design. It gave rise to the manufacture of a diamond pattern, known as argyle plaid, used on sweaters and socks. The pattern has appeared on articles sold worldwide.

ATLAS

The term *Atlas* is used chiefly for a book of maps, a size of paper, and the first vertebra of the neck. The name Atlas is attributed to a mythological character, one of the Titans who tried to overthrow Zeus but failed. The punishment meted out to him for his part in the conspiracy was to hold up the pillars of heaven for the rest of his days. Because he was an immortal god, his days went on forever.

Hercules graciously offered to support the heavens for a while if Atlas would obtain for him the golden apples guarded by the Hesperides. Atlas agreed and felt renewed without the heavens on his shoulders. He then stole the apples from the garden where they grew, returned to Hercules, and offered to take them back home for him. Hercules thought he detected a trick, and so he told Atlas to hold up the heavens while he found a pad for his shoulders. When Atlas took over, Hercules departed with the apples, never to return, leaving a raging Titan with his burden.

The story of Atlas and his mythic burden has many versions. One is that Atlas, after holding up the world for centuries, became faint from weakness. One day Perseus, carrying the head of Medusa, flew by. Atlas, knowing that anyone who looked at Medusa would be turned to stone, begged Perseus to let him look at her. Perseus agreed, Atlas looked, was petrified, and became the Atlas Mountains, which extend for 1,500 miles along the coast of North Africa.

In the sixteenth century, the Flemish cartographer Gerhardus Mercator put a figure of Atlas supporting the world on his shoulders on the title page of his first collection of maps. The idea appealed to other publishers of geography books, who then adopted a similar picture for the title page of their books.

AUGUST, AUGUSTAN AGE

Latin *Augustus* means venerable, a title conferred by the Senate in 27 B.C. on Gaius Octavianus, who thus became the first Roman emperor. He then changed his name to *Augustus Caesar* and was the founder of the Imperial Roman government. Augustus was the adopted son of Julius Caesar, for whom the month of July, consisting of thirty-one days, had been named. The month named for Octavianus was August, originally *Sextilis*, the sixth month in the old Roman calendar, which started in March. As Augustus Caesar, he resented the fact that July was longer than his month. He therefore stole a day from February so that August would also have thirty-one days.

The Augustan Age, which began approximately in 43 B.C. and continued to about A.D. 18, was marked by peace, the historic "Pax Romana," and was indeed the most illustrious period in Roman history. Its writers were brilliant, polished, and sophisticated. Vergil published his *Georgics* and completed the *Aeneid*; Horace, his *Odes*, Books I-III, and *Epistels*, Book I. Livy began his monumental history of Rome; Ovid, the author of *Metamorphoses*, a mythological history of the world from the creation to the Augustan Age.

"Augustan Age" came to be applied to the apogee of any nation's cultural achievements, primarily to its "classical" period in literature.

B

BABBITT, BABBITT METAL

A tin-based alloy, called *babbitt metal*, was invented by Isaac Babbitt in 1839. The metal, composed of a soft, silver-white alloy of copper, tin, and antimony, is widely used for bearings to reduce friction. For this invention, the United States Congress voted to grant Babbitt $20,000, a sum that enabled him to manufacture this alloy.

Isaac Babbitt (1799–1862) was born in Taunton, Massachusetts. Trained as a goldsmith, he made the first Britannia ware in America in 1824. He then took employment as a superintendent at the South Boston Iron Works and is credited with having helped make the first brass cannon in the United States.

The leading character in Sinclair Lewis's novel *Babbitt*, published in 1922, was George F. Babbitt, a prosperous real estate agent in Zenith, a Western city. He was "nimble in the calling of selling houses for more than people could afford to pay" and was the prototype of the narrow-minded, self-satisfied, materialistic, middle-class American. He represented the orthodox businessman with drives that laud his own middle-class existence and with no interest in cultural values. He placed great store on local esteem and outward prosperity. Babbitt was everything that the author hated about America. The word *Babbitt* now appears in American dictionaries to represent a person who unthinkingly conforms to group standards or a smug, schooled but uneducated businessman. *Babbittry* is middle-class conformity.

As the book closes, Babbitt's son tells Babbitt of his intention to "get into mechanics" rather than go to the university. He also tells him that he has been secretly married. Babbitt, who with age has come to understand his parochial outlook and virtues, felt that the time had come to give his son advice based upon his own flawed experiences. Babbitt "crossed the floor, slowly, ponderously, seeming a little old. 'I've always wanted you to have a college degree.' He meditatively stamped across the floor again. 'But I've never . . . I've never done a single thing I've wanted to do in my whole life! Well, maybe you'll carry things further. I don't know . . . Don't be scared of the family. No, not of Zenith. Not of yourself, the way I've been. Go ahead, old man! The world is yours!' "

BACCHANALIAN

In Roman mythology, Bacchus, the equivalent of the Greek Dionysus, was the respected god of wine and vineyards. It was he who planted the vine. The triennial festivals paying homage to the harvest were originally characterized by propriety and sobriety and were followed by dignified rituals. But with time the nature of the celebration changed. Bacchus's worshipers succumbed to the delights and effects of the wine, and the revelers became known for their drunkenness and licentiousness.

If it were not for Zeus, there might have been no Bacchus and no wine. According to legend, Bacchus was the son of Zeus and Semele. Foolishly, Semele asked Zeus to appear before her in all his glory, as he was wont to do before his wife Hera. Zeus complied and appeared in thunder and lightning. As Semele was being devoured by the flames, she gave birth prematurely. Zeus took the child (Bacchus) and sewed him into his thigh, where he remained until reaching maturity. Bacchus was one son who was truly raised at his father's knee.

A *bacchant* is a worshiper of Bacchus and a *bacchante* is a priestess or female admirer of Bacchus.

BAEDEKER

Baedeker, a travel guidebook, is an authoritative work first published in Germany by Karl Baedeker (1801–1859), born in Essen, Germany, the son of a printer and bookseller. He followed his father's footsteps and became a printer with a shop in Coblenz, publishing the first of his famous series of guidebooks, modeled on John Murray's *Handbook*, in 1839. The book, titled *A Rhineland Journey from Basle to Dusseldorf*, was immediately successful and was known for its reliability and thoroughness. Baedeker then prepared guidebooks covering other areas, which equally described in detail what a tourist might want to know about the important cities and places of historic interest or questions of cuisine. And so tourists throughout the world felt safer, were more knowledgeable, and were able to enjoy their vacations better with a *Baedeker* in hand.

Baedeker inaugurated the practice of marking with one or more stars the objects and places of interest according to their historic or aesthetic importance, which gave rise to the expression *starred in Baedeker*.

That *Baedeker* became an international generic term was exemplified by Chekhov when he said, in a letter, "Here I am alone with my thoughts and my Baedeker." Although with the proliferation of travel books over the last century *Baedeker* is not a word so often heard anymore, it still is an apt (albeit loose) replacement for "guidebook."

BAKELITE

Bakelite is the trade name of one of the first plastics to come into wide use. It is a phenolic invented in 1907, and it came to be employed for all kinds of household items and ornaments, but its main use today is in electrical installations because it is a good insulator against heat and electric current. *Bakelite* can be molded into many shapes and is relatively inexpensive. Its use for handles and enclosure elements on kitchen wares, irons, and similar products has been widespread.

Chemist Leo Hendrick Bakeland (1863–1944), born in Ghent, Belgium, came to the United States in 1889 and founded a company to manufacture paper called Velox. In 1909 he publicized the invention of *Bakelite*, a synthetic resin (a plastic used to harden rubber and celluloid) which he then manufactured for twenty years. Afterwards the name became generic for any phenolic plastic, regardless of the manufacturer.

This Flemish chemist is often spoken of as the father of the modern plastics industry because of the practical application of his discoveries.

BARMECIDE, BARMECIDE'S FEAST

According to the "The Barber's Story of his Sixth Brother" in the *Tales from the Arabian Nights*, Barmecide is an illusion, particularly one containing a great disappointment. The story begins in Baghdad, where a member of the Barmecide family decides to amuse himself. He invites Schacabac, a poor, starving wretch, to dinner. Having set before him a series of empty plates, the Barmecide asks, "How do you like your soup?" "Excellently well," replies Schacabac. "Did you ever see whiter bread?" "Never, honorable sir." When illusory wine is offered, Schacabac pretends to be drunk and knocks his host down. Barmecide sees the humor in the situation, forgives him, and provides him with a sumptuous meal.

A *Barmecide feast* is an empty pretense of hospitality or generosity. One who offers false and disappointing benefits is a *Barmecide*. The adjective *Barmecidal* means unreal, illusory.

BARNUM, BARNUMISM

"It's the greatest show on Earth." Very possibly. But who said it? Barnum himself, the mastermind of the Barnum & Bailey Circus, which later was merged to form part of Ringling Bros. and Barnum & Bailey Circus. Was Barnum being honest? Perhaps. But he is also reputed to have said, "There's a sucker born every minute." And he never denied getting people moved out of his exhibit to make room for others by shouting, "Here's the way to the egress." Those who followed his suggestion, expecting to see something, found themselves outside the exhibition hall and unable to return. And is it true that he whitewashed an ordinary elephant and paraded it as a white elephant from Siam? To be *barnumized* is to be classed as a sucker.

Phineas Taylor Barnum (1810–1891) was born in Bethel, Connecticut, the son of a farmer. He failed in several undertakings, but in 1835 he took the step that would make him one of the country's greatest impresarios. He began his career as a showman by successfully, but fraudulently, promoting Aunt Joice Heth as the nurse to George Washington. This made her at that time 162 years old, and yet thousands paid to see her. Barnum must have been right; a sucker *is* born every minute.

Barnum was first with many novel and exciting show pieces. He exhibited Tom Thumb, a twenty-five-inch midget. He brought over Jenny Lind, a Swedish soprano, calling her "The Swedish Nightingale." He showcased Jumbo, the biggest elephant on earth, so he said (and gave a new word, *Jumbo*, to the American language), and his exhibit of the Siamese twins Chang and Eng was a constant source of wonder.

Barnum, America's most famous showman, relished fleecing the public (*barnumism* is a synonym for "humbuggery") and didn't object to his title "The Prince of Humbugs."

BAROQUE

Baroque is a style of art and architecture of the early seventeenth to mid-eighteenth century, characterized by elaborate ornamentation, curved lines, and enormous size. The *Oxford English Dictionary* says the style pays tribute to Francesco Borromini (1599–1667), its chief exponent. But the French word *baroque* came from the name of the founder of the baroque style, Federigo Barocci (1528–1612), an Italian painter whose flamboyant art was thought to evoke the mood of a movement known as Counter-Reformation, which stirred a sense of religious enthusiasm in Europe and which expressed its drama and emotion. Barocci was regarded a master of tender sentiment with "a nervous, fluttering style and gay colors." Perhaps the most majestic portrayal of baroque is St. Peter's Basilica in Rome.

According to Klein's *Comprehensive Etymological Dictionary of the English Language* (and other authorities concur), *baroque* was not derived from the Portuguese word *barroco*, "irregularly shaped pearl," as has been generally assumed. The term *baroque* was used to describe musical compositions that were chromatically elaborate and had distinct ornamentation. The word was also used by Italian Renaissance philosophers to represent far-fetched arguments in Scholastic syllogisms.

By the eighteenth century *baroque* was considered a pejorative term to indicate an abandonment of the norm of nature and of classical antiquity.

BARTLETT PEAR, SECKEL

The *Bartlett pear*, long before its introduction into America, was grown and enjoyed in Europe, where it was called Williams, *Bonchrétien*, after a London farmer. The pear trees were imported to America from England by Captain Thomas Brewer in the 1800s, and were planted on his farm in Roxbury, Massachusetts. The farm was purchased by Enoch Bartlett (1779–1860) of Dorchester, Massachusetts, who, although the fruit deserved the name *Brewer pear*, distributed and promoted the fruit under the name *Bartlett*.

These delicious yellow pears have moved west to Oregon and Washington, where they can enjoy a healthier and longer growing season than they might have had in the East. Most Bartletts today come from that area but are a delight all over America. The *Seckel pear* was grown by a Philadelphia farmer whose name was *Seckel*. It is a good eating pear from an Asian variety, but is hard to bite into. It appeared on the American scene shortly after the American Revolution, and so had the jump on the *Bartlett*, but it couldn't keep up with Bartlett's edibility.

BARTLETT'S QUOTATIONS

American bookstores are blessed with many excellent quotation books, but one has been outstanding since its publication in 1855. This book, Bartlett's *Familiar Quotations*, has been a bedrock source of information for writers, speakers, and anyone else wanting a quotation to back up a point.

John Bartlett (1820–1905) was born in Plymouth, Massachusetts, and became the owner of the University Book Store in Cambridge. Students and Harvard professors gravitated to his store and were particularly grateful for his help in reference matters. Bartlett's memory was encyclopedic, and he answered many questions concerning the source of a quotation without having to check the source. Hence "Ask John Bartlett" became proverbial. His opus *Familiar Quotations* has been kept current over the years through several editions. Bartlett joined the Boston publishing firm of Little, Brown in 1863 and became a senior partner in 1878.

John Bartlett's *Complete Concordance to Shakespeare's Dramatic Works and Poems* is also a standard reference guide.

John Bartlett should not be confused with John Russell Bartlett (1805–1886), who made a great contribution to linguistics with his *Dictionary of Americanisms*. He assisted John Carter Brown in acquiring and cataloging his noted book collection, now in the John Carter Brown Library of Brown University, founded by his grandfather Nicholas.

BEAU BRUMMEL

George Bryan Brummel, born in England in 1778, believed in living the high style. As a student at Eton and later at Oxford, he began dressing the part of a fashion plate in high society. He gave up his study of medicine and resigned from the military. The only thing he really enjoyed was dressing elegantly and it is reputed that he spent an entire day dressing for a royal ball. He did not tip his hat at ladies lest he ruffle his coiffure, and he was conveyed from his quarters in a sedan chair to avoid stepping onto the dirty street.

Brummel's sartorial splendor enabled him to mingle with and be accepted by the aristocracy. After inheriting a sizable fortune, he lived in a luxurious bachelor apartment in exclusive Mayfair and became the undisputed arbiter of fashion. It has been reported that he invented the starched neckcloth and introduced long pants. The Prince of Wales, later George IV, sought his advice on matters of dress. Unfortunately, Brummel later fell out of favor with the king, when he reportedly met George and Lord Westmoreland as they were strolling at Bath. "Good morning, Westmoreland," said Brummel. "Who's your fat friend?"

With his good primary standing in society undercut, Brummel, in debt from gambling and extravagant living, left for France in 1816 seeking a haven from his problems. France did not turn out to be the green pastures that he expected. Instead he feuded constantly with creditors, suffered several paralytic attacks, and died alone at the age of sixty-two. Adversity had changed Brummel into a man unrecognizable from the person he had been. His confidence and lordly pretensions, along with his refined manners, had gone. Slovenly and unkempt, he spent his final days in a mental institution. When he died, he, once the most elegantly attired Englishman, was carted away in a beggar's shroud.

Although the man known as Beau Brummel has been long gone, his name is still an epithet for a fashionable dresser, a dandy, a fop. The title *Beau*, from the French for beauty, was an honorific bestowed on him by an adoring public.

BEEF, BEEF STROGANOFF, BEEF WELLINGTON, CHATEAUBRIAND

Beef has been a standard food for many, many centuries. The eating of beef was mentioned in the Greek epics the *Iliad* and the *Odyssey*. King James II reportedly was so delighted by a roast from the loin end of beef that he dubbed it "Sir Loin," and from that moment the heavy ends of the beef loin came to be known as *sirloin cuts*. This, of course, may be apocryphal.

From the cuts of beef have come many interesting and delectable dishes. One of the most famous comes from the eponym of a man not quite so famous—Count Paul Stroganoff, a nineteenth-century Russian diplomat. He favored thinly sliced beef fillets sautéed and served with mushrooms and sour cream. Another recipe calls for the beef to be cooked with onions and in a sauce of consommé. Tuleja reports, "As far as Mother Russia is concerned, it is his only memorial: the *Great Soviet Encyclopedia* gives the czarist functionary not a nod." But the dish *Beef Stroganoff* continues on the menus of some of America's finest restaurants.

Beef Wellington is a particularly favorite preparation. It not only honors the "Iron Duke," Arthur Wellesley, the first Duke of Wellington, but also is a gustatory delight of beef eaters. Added to a choice cut of beef are liver pâté, bacon, brandy, and condiments, all baked in a golden crust of puffed pastry.

Those beef eaters who prefer a double-thick tender cut of beef tenderloin might choose *chateaubriand*, generally served with mushrooms and béarnaise sauce. This mouth-watering dish has been attributed to the chef in the household of Vicomte Francois Renè de Châteaubriand (1768–1848), a writer of romantic novels and travel narratives.

BEGONIA

Michel Bégon (1638–1710) was appointed commissioner for Santo Domingo by Louis XIV after Bégon married Jeanne-Elisabeth de Beauharnais, sister of Marquis de Beauharnais, governor-general of New France. Although there is some dispute as to the nature of Bégon's duties, some historians believe that he served for a while as governor of Santo Domingo.

Bégon was an enthusiastic amateur botanist. He organized a detailed study of the plant life on the island and collected many specimens. One tropical plant that he collected was a genus of a flowering succulent herb with ornamental leaves and clusters of showy flowers of various colors. Bégon took the plant back with him to France and introduced it to botanists and horticulturists. Ever since, the *begonia* has been widely planted in gardens because it prefers shade. It is also a popular house plant, cultivated for its variety of blooms or for its foliage.

The plant was named for Michel Bégon by a French botanist, Charles Plumier, when it was first brought to England, sixty-seven years after Bégon's death. The name given the plant, appropriately, was *begonia*.

BERSERK

From Norse mythology has come the word *berserk*, meaning "deranged" or "raging" or "crazed." *Berserk*, a legendary Norse hero of the eighth century, always went into battle without armor and was famed for the savagery and reckless fury with which he fought. In old Scandinavian, *ber-serk* probably meant "bear-shirt," that is, one clothed only in his shirt and not protected by armor or heavy clothing. Berserk's twelve sons, who like their father fought ferociously and recklessly, were called Berserkers. Later *berserker* was applied to a class of heathen warriors who were supposed to be able to assume the form of bears and wolves. Dressed in furs, these lycanthropic creatures were believed to fall into a frenzied rage, foam at the mouth, bite their shields, and growl like wild beasts. They were dreaded for their prodigious strength and apparent invulnerability to fire and iron. To go *berserk* is to go into a frenzy of rage or to be frenetically violent.

BERTILLONAGE

Alphonse Bertillon (1853–1914) was born in Paris. Although he had no scientific training, he became the chief of the Department of Identification in the préfecture of police of the Seine, at Paris. In that capacity he designed an identification method known as anthropometry (but better known as *Bertillonage*) that was used with extraordinary results throughout France. His system, which he described in his book *Anthropologie métrique et photographique*, incorporated the classification of skeletal and other measurements and a complete physical description—color of hair, of eyes, and so on—and photographs. As a system of description, it was not infallible, and so with time it came to be superseded by fingerprints. Nevertheless, it is still useful to furnish descriptive portraits.

The first in anything marks a beginning and acts as a foundation of things to follow. Bertillon introduced to the world the value and plausibility of criminal identification. He may be considered the founder of forensic science.

BESSEMER PROCESS

The *Bessemer process*, which de-carbonizes melted pig iron into steel by means of a blast of air, was named after its inventor, Englishman Sir Henry Bessemer (1813–1898). The process was a boon to manufacturing, for it greatly reduced costs of production. Bessemer described the process in his paper "The Manufacture of malleable and steel Iron Without Fuel." In the *Bessemer converter*, the melted pig iron surrenders its carbon and other impurities through the action of air forced on the molten metal. Bessemer patented his discovery in the United States in 1857.

Meanwhile a certain William Kelly (1811–1888) discovered the same process accidentally at about the same time while working as a master of an iron furnace at Eddyville, Kentucky. He observed that a blast of air on molten metal raised its temperature greatly by oxidation. Kelly must have had great powers of persuasion, because he convinced the patent officials of the priority of his claim. He thereupon organized an ironworks near Detroit, Michigan, in 1864. Another American began operating with Bessemer's patents the following year at Troy, New York. This latter company and Kelly's became engaged in a prolonged lawsuit that finally was settled by consolidating the litigating companies. Kelly retired, and the *Bessemer converter* continued to convert and since then has remained unchallenged.

BIG BEN

Big Ben, the famous bell in the Clock Tower that strikes the hour over the British Houses of Parliament and is sounded by the British Broadcasting Company throughout the world, was originally cast in 1856. But the fifteen-ton bell showed a serious crack, justifying a recasting. The new bell was completed in 1858, and it weighed some thirteen tons. The first stroke of the bell marked the hour; four smaller bells the quarter hour, and these were first broadcast in 1923.

The bell was to be named "St. Stephen," but a whimsical use in the press of "Big Ben" caught the public's fancy, and that name persisted, honoring Sir Benjamin Hall (1802–1869), the chief commissioner of works at that time. Hall had nothing to do with the construction of the bell; it was just that the bell was cast during his term in office.

A strange incident occurred on the morning of March 14, 1861. As related, "the inhabitants of Westminster were roused by repeated strokes of the new great bell, and most persons supposed it was for the death of a member of the royal family. It proved, however, to be due to some derangement of the clock, for at four and five o'clock ten and twelve strokes were struck instead of the proper number." Within the next twenty-four hours, word came that the Duchess of Kent (Queen Victoria's mother) was dying. She died early March 16. Did the clock toll for her?

BIG BERTHA

The name of the heaviest siege guns ever built alludes to the Bertha Krupp von Bohlen und Halbach works in Essen. This large howitzer bombarded Liege and Namur in 1914, but the same name was used for the 142-ton cannon that shelled Paris in 1918 from the unbelievable distance of 76 miles, safely within the German lines. Soldiers noted the resemblance between the gun and the rotund owner of the great Krupp armament empire. The designation *Big Bertha* was not flattering, nor was it meant to be. It is a translation of *die dicke Bertha*, "the fat Bertha," the name given by the Germans to their large howitzer.

Bertha Krupp (1886–1957) took over as head of the Krupp works upon the suicide of her father, Friedrich Alfred Krupp (1854–1902). She was the sole heir to his immense fortune. In 1906 she married Gustav Bohlen und Halbach (1870–1950), whose petition for a change of name to Gustav Krupp von Bohlen und Halbach was granted.

In reality, the belief that the cannon was a product of the famous German armament firm was mistaken. "Big Bertha" was made at the Skoda Works in Austria-Hungary.

BIKINI

How the word *bikini* came to apply to the skimpy two-piece swimsuit has been a linguistic mystery since 1947, when bikinis were first seen on the beaches of the French Riviera, a year after the United States began testing atom bombs on the Bikini atoll of the Marshall Islands. Some shocked people said that the impact of the swimsuit on male beach loungers was like the devastating effect of the atomic bomb. Whoosh! And so they were called *bikinis*.

A simpler and more credible notion is that the daring swimsuits resembled the attire worn by women on the Bikini atoll.

BINET-SIMON TESTS

Back in 1905, a French psychologist named Alfred Binet (1857–1911) began a critical method of determining mental age versus actual age. As the director of the laboratory of psychology and physiology at the Sorbonne, he worked in association with Théodore Simon, and the tests that were invented bore the names of both men. The tests for measuring intelligence, called the *Binet-Simon Scale*, were designed for children ages three to twelve, and they have formed the basis for much of the scholastic intelligence testing done in Europe and America for nine decades.

The score of 150 is accepted as that of a genius and below 70 as an indication of mental deficiency. According to historical researchers the intelligence score of John Stuart Mill, who learned Greek at age three, was "over 200."

Binet was a pioneering figure in modern psychological research. Among his writings are *Psychology of Reasoning* (1886) and *Alterations of Personality* (1892). Since Binet's death, the tests have been revised several times.

BLOOMERS

Bloomers were designed, in 1850, by Mrs. Elizabeth Smith Miller, who also was the first to wear them. But this garment got its biggest impetus and its name from Amelia Bloomer, who dressed frequently in this attire and was its most consistent advocate.

Amelia Bloomer (1818–1894), born Amelia Jenks in Homer, New York, was the editor of a journal in Seneca, New York, titled *The Lily*, the house organ of the Seneca Falls Ladies' Temperance Society. Amelia had always been something of a maverick. For example, she had the word *obey* omitted from her marriage vows when she married Dexter C. Bloomer in 1840. When Amelia learned about the costume that ultimately memorialized her, she wrote about it in *The Lily* and described it as "sanitary attire."

In 1849, in New York, Amelia introduced this attire by wearing it at the lectures she gave and on other occasions, despite the derision of many onlookers. Amelia wrote that the upper part of the costume should follow the wearer's taste, but below "we would have a skirt reaching down to nearly half way between the knee and the ankle, and not made quite so full as is the present fashion. Underneath this skirt, trousers moderately full (in fair, mild weather) coming down to the ankle (not instep) and there gathered in with an elastic band. . . . For winter, also wet weather, the trousers also full, but coming down into a boot, which shall rise some three or four inches at least above the ankle."

Mrs. Bloomer's fashion was charged with immodesty. She rebutted with, "If delicacy requires that the skirt be long, why do ladies, a dozen times a day, commit the indelicacy of raising their dresses, which have already been sweeping the side-walks, to prevent their dragging in the mud of the streets? Surely a few spots of mud added to the refuse of the side-walks, on the hem of their garment, are not to be compared to the charge of indelicacy to which the display they make might subject them!"

The garment stirred a hubbub, with sides taking strong viewpoints. Some ministers forbade their congregations to wear bloomers in church.

One cited Deuteronomy 22:5 to show that women are forbidden to wear men's clothing. Bloomer's quick retort was, "Really, there was no distinction in the fig leaves worn by Adam and Eve."

BLUEBEARD

The eponym *Bluebeard*, a noun meaning "a man who successively marries and murders several wives" is the main character in Charles Perrault's story *Barbe Bleue*, published in *Contes du Temps* (1697). The adjective *bluebeard* means "not to enter or be explored," as in the bluebeard room in the house. The character Bluebeard was a murderous tyrant, a habitual wifekiller. Today he might be called a serial wifekiller.

Fatima, a pretty young woman, married the sinister Bluebeard against her brothers' wishes. Before leaving on a business trip, Bluebeard gave his new wife the keys to his castle, but forbade her to open a certain door. Curiosity got the best of her, and she disobeyed her husband's warning. There she found the bodies of Bluebeard's six former wives hung up like beef. On Bluebeard's return, he spotted a drop of blood on one of the keys, which told him of his wife's disobedience. Bluebeard was preparing to make Fatima number seven when her brothers rushed in and bestowed on Bluebeard the fate he had intended for their sister.

In Brittany, a real-life Bluebeard, French General Gilles de Retz, the Marquis de Laval, was burned at the stake for his crimes in 1440. This sadistic creature murdered six of his seven wives, but whether de Retz was the historical source for Perrault's Bluebeard has never been attested.

Perrault's *Contes du Temps* contains "Sleeping Beauty," "Red Riding Hood," "Puss in Boots," and other famous fairy tales collected from various sources.

BLUESTOCKINGS

The expression *bluestocking* took root in the mid-eighteenth century after a botanist and sometime poet, Benjamin Stillingfleet, wore blue silk stockings when attending a gathering of women who had decided to forgo card playing for literary pursuits and invite learned such as Samuel Johnson, Horace Walpole, and David Garrick to lecture before them. The usual stockings worn by men to such an affair—in fact it was de rigueur to wear them—were black. Stillingfleet had no black silk stockings. He was told to come anyway, and he wore blue stockings. The stockings have bestowed on members of this coterie the sobriquet "Bluestocking Society." It was, of course, a derisive expression because for women to acquire learning was regarded as ungraceful.

Today a *bluestocking* is, to borrow a statement from Rousseau, "a woman who will remain a spinster as long as there are sensible men on earth." Rousseau, of course, had never heard of the feminist movement or the attraction of sensible men to erudite women.

BLURB

Belinda Blurb was a fictional character who appeared on the dust jacket of a book written by Gelett Burgess (1866–1951) titled *Are You a Bromide?* Her name has been immortalized by its acceptance into the English language and by an entry in recent English dictionaries.

The publisher of the book, B. W. Huebish, in the summer 1937 issue of the publication *Colophon*, to report the history of the word *blurb*, wrote, in part: "It is the custom of publishers to present copies of a conspicuous current book to booksellers attending the annual dinner of their trade association, and as this little book was in its heyday when the meeting took place I gave it to 500 guests. These copies were differentiated from the regular edition by the addition of a comic bookplate drawn by the author and by a special jacket which he devised. It was the common practice to print the picture of a damsel—languishing, heroic, or coquettish—on the jacket of every novel, so Burgess lifted from a Lydia Pinkham or tooth-powder advertisement the portrait of a sickly sweet young woman, painted in some gleaming teeth, and otherwise enhanced her pulchritude, and placed her in the center of the jacket. His accompanying text was some nonsense about 'Miss Belinda *Blurb*,' and thus the term supplied a real need and became a fixture in our language."

Burgess was born in Boston, attended Massachusetts Institute of Technology, and in the late 1800s moved to San Francisco. After a stint at teaching at Berkeley, he became an associate editor of *The Wave*, a society paper. He was a prolific writer, known for a briskly satirical style, as exemplified by the titles of some of his books. Aside from *Are You a Bromide?* (1906) he wrote *Why Men Hate Women* (1927) and *Look Eleven Years Younger* (1937), and several other books in the same vein.

Burgess, in 1895, wrote a four-liner that plagued him all the rest of his life. His whimsical quatrain—"*I never saw a Purple Cow,/I never hope to see one;/But I can tell you anyhow,/I'd rather see than be one*"—was gleefully shouted at him wherever he went. In retaliation, in 1914, Burgess wrote this rebuttal—"*Ah, yes I wrote the Purple Cow,/I'm sorry now, I wrote it!/But I can tell you anyhow/I'll kill you if you quote it!*"

BOBBY, PEELERS

The great British statesman Sir Robert Peel (1788–1850) was born into a wealthy family in Lancashire, England. He attended Harrow School and Oxford University. In 1812 he was appointed chief secretary for Ireland. There he established the Irish Constabulary, which the Irish first nicknamed *Orange Peel*, for his support of the Protestant "Orangemen" and then *peelers* after the secretary's surname. In 1829, as home secretary, Peel created the Metropolitan Police. The common nickname for

London policemen became *bobby*, after Peel's given name, and it has been in use ever since.

Peel became Britain's prime minister in 1834 and again in 1841. He abolished capital punishment for petty crimes and was responsible for the enactment of the Catholic Emancipation Bill (1829), which allowed Catholics to sit in Parliament. He lost office in 1849. The following year he was thrown from a horse in a freak accident; he died two days later.

BOGUS

Be careful of those who think they know the etymology of *bogus*. The dictionary defines *bogus* as counterfeit or spurious. No matter how you consider it, that which is bogus is a fake. The prestigious Oxford English Dictionary backs an ex-Vermonter's story of a machine that made counterfeit coins that was dubbed a "bogus" in Ohio in 1827; and then connects it with *tantrabogus*, a Vermont word for bogeyman. Or did it derive from a Scots-gypsy word for counterfeit—*boghus*? H. L. Mencken surmised that *bogus* might be of French origin, possibly coming from *bagasse* or *bogüe*. Another opinion appeared in the *Boston Daily Courier* on June 12, 1857: "The word *bogus*, we believe, is a corruption of the name of one Borghese, a very corrupt individual, who, twenty years ago, did a tremendous business in the way of supplying the great west, and portions of the southwest, with a vast amount of counterfeit bills, and bills of fictitious banks, which never had an existence out of the forgetive brain of him, the said Borghese. The western people who are rather rapid in their talk, when excited, soon fell into the habit of shortening the Norman name of Borghese to the more handy name of *Bogus*, and his bills and all other bills of like character were universally styled *bogus* currency."

It might be that among these conjectures is the real thing—the genuine *bogus*.

BOLOGNA, FRANKFURTER (HOT DOG), HAMBURGER

Three fine European cities have become eponyms for common American edibles. Bologna, a gastronomic center in northern Italy, has been credited with many delectable dishes that have spread throughout the world; Venus's navel, better known as tortellini, is served in the best of European and American restaurants. But the eponymous food that has made the city famous is the sausage. This everyday meat was called *bologna* and was so ubiquitous that the city of its origin was on everyone's lips. The name of the sausage has been corrupted to "baloney," and the name has received other usages. An ordinary way of expressing disbelief is to say, "You're full of baloney." "Baloney" has become the equivalent of nonsense. The phrase proliferated during the early '30s, and it may have had its genesis in a jingle: "Dress it in silks and make it look phoney, / No matter how thin you slice it, it's still baloney."

The *frankfurter* is a sausage originally made in Frankfurt, Germany. During World War I, the American soldiers called this snack a "victory steak," but in America, where it found a warm home, the frankfurter received a new name: "hot dog." The name giver was T. A. Dorgan, "Tad," the most prominent sports cartoonist of the era. According to H. L. Mencken, the first person to heat the roll, and add mustard and relish, was Harry Stevens, concessionaire at the Polo Grounds, home of the New York Giants. The hot dog has become America's basic food delight at a baseball game. According to William Morris, the hot dog in the Midwest is called a *Coney Island*, and it is piled high with all kinds of culinary treats, but it has ketchup. Ketchup is unheard of on Coney Island, New York; there the hot dog is drenched with mustard. From Laurence J. Peter, *Quotations for Our Time* (1977), has come the warmest tribute to a hot dog: "The noblest of all dogs is the hot-dog; it feeds the hand that bites it."

The meat pattie known as the *hamburger* originated in the city of Hamburg, Germany. In the early days in the United States, chopped beef was known as *hamburger steak* and was served like any other steak. With time, hamburger steak degenerated from the estate of a steak to the level of a sandwich. It then became known as *hamburger*, the biggest selling fast-food item in America. The National Restaurant Association reported that ninety percent of all table service restaurants offer the hamburger and that the hamburger is America's number one choice for eating away from home. Over five billion hamburgers were purchased or sold in 1995.

BONIFACE

The Beaux' Stratagem was the title of a play written in 1707 by the Irish comic dramatist George Farquhar (1678–1707). In that play an inn-keeper was called *Boniface*, Latin for "do good," because it was believed that Pope Boniface VI, whose reign in 896 of only fifteen days, promised an indulgence for anyone who would drink to his health. This may have been the reason an innkeeper in the play was called *Boniface*. During the early times of stagecoach travel, the innkeeper was likely to greet guests at his door to welcome them. The word *Boniface* was given the innkeeper, and it stuck. The word applies equally well to proprietors of nightclubs, hotels, or restaurants.

Many practices of times gone by are no longer respected. Even though an innkeeper may not greet his guests with warm hospitality, the name for an innkeeper has remained. Ebenezer Cobham Brewer extends the meaning of *boniface* to include any sleek, well-mannered, jolly land-lord.

BOOZE

Booze, meaning an alcoholic drink, is a barroom term not found in the vocabulary of the genteel. Yet for centuries it enjoyed credentials that made it, in one form or another, a commonplace word in the English language. With time, however, it degenerated into slang, so much so that in the sixteenth century it was regarded as thieves' cant. Its level of acceptance has risen since then, but not enough to enter literary circles.

Those who believe that *booze* is an eponym for E. G. Booz, a Philadelphia distiller who purveyed whiskey in a bottle bearing his name and shaped like a log cabin, are behind the times. During the 1840 presidential campaign, the bottle was widely distributed to impress people that William Henry Harrison, the successful Whig candidate (Tippecanoe and Tyler, too) had been born in a log cabin. The full imprint on this bottle was "Booz's Log Cabin Whiskey."

Booze traces back to Middle English *bousen*, to carouse, to guzzle liquor, or to drink to excess. The term has been given various forms (Edmund Spencer in 1590 in *The Faerie Queen* spoke of a "boozing can"). Some etymologists attribute its origin to the Hindustani *Booza*, drink; others to the Turkish *boza*, a kind of liquor favored by gypsies.

The confusion concerning this word even extends to the correct provenance of the log-shaped bottle of Harrison's campaign. Some say it did not come from the Philadelphia distiller but from E. S. Booz of Kentucky. The ploy with the log cabin bottle did so well that Daniel Webster was wont to say, "I wish I had been born in a log cabin." It certainly didn't harm the candidacy of Abraham Lincoln.

In any event, *booze*, with a lower-case *b*, has a fixed place in the English language.

BORGIA, NEPOTISM

Lucrezia and Cesare Borgia, sister and brother, were members of an unscrupulous family in which compassion and humane behavior played no part. There is little doubt in the minds of historians that they committed many murders, usually by poisoning, although this belief has never been proved by hard evidence. The Borgias were supposed to have possessed a secret, fatal recipe that they served to foes and unwanted guests alike. Drinking a toast to the health of the Borgias was chancy because the drinker might be about to lose his.

Cesare (1476–1507) and Lucrezia (1480–1519) were children of Pope Alexander VI. The English word *nepotism*, "favoritism shown on the basis of family relationship," can be traced directly to this misuse of official position. The Latin word *nepos*, "a descendant, especially a nephew," was given to the illegitimate children of popes. Pope Alexander VI in civilian life was Rodrigo Borgia, and he turned out to be a good family provider. He installed his son Cesare as an archbishop when the boy was only sixteen years old. His young nephew Giovanni was given a cardinal's hat. Talk about family favoritism!

To dine at the Borgias became known as a great but sometimes fatal honor. Sir Max Beerbohm noted in *Hosts and Guests*: "I maintain that though you would often in the fifteenth century have heard the snobbish Roman say, in a would-be off-hand tone, 'I am dining with the Borgias tonight,' no Roman was ever able to say, 'I dined last night with the Borgias.'"

BOSWELL, BOSWELLIZE

James Boswell (1740–1795) has been regarded as the foremost biographer in English literature. His great masterpiece was *The Life of Samuel Johnson*, the great compiler of the English dictionary. Thomas Macaulay ranked the biography first among biographies of all time.

Boswell was born in Edinburgh and educated there and in Glasgow, and the University of Utrecht in Holland. He met Johnson (1709–1784) in 1763 and became such a devoted admirer that his life was shaped around Johnson. Boswell toured the Hebrides with Johnson and published the *Journal of a Tour to the Hebrides with Samuel Johnson, L.L.D.*

Ten years after the men met, Johnson arranged for the admittance of Boswell into the Literary Club that Johnson had founded. There Boswell was introduced to some of the greatest minds of England: Edmund Burke, Oliver Goldsmith, Sir Joshua Reynolds, and David Garrick.

The Life of Samuel Johnson (1791) was not published until seven years after Johnson's death.

Boswell inherited a substantial estate, which enabled him to do as he liked. And what he liked were matters of questionable morality. He was a man of intemperate habits, and it is said that his vanity often took him to the point of absurdity.

A biographer is often called a *Boswell*, and from Boswell's name has come the verb *Boswellize*, meaning "to write a hero-worshiping biography."

BOUGAINVILLAEA

The story behind the naming of the *bougainvillaea* started in 1766 with a three-year journey of discovery around the world, from which the woody vine of the four-o'clock family was brought home to France. This plant, which was named for the explorer Louis Antoine de Bougainville, is recognized by its inconspicuous flowers surrounded by brilliant red or purple bracts. Many people regard the bougainvillaea as the handsomest of subtropical vines. The plant is often cultivated in greenhouses but can be grown outdoors in the semi-tropical parts of the United States.

Bougainville (1720–1811) was head of the first French naval forces to circumnavigate the world (1766–1769). He was accompanied on his journey by astronomers and naturalists who named the woody climbing plant

Bougainvillaea in his honor. They visited Tahiti, the New Hebrides, and the Solomon Islands, the largest of which is named *Bougainville* after him.

Bougainville served as aide-de-camp to General Louis de Montcalm in Canada during the French-Indian War and under François Joseph Paul, Comte de Grasse in the American Revolution. Bougainville was a man of many interests and abilities. His two-volume work on integral calculus earned him a membership in the Institut de France. In later years, Napoleon made him a senator, count of the empire, and member of the Legion of Honor.

BOULANGISM

Boulangism is a wave of political hysteria that swept over France, especially in Paris, during the years 1886–1889. Its purpose was to support General Georges Ernest Jean Marie Boulanger (1837–1891), a military leader who advocated revenge on Germany. As Minister of War (1886–1887), he achieved some popularity for army reforms, but more particularly for his handsome military figure. When he was relieved of his command, his approval rating did not drop; it increased. Boulanger acquired the title *Man on Horseback* because he habitually appeared before the public mounted on a magnificent charger. He became a favorite with the royalists, and the movement called *boulangism* to punish the Germans for what they had done to France during the war of 1870 developed a long line of followers.

When Boulanger was not reappointed to his cabinet post, his popularity was such that almost everyone believed that he could make himself dictator of France whenever he wanted. But the golden opportunity slipped by and disappeared when he was publicly proved a liar and a coward. When a warrant for his arrest was signed, Boulanger fled the country. His crimes against the Republic and subsequent flight lost him his supporters. Two years later the *Man on Horseback*, who might have been dictator, on a blustery day and all alone, went to the cemetery in which his mistress was buried in Brussels and there shot himself, falling dead over her grave.

BOWDLER, BOWDLERIZE

Thomas Bowdler (1754–1825) was born near Bath, England. His father was a strict disciplinarian who prescribed that his son be a physician. The father's prescription was filled only partly, however. Although Thomas became a physician, he could not bear to see anyone in pain—and so gave up his practice.

Young Thomas then spent his time crusading against immoral activities and influences by, among other things, joining anti-vice organizations, which became a natural foundation for his lifework on the Isle of

Wight. He had concluded that modest ladies should be enabled to read Shakespeare without blushing.

In 1818 Bowdler published a diluted ten-volume edition of Shakespeare's works "in which nothing is added to the original text; but those words are omitted that cannot with propriety be read aloud in a family." He had toned down suggestive dialogue and snipped off scenes that he thought were too explicit, insisting that only references that might "raise a blush on the cheek of modesty" had been excised.

Bowdler believed that the language of the seventeenth century was not necessarily acceptable in the nineteenth. For example, the words of Hamlet—"transform honesty from what it is to be a bawd"—were changed to "to debase honesty from what it is," and his words with Ophelia became decorous. Lady Macbeth's poignant "Out, damn'd spot!" became "Out, crimson spot!" The speeches of some main characters—Hamlet, Macbeth, Falstaff—were dismembered beyond recognition, whereas others were so diminished that they fell into oblivion (the lascivious Doll Tearsheet, for example, who makes her appearance in *Henry IV*).

This expurgated version of Shakespeare's works, *The Family Shakespeare*, was published in Bath in 1818 and contained no name in the preface and no name of an editor. A reader did not know to whom to attribute the revision. In future editions, Thomas Bowdler was listed as editor. And yet the Bowdler family and friends knew that Henrietta Maria, or Harriet, Thomas's sister, was the phantom author of the original volume. Why the anonymity? It has been suggested that because Harriet was a prim and proper spinster, she would not be expected to know, and would not want anyone to know, that she understood obscene words and expressions. Hence she hid her authorship.

Although Bowdler thought that the public would be pleased with his purge of Shakespearean obscenities, he was quite shocked to learn that his excisions did not receive universal acceptance. He replied to his critics: "And should I be classed with the assassins of Caesar, because I have rendered these invaluable plays for the perusal of our virtuous females?" He added, in capital letters, "IF ANY WORD OR EXPRESSION IS OF SUCH A NATURE THAT THE FIRST IMPRESSION WHICH IT EXCITES IS AN IMPRESSION OF OBSCENITY, THAT WORD OUGHT NOT TO BE SPOKEN, OR WRITTEN, OR PRINTED, AND IF PRINTED, OUGHT TO BE ERASED."

Bowdler's eraser skipped none of Shakespeare's works. He expurgated all of them. He then turned his purifying scalpel on Gibbon's *History of the Decline and Fall of the Roman Empire*, excising that marvelous masterpiece by removing "all passages of an irreligious or immoral tendency."

For attacking the classics of literature, Bowdler has been immortalized as the world's best-known self-appointed literary censor. His name lives in the language in many forms. The dictionary definition of *bowdlerize*, a verb sprouted from his name (other growths are *bowdlerism* and *bowdlerization*), is "to radically expurgate or prudishly censor" a book by omitting words or passages regarded as indecent, which, of course, removes its vitality and "spice."

BOWIE KNIFE

The Bowie knife, once called an Arkansas toothpick, is a dangerous weapon. It is a dagger, strongly made, with a one-edged blade of some twelve inches in length that curves to a point. It has a heavy guard of horn between the hilt and the blade. Whether James Bowie or his brother Rezin dreamed it up is uncertain. James is given credit for it because he made the weapon famous when he, armed with only his knife, fought and killed a man in Natchez who wielded a pistol.

Bowie became a national hero in 1836 when he, together with Davy Crockett and some two hundred other soldiers, fought gallantly against the overwhelming Mexican forces that stormed the Alamo, an abandoned mission house in San Antonio. For thirteen days these brave men fought and suffered. Bowie, confined to a sick-bed, fought from his cot with only a knife in hand. But sheer numbers finally triumphed. Bowie, Crockett, and everyone else at the Alamo was killed in hand-to-hand combat by General Santa Anna's troops; they died bravely.

Bowie, born in 1799, settled in Texas in 1828, when it was still Mexican land. He became friendly with the Mexican vice-governor, married his daughter, and acquired Mexican land grants. He became a Mexican citizen. Bowie was known to be unethical; he did not hesitate to dupe Mexicans. Bowie became interested in the restrictions Mexico imposed on American migration. He became a colonel in the Texas Rangers and fought with distinction in several battles. He joined up with Colonel William B. Travis in his last gallant hurrah—the Alamo.

Bowie has become a legend through Western song and folk tales. The knife that he or his brother Rezin designed continued in demand long after Bowie's death. The famous Sheffield steelworks in England marketed large quantities for use in Texas.

BOYCOTT

A boycott is a refusal to do business or have other contacts with a person, a corporation, or a country. The word *boycott*, with a small "b," surfaced in 1880 when Captain Charles Cunningham Boycott (1832–1897), an English land agent for the estates of the Earl of Erne at Connaught in County Mayo, Ireland, evicted poverty-stricken tenant farmers who could not pay their rent. The farmers had been struck by a ruinous failure of crops and had little money.

Captain Boycott was made a test case by the great Irish nationalist leader, Charles Parnell. Parnell's strategy was to ostracize any landlord who refused to lower rents or any tenant who took over a farm of an evicted tenant "by isolating him . . . as if he were a leper of old . . . by leaving him strictly alone." Boycott then found himself the target of total ostracism. His servants left, his farmhands left, and he was deprived of all mail delivery. Storekeepers refused to sell to him; people jeered at him and hung him in effigy. Further, marauders tore down his fences and turned his cattle loose. Life became unbearable, so miserable, that Boycott finally gave up and fled to England. Thus Boycott was responsible for the first boycott.

People came to call this action a *boycott*, which became a very powerful term, especially when used by unions against employers regarded as unfair. A refusal to do business with the employer was called a primary boycott. Influencing other people to join the boycott was termed a secondary boycott. However, this latter maneuver was declared illegal by Federal United States courts.

Boycott's fortitude must have returned to him or else he became lonely for Ireland, for he later visited Ireland on one of his holidays. At a public gathering in Dublin, Boycott was recognized—and cheered!

Although to *boycott* and *to send to Coventry* mean the same thing, the latter expression arose much earlier in time. At the beginning of the war between Charles I and Parliament, Royalist prisoners were sent to the Cromwell stronghold of Coventry for safekeeping. The citizens of Coventry, especially the women, shunned them; they were soundly ostracized.

BRAILLE

The system of writing and printing for the blind, known as *Braille*, is eponymous for Louis Braille, its inventor (1809–1852). Braille was blinded at age three. While playing in his father's harness-repair shop in Coupvray, near Paris, he drove an awl through an eye. Soon after the other eye lost its sight.

There weren't many useful jobs for blind people, but Braille's father was determined to help his son find a life of usefulness; accordingly the boy needed a good education. To this end, Louis, until age ten, attended his village school with sighted children. His father then enrolled him in the Institution Nationale des Jeunes Aveugles for blind youth in Paris. Braille had learned the alphabet by feeling twigs formed in the shape of letters.

Books for the blind were scarce in those days, and those in the school library were very heavy. From those oversized books, some weighing twenty pounds, young Braille learned to read. The books had been developed at the Institution and consisted of enlarged, raised Roman letters, which was the only touch-reading technology then in existence. About half the blind children who tried to learn this method found it too difficult. Braille was a distinguished student and, in 1829, became a professor at the Institution.

The army at the time used a system of communication based on touch rather than sight, a primitive form of "night writing" invented by Charles Barbier, a captain of artillery in the army. The system consisted of twelve raised marks on paper that in the darkness could be passed along with no spoken word or illumination and which fingers could "read." The message was clear but simple, such as one dot for advance, two dots for lie low, three dots for take cover, and so on. It ignited Braille's imagination.

Braille, when only fifteen years old, refined the system by using a six-dot cell, his pattern being two dots across and three down. This pattern lent itself to sixty-three combinations, which represented all the letters in the French alphabet, except "W" (French like Latin had no "W," although later at the request of an Englishman one was added), together with punctuation and contractions and a system for musical notations. A whole world opened up for the blind.

Braille's system of communication received a warm reception throughout France, and he was also hailed for his musical compositions. (Braille displayed some talent with the piano, but he became an accomplished organist.) Nonetheless, doom set in when a new director at the institution decreed that the old system had to be used and not Braille's. Despite that setback, Braille continued improving his system, including notational variations for music.

Perhaps Braille's system might have passed into oblivion but for a young blind girl, Thérèse von Kleinert, who, after performing at the organ before a large gathering of cultured people, announced, as the applause subsided, that the applause really belonged to Louis Braille, the inventor of the system that she used. By then he had already died, unheralded, of tuberculosis, two days after his forty-third birthday.

Braille's body was borne to Coupvray for burial. The newspapers in Paris ignored Braille's death and made no mention of it. The task of educating the blind came to a dismal standstill. But fortunately there was a turnaround in favor of Braille's method, including adoption of the Braille system by the Institution in 1854, two years after Braille's death, so that today the magic dots convey a truly universal language for the blind.

On June 30, 1952, Braille's body was exhumed and transported to Paris and carried up the steps of the Pantheon, to receive the highest honor that France can bestow upon its dead—burial among the most famous heroes of the nation.

BRILL

Abraham Arden Brill (1874–1948) was born in Austria but came to the United States at an early age. He studied medicine at Columbia University and received his M.D. degree in 1903. Brill pursued his interest in psychoanalysis during his university studies, and, after graduation, went to Europe to train under the master Sigmund Freud. As a proponent of psychoanalysis, he practiced in the United States for forty years.

Dr. Brill introduced Freudian psychoanalysis to the American medical profession. He sought to revolutionize the treatment of the mentally ill. Although Brill met with great resistance, he persisted. As a result, psychoanalysis became accepted as a new treatment technique. He founded the Psychoanalytic Society in 1911 in New York and served as its first president. In 1934 he became the first president of the Psychoanalytic Section of the Psychiatric Association.

Brill remained a close friend of Freud and for fifteen years translated most of his major works into English as well as some of Carl Jung's works. Brill was also the author of several notable texts on psychoanalysis.

BRODIE, DO A BRODIE

Steve Brodie, a newsboy did on July 23, 1886, what people thought was impossible to do and still live. He jumped from the Manhattan side of the Brooklyn Bridge. And for that foolhardy leap, won a bet of $200.

According to *The New York Times*, Brodie sneaked around the Brooklyn Bridge guards, climbed to the lowest chord, and plunged into the water 135 feet below. Friends in a rowboat were waiting to rescue the twenty-three-year-old daredevil. Brodie was arrested for endangering his life and was severely reprimanded by a judge. One should bear in mind, however, that Brodie's claim to have jumped off the bridge is questionable; although he was pulled from the water, no one actually saw him jump. Many people believe he never did it. The opinion of Boxing Commissioner William Muldoon, as reported in the *New York Times*, July 23, 1986, the 100th anniversary of the day Brodie supposedly jumped, was that his so-called exploit "was a fake and that an unbiased investigation had shown that by a clever bit of trickery with a dummy it had been made to appear that Brodie had made the leap." However, he used his fame from this purported leap to branch into acting (he was the subject of a hit play called *On the Bowery*) and other money-making ventures that kept him in the public spotlight for the rest of his life. In the 1983 gangster cinema *The Bowery*, Brodie was portrayed by the late George Raft. Brodie has been immortalized by the phrase *to do a brodie*, which is now proverbial for "to take a chance."

The slang term *brodie* represents a suicidal leap. A story that made the rounds is that Brodie met Jim Corbett's father sometime before the Jim Corbett-John L. Sullivan prizefight and predicted that Sullivan would knock out his son. Mr. Corbett looked down at little Brodie and sneered, "So you're the fellow who jumped over the Brooklyn Bridge." Brodie's riposte was, "No, I jumped *off* of it." To which the senior Corbett remarked, "I thought you jumped *over* the bridge. Any damn fool could jump off of it."

BROUGHAM

Some automobile manufacturers make a model they call a *brougham*. It's usually a distinguished, more expensive model. At one time broughams were built with no roof over the chauffeur's section. It was quite a snazzy-looking car, even though the chauffeur had a problem when it rained.

The car style derived from a carriage style. The horse-drawn *brougham* was one of the most popular styles during the days before the gasoline-fired motor. It consisted of a four-wheel carriage—a closed, low-slung cab for two passengers—drawn by one horse, with the driver's seat high above the wheels. It was named in honor of Henry Peter Brougham, Baron Brougham and Vaux (1778–1868), a leading legal reformer in the nineteenth century. Brougham, born in Scotland, was a versatile and brilliant man—a noted lawyer, orator, politician, writer, and a remarkable wit. He was most remembered for his defense of Queen Caroline against the charge of her husband, the regent and later King George IV, that she was guilty of adultery.

Some people say that the four-wheeled carriage with an open driver's seat got its name because Brougham was frequently seen in this "garden chair on wheels," often in the company of Disraeli or Gladstone. As they drove by, the townspeople would say, "There goes Brougham." It didn't take long before the vehicle itself was called a *brougham* after its distinguished occupant.

The brougham became a public service vehicle and was London's most popular means of transport until eclipsed by the hansom cab.

BUDDHISM

Buddha was the title given to a young man named Gautama, the founder of Buddhism. Buddha was born about 563 B.C. at Kapilavastu, a town in northern India; when he grew to manhood, he developed a great desire to help his people and to save them from mental and physical problems. To this end, he gave up his palace and his inheritance to search for the truth and to bring peace to India. After seven years of searching, the truth came to his mind as he sat under a sacred fig tree, called a *pipal* or *bo* tree. This was at Buddh Gaya, India, from which the name *Buddha* was taken.

Buddha taught that the secret of life was brotherly love and that selfishness causes the world's woes, which can be eradicated only by the system known as the "Eightfold Paths—right beliefs, right ideals, right words, right deeds, right way of earning a living, right efforts, right thinking, and right meditations." He believed that hatred will never stop until it comes under the power of love. The well-trained mind holds a kindly attitude toward those around, above, or below it. And the love of one's enemies is the crowning jewel of Buddhist life. The Buddhist goal is

Nirvana, a condition of the mind of complete love and peace. A man may hope for *Nirvana* only if he has perfect self-control, unselfishness, knowledge, enlightenment, and a kindly attitude. He must also reject all anger, passion, fear, and sin.

Buddhism is a worldwide religion, but it is practiced primarily in India, Indochina, China, and Japan.

BUFFALO BILL

It is hard to believe that a person could put so much into one life as Buffalo Bill did. William Frederick Cody (1846–1917) was born in Scott County, Iowa, and orphaned when eleven years old. His first job was in Kansas as a mounted messenger, and before he was twenty he excelled as a wrangler, hunter, plainsman, and Indian fighter. After serving in the Civil War, he worked for the U.S. Army as a civilian scout and messenger. For the next two years he hunted buffalo for the Union Pacific Railroad; he reportedly slew 42,800 head.

No one knows for certain how he came to be dubbed Buffalo Bill, but after being engaged in an eight-hour shooting match with another scout, he was regarded as the champion buffalo killer.

Cody was involved in sixteen Indian fights, including the scalping of the Cheyenne warrior Yellow Hair, all done at the behest of the U.S. Fifth Cavalry, which was assigned the task of wiping out Indian resistance to the coming of the white man.

Cody organized his first Wild West exhibition in 1883. It was a spectacular show with much shooting and riding by cowboys. Annie Oakley, the champion marksman, became a highlight. And Sitting Bull, the American Dakota Indian leader, was an outstanding attraction. But as happens to many celebrities who were once legends in the entertainment field, Buffalo Bill developed mounting financial problems that reduced him to poverty level. Gone were his glorious shooting days. Gone were Annie Oakley and Sitting Bull. And gone was the life Buffalo Bill had known. Bill Cody, alias Buffalo Bill, died in relative obscurity.

BUNSEN BURNER, BUNSENITE

Robert Wilhelm Bunsen (1811–1899) was a professor of chemistry at the University of Heidelberg for thirty-seven years. He is credited with having invented the *Bunsen burner*, but other scientists helped in its design. Together with Gustave Kirchhoff, Bunsen also developed the spectroscope, which enables scientists to engage in spectrum analysis. Utilizing spectrum analysis, these men discovered the chemical elements cesium and rubidium. Bunsen in addition invented the calorimeter and the carbon-zinc electric cell, which is called a *Bunsen cell*.

The *Bunsen burner*, from a design by Michael Faraday, has been the burner in science laboratories ever since its invention. It is a gas burner consisting of a metal tube on a stand and a long rubber hose that connects the metal tube to a gas jet. Two openings at the bottom of the tube control the amount of air that mixes with the gas before burning so that it produces a flame without smoke. This principle has been applied to the common gas stove.

Bunsen has been further honored by having a nickel monoxide named for him—*bunsenite*.

BURNSIDE, SIDEBURNS

Technically, this essay does not belong in the book because the subject does not consist of a proper noun used as an ordinary word. The proper noun is *Burnside*; the ordinary word, *sideburns*. Clearly *sideburns* is not a derivative. Let's clarify the mixup.

Ambrose Everett Burnside (1824–1881) went from being an apprentice tailor in Liberty, Indiana, to a Union general and ultimately commander of the Army of the Potomac. He was a dreamer of bizarre schemes to win the Civil War.

No one would disagree that Burnside looked the part of a general, what with his striking figure, his bushy side whiskers, and smooth chin. His greatest pleasure was to lead a parade and maneuver his Rhode Island volunteers, for he was always warmly applauded. Astride a horse, and with whiskers flowing and the bands playing, he was the dashing general that people expected to see. This was the spectacle of Burnside at his best.

Militarily, Burnside was a different kind of spectacle. At the battle of Fredericksburg, Burnside instigated a surprise strike by crossing the river. More than 100,000 Union soldiers were killed. This debacle was followed by others, including a plan to tunnel under the enemy lines. Kindhearted historians report simply that Burnside had his ups and downs. Abraham Lincoln said that he was the only man he knew who could snatch defeat from the jaws of victory. Burnside was bumble-headed and undoubtedly the least distinguished general in the Union Army. He committed so many military errors that the war would have been lost had he not been replaced before resigning his commission.

But Burnside lived on, not because of his surname but because he had cultivated side whiskers, a luxuriant growth of muttonchop whiskers called *burnsides*. Men, particularly young men, liked the look. *Burnsides* became a popular fad. However, because of a semantic shift the name for side whiskers was sensibly turned around to *sideburns*, a logical generic term because such whiskers grow on the sides of the face. The continuation of hair down the side of a man's face is still called *sideburns*, making Burnside's name, anagrammatically speaking, one of the best eponymous words.

Being bumble-headed doesn't prevent a person from rising to high office. Burnside, with his winning personality and imposing presence, was elected governor of Rhode Island three times and then served as a United States senator for two terms. The people of Rhode Island were more compassionate than Burnside's first wife-to-be. When the minister asked whether she would take this man as her husband, she took a quick look at him, shrieked a resounding "No," and ran out of the church.

CAESAR, CAESARIAN

This great soldier and statesman is responsible for many words in English and many expressions that have become commonplace. Caesar (100–44 B.C.) was named Gaius Julius at birth. He later assumed the cognomen *Caesar,* which became synonymous with "emperor," a title with the connotation of "leader" that spread in usage to other lands. It was adopted by Ivan the Terrible in 1547 in the form *czar.* The German emperor also called himself *caesar* but spelled it *Kaiser.* Caeser's adopted son, who succeeded him as ruler, took the name Augustus Caesar. There were, including Julius, twelve Caesars.

Caesar, a punster might say, although not historically correct, became important at birth. A new method of giving birth was named after him. Rather than being born through the birth canal, Caesar was born when the walls of his mother's womb were cut, a procedure that has ever since been called a *caesarian section.*

Young Julius became prominent in Roman politics. Following the *cursus honorum* (rungs of the political ladder), he reached the pinnacle when named consul in the year 59 B.C. Caesar then turned to military affairs, conquering Gaul in numerous campaigns from 58 to 50. In 49 the Senate ordered him to disband his army; instead he crossed the Rubicon River into Italy, thus initiating the Roman Civil War (49–45). It was at this time he declared "*Alea iacta est*" (the die is cast). At war's end he acquired the title dictator, but many in Rome opposed him. On March 15, 44 B.C. (the Ides of March), he was assassinated in the senate house (known as the Curia), falling at the base of the statue of Pompey, where he uttered those immortal words, "Et tu, Brute?" first recorded by the Roman historian Suetonius (69–122) in *The Lives of the Caesars,* and borrowed later by Shakespeare. Shakespeare and other Elizabethan writers were largely responsible for the impression that Caesar was murdered in the Capitol.

The expression "Caesar's wife must be above suspicion" followed the unveiling of a certain Clodius, a man who dressed in female garb and attended an affair for women. Caesar's second wife, Pompeia, was the hostess, and although Caesar didn't think his wife was guilty of infidelity, he nonetheless divorced her. Though the affair has given us the basis for the foregoing expression, no one knows what Caesar actually said.

Possibly the best-known of his expressions was the terse message he sent to Rome after his defeat of Pharnaces at Zela in 47 B.C.: "*Veni, vidi, vici*" ("I came, I saw, I conquered").

Many places have been named for the great emperor, particularly *Caesaria,* a seaport in Israel dating back to ancient times.

Caesar salad was not named for the Roman statesman. It was the creation, in 1924, of Italian-American chef Caesar Cardini. Chef Cardini operated restaurants in Tijuana.

CALAMITY JANE

A *Calamity Jane* is a woman who constantly complains of her troubles or one who brings trouble with her. Martha Jane Canary (1852–1903) was born in Princeton, New Jersey. Her parents moved to Virginia, where they separated and left their daughter to drift on her own. That she drifted is apparent from the many places where she spent time, usually dressed like a man and with a gun by her side. Eventually she found herself in the Black Hills of South Dakota, where she spent the rest of her years.

Many unverifiable stories have been circulated about her. For example, it is claimed that she was a prostitute in Kansas, that Wild Bill Hickock was her lover, and that she acted as a scout for General Custer. That she acted like a man, befitting her attire, has been attested. She was a bullwacker and an Indian fighter.

Calamity Jane was a superior marksman with both rifle and revolver. She was dubbed with her lugubrious name when she warned that anyone who offended her would be inviting "calamity." Some reference books refer to her surname as Burke, the name of one of her husbands. But then again, she had twelve of them. Her unusual marksmanship and her many forays into the nuptial field, however, could not save her from financial disaster. Although her nickname enriched the English language, financial richness did not accompany her to her end.

William Morris reported that an admirer of Calamity Jane paid her the ultimate frontiersman's tribute: "She'd look like hell in a halo."

CANDY, PRINCE CONDÉ

Everyone likes candy. It's hard to believe that a person would not enjoy a piece of chocolate after a meal. Candy is a food that supplies quick energy. Admiral Byrd took about a hundred pounds per man with the exploring party to the South Pole. During World War II, soldiers were given small amounts of candy in their field rations.

But how candy came to be an important food among the people of the world is in dispute. The children of Israel ate *manna*, a wafer with honey, during their forty years of wandering. Ancient Egyptians and Romans ate sweets after large banquets. According to some authorities, a Venetian, in 1470, learned how to refine sugar imported from the Orient. The use of this sugar for making expensive sweets was the beginning of the candy industry. Apothecaries in England coated their pills with this sugar, and, as time went on, their shops became the forerunner of the modern candy store.

Authors of eponymous stories attribute the founding of the candy industry to another source. Prince Charles Phillipe de Condé, grandnephew of Louis XIII, King of France, during the late 1600s loved sugary treats. His passionate fondness for sweets directed his toddling steps to the royal kitchen for such confections. When the royal chef realized that the Prince was not eating healthful foods and that his health could be damaged, he hit on a brilliant idea of glazing meat, vegetables, and fruit with sugar. The chef's idea worked. The King one day sampled the glazed food, smacked his lips and pronounced it delicious, and ordered that this sweet coating be named for the youngest member of the Condé family. Later, as the public came to eat this glazed food without the filling, just the coatings of the Prince's sweet treats, it adopted the name *candy*.

Despite the many stories concerning the naming of this confection, word sleuths say that the word *candy* has come from Sanskrit *Khaṅdakaḥ*.

CANT, JARGON, CANTING CREW

Some people believe that the word *cant* is eponymous for Andrew Cant (1590–1663), a Presbyterian minister in Aberdeen, Scotland. The Reverend's speech was hard to understand because of the dialect he used. The *Spectator* observed in 1711 that he talked "in the pulpit in such a dialect that it's said he was understood by none but his own congregation, and not by all of them."

Cant was a staunch supporter of the Royalist cause. Once when he spoke before a group of officers dedicated to Cromwell, the officers advanced with swords drawn, whereupon the intrepid minister opened his breast and said, "Here is the man who uttered those sentiments," urging them to strike him if they dared. Though he seemed to be a zealous leader of the Scottish Covenanters, supporting the reformation of religion, he was known as a bigot and a hypocrite. Cant and his brother believed in persecuting religious opponents ferociously while praying at the same time.

The name has stuck for all ravings of this kind in the name of religion. The term has also come to be applied to the whining speech of beggars, who were known as the *canting crew*. *Cant* has also become equated with *jargon*, which today means the special vocabulary shared by members of a trade or profession.

CARDIGAN, CARDIGAN SWEATER

James Thomas Brudenell (1797–1863), who became the seventh Earl of Cardigan upon his father's death, and for whom the cardigan sweater was named because he was frequently seen wearing that collarless sweater with buttons down the front, was the sole heir to a fortune and a famous English name. Brudenell was vain and overbearing, unfit for any profession but the military because of his uncontrollable temper. He therefore purchased for £40,000 a lieutenant colonelcy in the 11th Light Dragoons.

Cardigan was a foolish and harsh officer, subject to unreasonable fits of rage. He was such a strict disciplinarian that he imposed rules for all kinds of conduct and, martinet that he was, demanded rigid field drills. He often punished his soldiers with imprisonment and once had a soldier flogged in front of the soldier's regiment. In his first two years as a commissioned officer, he made 700 arrests and held 105 courts-martial.

He was, as one might imagine, thoroughly despised by his troops and the English people. He had to avoid stones thrown at him when he attended theater in London and needed police protection just to walk on the streets. He was hissed wherever he went.

Cardigan's life in 1854 took a new turn, and a disastrous one. The Crimean War erupted, and Cardigan immediately applied to serve under Lord Raglan, the commander in chief. Because of his prestigious name, Cardigan was appointed major-general. He was unable to function in this high position not only because he had no previous active military field service, but also because he had an extreme dislike for his superior officer, Lord Lucan, who happened to be his brother-in-law.

Cardigan made extravagant arrangements for his post, which included making the soldiers' uniforms more attractive and having a renowned cutler sharpen the brigade's swords. But when the brigade sailed for Scutari, Cardigan did not sail with it. Instead he went to Paris to pay a social call on Napoleon III and Empress Eugenie.

Cardigan did little to keep his men in fighting condition. He was wrapped up in his hatred of Lord Lucan. His spirits, however, took a turn for the better when his yacht, the *Dryad*, arrived in Balaclava, a seaport on the Crimean Peninsula, with his French cook on board. Understandably an officer living on an elegant yacht while his men slept in mud and ate army chow would upset the most hardened soldier. This it did. The men were enraged.

Historians have agreed that Cardigan was bumble-headed and not militarily equipped to be a commander. On October 25, 1854, the Battle of Balaclava began. In the middle of the battle, Lord Lucan issued an imprecise order: "Attack anything and everything that shall come within reach of you." Cardigan was not sure what to do. Then down came Lord Raglan's directive to send the Light Brigade through the length of the valley, an order that superseded Lucan's.

Cardigan, who was never accused of cowardice (in fact he had great personal courage), with sword flashing and in his brilliant cherry and royal blue uniform, led his troops in that famous charge. Cardigan himself was unscathed, although he left two-thirds of his cavalry dead in the battlefield.

Cardigan's tragic assignment can be laid at the doorstep of military incompetence and faulty communication. The brave soldiers under his command marched ahead unflinchingly, as Lord Alfred Tennyson so poignantly relates in his famous elegy "The Charge of the Light Brigade."

Forward, the light Brigade!
Was there a man dismayed? . . . Someone had blundered
Theirs not to make reply,

Theirs not to reason why,
Theirs but to do and die . . .
Into the jaws of death,
Into the mouth of hell,
Rode the Six Hundred.

CARTESIAN PHILOSOPHY

The philosophical system of René Descartes (1596–1650) was based on doubt, because to doubt is to think. His system became known as *Cartesian* philosophy, derived from the Latinized form of his name. His most famous conclusion was expressed in three words: *Cogito, ergo sum* ("I think, therefore I am"). His theory of the importance of doubt is based on the assumption that all existing knowledge rests on an unstable foundation; therefore everything that can be doubted should be doubted. The only fact that he could not doubt was that he was doubting. He reasoned that to doubt is to think, and to think is to exist. Hence the above three-word conclusion.

Descartes provided many expressions that have been passed down through the ages; for example, "Common sense is the most widely distributed commodity in the world, for everyone is convinced that he is well supplied with it." And another: "The reading of all good books is like a conversation with the finest men of past centuries."

Descartes was born at La Haye in Touraine, attended the Jesuit College at La Flèche, and was graduated in law from the University of Poitiers. After ten years' service in the army, and then travel throughout Europe, he settled in Holland where he remained the rest of his life and where he did his most important work. In 1649 he accepted an invitation to teach philosophy to Queen Christina of Sweden. He died a few months after arriving at the court at Stockholm.

Descartes was an eminent mathematician. He is often called the father of modern philosophy. His two chief works are *Discourse on Method* and *Meditations*. Descartes' explanation of heavenly bodies has been replaced by Newton's theory of gravitation.

CASANOVA

A *casanova* in today's usage is an unprincipled ladies' man, a libertine, a rake, dedicated to the gratification of his lust. Such a person was Giovanni Jacopo Casanova de Siengalt (1725–1798), born into a theatrical family. As a young man he played the violin in a Venetian restaurant, but then matriculated at a seminary, from which he was expelled for making licentious remarks and for immoral conduct. After a few more efforts to adjust to gainful employment, he became a traveler from capital to capital, displaying a charm that made women easy prey. Casanova meant no harm; he was a pleasant, likable person. All he wanted to do was make love to women. He bragged about his prowess and claimed to have bedded thousands of willing women.

His engaging personality and incisive wit gave him access to such distinguished giants as Voltaire, Catherine the Great of Russia, and Prussia's Frederick the Great. He became secretary and librarian to Count von Waldstein of Bohemia, a position that gave him the opportunity to write his *Memoirs* (in twelve volumes). The memoirs were racy and described his amorous adventures and intrigues.

With the exception of Don Juan, Casanova was the unrivaled "Lover of Women," on whom he thrived. He employed bizarre tricks to lure them, such as the "oyster game," in which he and his woman friend would eat oysters from each other's mouths. As long as he could, he thrived on seduction, but death took away his pleasures at age seventy-three.

CASSANDRA

In Greek legend, *Cassandra*, the daughter of Hecuba and Priam, the king of Troy, was given the power to prophesy by Apollo; but the god, being sexually greedy, was keenly disappointed by Cassandra's refusal to let him partake of her favors. And so he brought it to pass that, although she could retain the gift of prophecy, no one would ever believe her. Thus her warnings about Troy's plight were ignored; and even though she foretold the fall of Troy, her prophecies were disregarded.

Before uttering her prophecies, Cassandra went into an ecstatic trance; her family believed her to be mad. When Paris, Cassandra's brother, first came to Troy, she realized his identity, although he had been exposed on Mount Ida as an infant and was unknown to his parents. She foretold the harm that Paris would do by going to Sparta (where he abducted Helen), and she also knew the dangers concealed within the Wooden Horse. But her warnings went entirely unheeded by the Trojans. And so the story ends; Troy was captured and burned.

In today's usage, a Cassandra is still regarded as a person whose prophecies go unheeded, but also is considered one who prophesies disaster.

CATHERINE WHEEL

St. Catherine of Alexandria in the year 307 A.D. supposedly suffered martyrdom when she protested the persecutions of Christians during the reign of Emperor Maximinus. She had adroitly defended the Christian faith at a public disputation with certain heathen philosophers, whereupon the emperor sentenced her to imprisonment. He became further incensed, however, upon learning that Catherine had won over to Christianity both his wife and the Roman general who escorted Catherine to prison. She was then ordered broken on the spiked wheel. According to one story, however, the wheel broke, and Catherine was then axed and her body carried to Mount Sinai by angels. Whether Catherine ever lived is a matter of dispute. Catholic scholars no longer give credence to the fabulous story of her martyrdom. But the name of a spiked wheel memorializes her, as does any circular window with radiating spokes, sometimes called a *rose window*.

A *Catherine wheel* is a kind of firework in the form of a wheel. It is driven round by the recoil from the explosion of the various squibs of which it is composed.

CELSIUS, CELSIUS SCALE

The centigrade thermometer has two constant degrees, a freezing point of water, namely 0°, and its boiling point, 100°. It is sometimes called the *Celsius scale* in honor of the person who simplified the Fahrenheit scale, which has a freezing point of 32° and a boiling point of 212°.

The centigrade temperature scale (its name was changed to Celsius in 1948 by a world conference on weights and measures) was an invention of Anders Celsius (1701–1744), born in Uppsala, Sweden. The son of an astronomy professor, young Celsius, after teaching mathematics, followed in his father's footsteps: He became a professor of astronomy at the University of Uppsala, where he devised the scale that bears his name. Celsius published a collection of 316 observations of the aurora borealis, or northern lights, and in 1744 built the Uppsala Observatory. He subsequently was able to verify through the measurement of a meridian in Lapland that Newton's hypothesis that the poles were somewhat flattened was correct.

Celsius first described the *Celsius scale* in a paper he read before the Swedish Academy of Science in 1742. Today the mercury thermometer patterned on this thermometric scale is the favored method in Europe of determining meterological temperature as well as the temperature of human beings.

Centigrade temperature can be converted to Fahrenheit by multiplying the centigrade reading by 1.8 and adding 32 to the result.

CERES, CEREAL

Ceres, the ancient Roman goddess of agriculture (identified with Greek Demeter), was patroness particularly of grain, or cereal, and plants. The Latin adjective form is *cerealis*, "relating to Ceres." She was especially the corn goddess, and, despite her many celestial responsibilities, found time to have a daughter by Jupiter, Proserpine. One day while playing in a field of daffodils, Proserpine was abducted by Pluto, king of Hades, who carried her off to rule as his queen. Ceres was frantic and could not be consoled. She neglected the fruits and grains and all withered and died.

The problem was confounded when a prolonged drought struck. The people prayed to Jupiter, the king of the gods in Roman mythology, for rain, and their prayers were answered. The rains came. Then Jupiter ordered Pluto to release Proserpine so that she could spend six months of the year with her mother. Ceres was so delighted that she let the grains grow high during Proserpine's period with her. The people were delighted, too, and they showed their gratitude by building temples in her honor and worshiped her in festivities called *Cerealia*.

We don't know whether Kellogg, Post, and the other manufacturers of American cereals pay homage to Ceres, but certainly the American people do as they eat their breakfast *cereal*.

CHAUVINIST, CHAUVINISM

Chauvinist and *chauvinism* were derived from the name of an overzealous French patriot named Nicolas Chauvin, of Rochefort. Chauvin, a veteran trooper in La Grande Armée, was wounded seventeen times while serving the First Republic and then the Empire under Napoleon. He had an exaggerated, almost fanatical admiration for the Corsican. He would not stop singing Napoleon's praises and the glories of France, and he was ridiculed for his unbridled boasting. He was caricatured by French playwrights Charles and Jean Cogniard, who were brothers, in *La Cocarde tricolore* ("Je suis français, je suis Chauvin"—I am French, I am Chauvin) and by Eugène Scribe in *Le Soldat Labourer*. The character of Chauvin was depicted in a number of other works, including *Conscript Chauvin* by Charet and *The Scarlet Pimpernel* by Baroness Orczy.

Chauvin would not recognize what has happened to the word denoting his adoration of Napoleon. Today a *chauvinist* may still of course refer to someone who mouths unreasoning patriotism, but it is far more frequently used by feminists to deride dispositions of male supremacy. Or it may represent a person who is an overzealous supporter of any cause.

Eugene Maleska, former crossword puzzle editor of *The New York Times*, cites this doggerel without attribution:

Poor Nicholas, how fickle is
The world you loved a lot;
Now you're condemned by angry femmes
For all that you were not.
But, sir, you rate some hoots of hate
As superpatriot!

CHESTERFIELD OVERCOAT

A *chesterfield coat* is a velvet-collared, single-breasted overcoat with concealed buttons reaching to the knees. The coat was designed by an Earl of Chesterfield. But which earl? There were at least five. A Chesterfield also gave his name to an overstuffed sofa and to a popular brand of cigarettes.

Philip Dormer Stanhope (1694–1773), the fourth Earl of Chesterfield, was the more prominent of the earls and probably the one for whom the foregoing items were named. Stanhope was an English writer and statesman whose name became a symbol of elegant manners and good breeding. But he is chiefly remembered for the *Letters* to his son written for his illegitimate son Philip Stanhope, published in 1774, a year after the earl's death. The work offered advice on affairs, courtly etiquette, and women.

Dr. Samuel Johnson, who thoroughly disliked the earl because he refused to become a patron of Johnson's *Dictionary*, described the *Letters* as "teaching the morals of a whore and the manners of a dancing master." When Chesterfield wrote favorably on the *Dictionary*, Johnson retorted: "Is not a patron, my lord, one who looks with unconcern on a man struggling for life in the water, and when he has reached ground encumbers him with help? The notice which you have been pleased to take of my labours, had it been early, had been kind; but it has been delayed till I am indifferent, and cannot enjoy it; till I am solitary, and cannot impart it; till I am known, and do not want it." Charles Dickens caricatured Chesterfield as Sir John Chester in *Barnaby Rudge* (1871). The opinions of these two popular writers contributed to Chesterfield's image as a cynical man of the world and a courtier. Careful readers of Chesterfield's letters, nevertheless, consider these opinions unjustified. Johnson's diatribe was not well-received by the literati.

The *Letters* contains homely counsel written in a witty and epigrammatical style. Among his quotations are "No idleness, no laziness, no procrastination; never put off till tomorrow what you can do today" and "Advice is seldom welcome; and those who want it the most always like it the least."

CHICKEN À LA KING

The origin of this dish, tasty enough for a king but not named in honor of one, is so controversial that word sleuths can make no sense of it. However, two possibilities seem to have attracted more "origin hunters" than any other.

The stronger possibility—diced chicken in a sherry-cream sauce—was served at the Claridge Hotel in London. This dish was dreamed up by its chef to honor J. R. Keene, who had won the Grand Prix in 1881. The name of this delectable comestible may have been *Chicken à la Keene*, a name later corrupted by changing *Keene* to *King*. But who knows?

And then again, some people attribute the invention to another Keene, the son of J. R. This Keene, with a forename of Foxhall, who modestly claimed that he was the world's greatest amateur athlete, may have suggested the recipe to the chef at New York's Delmonico, where presumably the name of the dish ended with a flourish of *à la Keene*, but not for long. The public lost interest in the Keenes, and *Chicken à la Keene* became *Chicken à la King*. However the dish got its name, first mentioned in print in 1912, it became a standard luncheon item, served from a chafing dish with rice or on a pastry shell.

CHIMERIC, CHIMERICAL

In today's language the adjective *chimeric*, or *chimerical*, means visionary, fantastic, unreal, or wildly improbable. The word stems from a mythological story of a she-monster named *Chimera*. This fire-breathing monster was represented as spewing flames and usually as having a lion's head, a goat's body, and a dragon's tail.

Chimera's doom stemmed from the fury of a woman scorned. Chimera was ravaging Lycia, in Asia Minor, and King Iobates sought a hero to destroy the monster. Coincidental with the king's search for a dragon slayer was the arrival of Bellerophon. He had been sent there with a sealed message from King Proteus of Argos demanding that Bellerophon be slain. King Proteus's wife had fallen in love with Bellerophon, but when he spurned her, she accused him of trying to seduce her. King Proteus was unwilling to kill him because he was a guest in Proteus's court. Hence his plan to have King Iobates execute the letter-bearer. Iobates figured out a good way to dispose of his guest and the Chimera simultaneously. He pitted Bellerophon against Chimera, fully expecting him to perish. But the ingenious youth had captured and tamed the winged Pegasus, surprised Chimera by riding above the dragon, and slew it with his bow and arrows.

CHURCHILL, CHURCHILLIANS

So much has been said and written about this greatest political figure in twentieth-century Britain that no one should expect anything original. Winston Leonard Spencer Churchill (1874–1965) was born at Blenheim Palace, in Oxfordshire, England, third son of politician Lord Randolph Churchill and his American wife, Jennie Jerome. He attended Harrow and Sandhurst and was commissioned in the Fourth Hussars. Churchill led an exciting life in different capacities and in different places. He changed his politics as he saw fit and, through the Liberal Party, was appointed lord of the admiralty in 1911. After active service in France, he became Lloyd George's minister of munitions and then secretary for war and air. He supported the Irish Free State and affirmed Palestine as a Jewish homeland. Churchill was out of the cabinet (but in Parliament) from 1929 to 1939, returning as the first lord of admiralty under Neville Chamberlain. The Germans invaded and conquered Norway, and he became prime minister on May 10, 1940. His refusal to consider Britain's defeat and his rallying phrases bolstered the spirit of Britons.

Churchill's rhetoric was well chosen, clear, and poignant. He was a scholar, and his words came from an unlimited mental library accumulated throughout his life. Among the outstanding Churchillians are "I have nothing to offer but blood, toil, tears and sweat"; "Never in the field of human conflict was so much owed by so many to so few"; and "the soft underbelly of the Axis." At Westminster College in Fulton, Missouri, where Churchill spoke at the invitation of President Truman, he declared that there had descended upon Europe "an iron curtain," cutting off the East from the rest of Europe. That phrase caught on and was repeated on innumerable occasions. Chagrined by the fall of France, he exclaimed, "Let us therefore brace ourselves that, if the British Empire and its Commonwealth last for a thousand years, men will say, 'This was their finest hour.'"

As happens to few persons, Churchill was made a citizen of the United States by a presidential proclamation issued by President Kennedy. It read: "In the dark days and darker nights when Britain stood alone—and most men save Englishmen despaired of England's life—he mobilized the English language and sent it into battle. The incandescent quality of his words illuminated the courage of his countrymen. Given unlimited powers by his fellow citizens, he was ever vigilant to protect their rights. Indifferent himself to danger, he wept over the sorrows of others. A child of the House of Commons, he became in time its father. Accustomed to the hardship of battle, he has no distaste for pleasure. By adding his name to our rolls, we mean to honor him—but his acceptance honors us far more. For no statement or proclamation can enrich his name—the name Winston Churchill is already a legend."

Churchill's Conservative Party was returned to power in 1951, with Churchill as prime minister. He resigned in 1955. His masterpiece *The Second World War* was published in six volumes.

In 1965 Queen Elizabeth and the royal family attended the funeral of Mr. Churchill. This was an unprecedented honor, as the queen does not attend funerals save those of family.

CLERIHEW

Edmund Clerihew Bentley (1875–1956) was a British journalist who became a detective-fiction writer; his best-known novel was *Trent's Last Case*. But Bentley was immortalized not by his novels, but by his humorous quatrains about a person or thing that he mentions in the first line. Bentley, according to G. K. Chesterton, could "write clear and unadulterated nonsense with . . . serious simplicity."

Bentley wrote the first clerihew when he was sixteen years old: "Sir Humphrey Davy/ Abominated gravy./ He lived in the odium/ Of having discovered sodium." Possibly the most well-known clerihew is "Sir Christopher Wren/ Said 'I'm going to dine with some men./ If anybody calls/ Say I'm designing St. Paul's.'"

Eventually Bentley published his clerihews as a book. It included: "George the Third/ Ought never to have occurred./ One can only wonder/ At so grotesque a blunder." And: "The art of Biography/ Is different from

Geography./ Geography is about Maps, / But Biography is about chaps."
Another: "It was a weakness of Voltaire's/ To forget to say his prayers, /
And which, to his shame, /He never overcame."

COLOGNE

The river Rhine, it is well known
Doth wash your city of Cologne;
But tell me, nymphs, what power divine
Shall henceforth wash the river Rhine?
    Coleridge

Cologne, a city on the Rhine, where "eau de cologne" was first made,
was founded in 38 B.C. as Ara Ubiorum. When the city became a Roman
colony in A.D. 50 its name was changed to *Colonia Agrippina* in honor
of the Roman empress Agrippina Minor (A.D. 15–59), who was born
there. Later the French modified the name to *Cologne*, and that is the
way it has remained in English.

Historians studying the life of Agrippina would all agree that the
city was entitled to a breath of fresh cologne, for the empress adulter-
ated everything around her during her brief (43 years) life. She poisoned at least one of her husbands, committed incest with her brother,
the emperor Caligula, and married her uncle, the emperor Claudius.
She was the mother of Nero by one of her husbands and was as ruthless as her son. Nero came to hate her, charged her with an attempt
on his life, and had her put to death. The empress, one might say, had
lived a pretty active life but suffered a ghastly end. The stench of her
nefarious activities, fortunately, has not affected the fragrance of the
city's colognes.

The cathedral of Cologne is famous because, according to medieval
legend, it houses the bones of the three Wise Men of the East, the
Magi.

COLOSSUS, COLOSSAL

Colossal is an ordinary word used by ordinary people, even though it
doesn't describe ordinary things. Its meaning, of course, is enormous in
size, extent, or degree. Its closest synonym is gigantic.

In ancient times the Colossus referred to the bronze *Colossus of
Rhodes*, a representation of the sun god Helios, built to commemorate
the successful defense of Rhodes against King Demetrius Poliorcetes of
Macedonia in 305 B.C. The Colossus was a huge statue erected across
the entrance of the harbor of Rhodes. Pliny, the Roman historian, tells
us that the statue was 70 cubits or more high, which, according to today's
measurements, means that it reached 120 feet heavenward and was so
large that ships could sail between its legs. The word *Colossus* (Latin,

from the Greek *Kolossos*, "large") referred only to the Colossus of Rhodes, one of the Seven Wonders of the Ancient World. English has acquired the word *colossal* from this humongous figure designed in 280 B.C. by a sculptor named Chares. In 224 B.C. disaster beset this monumental artwork when an earthquake toppled it.

Shakespeare's *Julius Caesar* immortalized this ancient statue when Cassius described the title character to Brutus:

> Why, man, he doth bestride the narrow world
> Like a *Colossus*; and we petty men
> Walk under his high legs, and peep about
> To find ourselves dishonorable graves.

COLT, COLT REVOLVER

Samuel Colt (1814–1862) was born and raised in Hartford, Connecticut. He received little education, and at the age of sixteen (some say thirteen) he ran away from home and became a seaman. The story is that he spent his nights on deck whittling a pistol that turned out to be the model for the *Colt revolver*, which he patented in 1835 and then manufactured.

His patent covered the first practical revolver, a single-barreled pistol with a revolving cylinder. The general idea was not original, but Colt used a rotating barrel of six chambers, and his cocking device is still used as a model for revolvers. His gun became the universal pistol: the gun of the Midwest; the gun of the cowboys; the gun for military service. It came to be known as the gun that won the West.

Colt was not immediately successful. His firearm was used in the Seminole War (1837) and then in the fracas between Texas and Mexico. Thereafter the demand for the gun lay dormant.

What turned things around in Colt's favor was a large order for guns from the United States Army during the Mexican War (1846–1848). Colt then went from strength to strength, becoming one of the world's biggest manufacturers of pistols and one of the wealthiest men in America. His revolver came to be known as "the six-shooter," and that term became generic for all revolvers, no matter who manufactured them.

COMSTOCKERY

Comstockery, an overzealous censorship of literature and other forms of art, was coined by George Bernard Shaw in reference to Anthony Comstock (1844–1915). People in this day and age may have a hard time believing that one narrow-minded person had the power to ban all the books and plays he felt were corrupting. But Comstock succeeded at doing it. And not simply banned: About 160 tons of books, stereotyped plates, magazines, and pictures were destroyed.

Comstock was the founder of the New York Society for the Suppression of Vice, an organization that advocated the banning of all literature deemed to be salacious or corrupting. Comstock did the deeming—he was the self-appointed censor of books, plays, and pictures. He also led many campaigns against abortion, birth control, and pornography. Through his influence certain types of literature, especially that concerning birth control, were excluded from the mail by federal passage of the *Comstock laws*. Appointed special agent of the Post Office Department, he arrested more than three thousand persons supposedly in violation of the laws that bear his name. The *Comstock Postal Act*, in H. L. Mencken's words, "greatly stimulated the search for euphemisms": Pregnant became "enceinte," syphilis and gonorrhea were changed to "social diseases," and so forth.

The inquisitor took aim at Shaw's play *Mrs. Warren's Profession*. Shaw retaliated when he coined the word *comstockery*. Thus the self-righteous moral censor has attained a dubious immortality.

Inspired by Comstock's censorious repression of thought and with Comstock as the guiding spirit, Boston's *Watch and Ward Society* was organized in 1876. The society proved to be ever vigilant in guarding the morals of the good burghers of Boston. Publishers were pleased to have their books banned because to advertise that a book was "banned in Boston" was a sure way of spurring sales throughout the nation.

CONFUCIAN, CONFUCIANISM

Confucius, known by the name of Kung Chiu, was a great Chinese philosopher, a recognized sage of China. His most famous remark, as apt today as it was when first uttered, was "What you do not like done to yourself, do not unto others." The ethical concepts of this man of tremendous influence are still the ideals of millions of people. His maxims dealt not with religion, but with morals (emphasizing one's virtue), the family (including remembrance of one's ancestors), social reforms, and statecraft.

The father of Confucius, a courageous soldier of royal descent, died when his son was three years old. The boy's mother had little money, but she gave him the best education that she could. At fifteen, Confucius mastered the teachings of the holy sages whose influence had made China a wise and united nation.

Confucius taught his followers that the secret of good government was in choosing honest and educated officials. At one time Confucius was appointed to a high position in the government of Lu, and he performed so well that he was considered the premier statesman in all of China. But he was subsequently forced to resign by a jealous duke. Confucius then traveled from place to place to find a prince who would listen to him. But his principles of good government were misunderstood or ignored by the rulers of his time.

Confucius taught for fifty years, yet died practically unknown. The publication after his death of the *Five Classics*, which recorded his wise teachings, became the bible of *Confucianism* and the ethical guide for his followers, which then grew in number.

Today the grave of Confucius is a place of homage.

COPERNICAN SYSTEM

The heliocentric or sun-centered theory of the universe was postulated by a great Polish astronomer, Nicolaus Copernicus (1473–1543). For more than fourteen hundred years people had accepted the system of Ptolemy, namely, that the sun moved round the earth. That the opposite is true—that the planets revolved round the sun—had been considered many years before by the School of Pythagoras. Thanks to Copernicus, scientists have all come to agree that the sun is the center of the system of planets (the heliocentric theory), and that knowledge has become the foundation of modern astronomy.

Although friends of Copernicus urged him to publish his masterwork *Concerning the Revolution of the Celestial Spheres*, he hid his publication for many years, for he knew that, although he was dedicating his work to Pope Paul III, a mind dominated by theology could not admit into its thinking scientific facts that might conflict with his beliefs. He was right, of course. The book was published when Copernicus was lying on his deathbed, and it was promptly placed on the Index of Forbidden Books.

Copernicus was born in Thorn, Prussian Poland. He studied astronomy and mathematics at the University of Cracow, and then spent three years at the University of Bologna, where he also studied Greek and philosophy. He decided on a career with the church, becoming a canon at the Cathedral of Frauenburg, East Prussia. Although he remained at that post until his death, his chief interest was in astronomy.

COUÉISM

Emile Coué (1857–1926) was born at Troyes, France, and worked as a pharmacist from 1882 to 1910. During that period he studied hypnotism and autosuggestion. He acquired an unshakable belief that people could control their health, and possibly improve their personalities, by convincing themselves that they were improving. Mind over matter, some might say.

Coué accordingly established a free clinic at Nancy where he practiced a form of psychotherapy dependent upon autosuggestion, a method known as *Couéism*. "This method," he declared, "clears the mind of the causes of mental and physical ailments." Coué became well-known and lectured extensively in the United States and England. He advocated that distressing ideas be eliminated from the subconscious and suggested the repetition of his key phrase: "Every day in every way, I'm getting better and better." He explained his theories in several books, the best-known one, published in 1922, was titled *Self-Mastery Through Conscious Auto-suggestion*.

COULOMB, COULOMB'S LAW

Charles Augustin de Coulomb (1736–1806), born into a French noble family, had available all the advantages for a good education. He attended the engineering school at Mézieres, the first school of its kind, where he showed a remarkable aptitude in mathematics. He received an excellent practical and theoretical education and decided on a career as a physicist with the Royal Corps of Engineers, one of the few careers open to a person of his noble birth. He retired as a physicist from the French military at age fifty-three because of poor health.

Coulomb pursued his interest in experimentation with electricity and magnetism, work he had begun while in the military, and invented a torsion balance system for measuring the force of magnetic and electric attraction. To understand his many findings, one must be an astute student in his field. For example, a *coulomb* is the quantity of charge transferred in one second by a current of one ampere. By international agreement, one coulomb is the quantity of electricity that deposits 0.00118 of a gram of silver. Coulomb published a treatise on the strength of materials which introduced methods still in use today.

In 1777, Coulomb's magnetic compasses won a prize offered by the French Academy of Sciences, one of the world's most prestigious institutions.

COXEY'S ARMY

Jacob Sechler Coxey (1854–1951), the wealthy owner of a quarry in Massillon, Ohio, had bills introduced in Congress to stimulate employment. The year following the Panic of 1893, a time when many people were unemployed, Coxey wanted Congress to enact bills for road building and public construction to put the unemployed to work. To publicize his ideas, he arranged for a march on Washington that would dramatize the need for congressional action and exert pressure on congressmen to vote for the bills.

Coxey began his march with a band of unemployed workers from Massillon on Easter Sunday, 1894. About 100 marchers and a six-piece band began the trek. The group swelled to about 500, but not the 100,000 that Coxey had expected. In any event, upon reaching the capital, about 50 marchers were clubbed by the police, and Coxey, who sought to read a speech that he had prepared, was denied the privilege. He was arrested for carrying a banner and walking on the Capitol lawn and was sentenced to twenty days. That was the grand finale of this makeshift army that was given the name *Coxey's army*. The bills died in committee.

Coxey was obsessed with a desire to hold public office. Although a perennial candidate, he was elected only once, as mayor of Massillon, 1931–1933. But his ideas were similar to those adopted by the New Deal under President Roosevelt, and on May 1, 1944, on the Capitol steps, Coxey achieved his long-delayed goal: He delivered his speech. And this time without interference.

People sometimes call a motley, ragtag group "Coxey's Army." The name is particularly evocative when a bunch of kids with bats slung over their shoulders, with torn pants, with their caps turned backwards, are seen marching off to the baseball field.

Coxey, who lived for ninety-seven years, had at one time become so fascinated with monetary problems that he wrote several books on the subject and named one of his sons Legal Tender.

CRAPPER

The person to whom we are indebted for the flushing toilet is Thomas Crapper, the scatologists' favorite son.

Sir Thomas Crapper (1837–1910) was born in Yorkshire, England. In the 1870s, he invented the modern toilet bowl, which consisted of a float, a metal arm, and siphonic action to empty the reservoir, enabling the bowl to be flushed without having the water run continuously. Crapper was known as the inventor of the water-waste preventer, and that became the name of this product when first used in England.

An invention by the ancient Romans carried away human waste. Crapper's invention made the use of the bowl more efficient in that it shut off the running water after it had served its purpose, and he thus made a lasting contribution to our comfort.

Crapper's name is an unlucky coincidence. The Dutch, through their word *krappe* ("scraps"), gave us *crap*, which for centuries has been used for excrement. But *crap* is more often used to mean nonsense: "What you're telling me is a lot of crap."

CROESUS

Croesus, the last king of Lydia, reigned from about 560 to 546 B.C. He was reputed to be the wealthiest man in the world, and from this reputation we have the eponym *Croesus*, meaning an extremely wealthy man. He had subjugated the Ionian cities and made the Greeks in Asia Minor tributary to him. The fame of his power and wealth drew many of the wisest Greeks to his court at Sardis, among them Aesop and Solon. His interview with Solon was celebrated in antiquity. In reply to Croesus's question, "Who is the happiest man you have ever seen?" Solon taught the king that no man should be deemed happy till he finishes his life in a happy way.

In a war with Cyrus, king of Persia, the army of Croesus was defeated, and his capital, Sardis, was taken. Croesus was condemned by the conqueror to be burned to death. As he stood before the pyre, the warning of Solon came to his mind, and he thrice uttered the name *Solon*. Cyrus inquired who it was whom he called on. Upon hearing the story, he reprieved his victim, and not only spared his life but made him his friend. Croesus survived Cyrus and, in a show of his friendship in return, accompanied Cambyses, son of Cyrus, in his expedition against Egypt.

In Mark Twain's *Tom Sawyer*, Huck Finn said, "Rich as creosote." Tom replied, "Rich as Croesus, you mean."

CURIE, CURIUM, POLONIUM

Pierre and Marie Curie deserve a place in the scientific heavens. They refused to patent their inventions or receive any money from them. Their interest was in pure science and the good that could come to people from it, *pro bono publico*.

Pierre Curie (1859–1906) was born in Paris. He taught at the Paris School of Physics and Chemistry and then became professor of physics at the Sorbonne. In 1895, Pierre married Marie Sklodowska (1867–1934), a twenty-eight-year old student born in Warsaw, Poland, where her father taught physics.

Marie had achieved a brilliant record at high school, but could find no outlet for her talents in her native country; the University of Warsaw did not admit women. She began research, nevertheless, on the magnetic properties of different kinds of steel. Marie had financed her sister Bronia's medical studies in Paris, and Bronia, in turn, invited Marie to come to Paris. She did in 1891 and resumed her studies in mathematics, physics, and chemistry at the Sorbonne. There she met many prominent physicists, including the man she was to marry, Pierre Curie. After her marriage, she and Pierre combined their scientific interests.

The Curies were responsible for so many discoveries and laws of nature that it would take a large volume to document and explain them. It took the Curies four years of work to extract one gram of radium salt from pitchblende, to prove that radium was a new radioactive substance. Together with Antoine Henri Becquerel (1852–1908) in 1903 they received the Nobel Prize in physics for the discovery of radioactivity. In 1898, while working with pitchblende, Marie found a new metal, which she named *polonium* (atomic number 84) in honor of her native Poland.

A few years after their discovery of radium, Pierre was run over by a wagon on the rue Dauphine in Paris. He died instantly. Marie succeeded her husband as physics professor at the Sorbonne, the first woman to hold that distinguished position. She continued her research and in 1911 became the first person to receive the Nobel Prize twice, this time in chemistry for isolating radium. She also was the first woman honored by membership in the French Academy of Medicine. No scientist has received more honors in a lifetime than Marie Curie, and no one has received honors more graciously. She was the most celebrated woman of her time.

When, in 1921, Marie made a triumphant visit to the United States, President Warren G. Harding presented her with a gram of radium bought as the result of a collection among American women. Its value at that time was $100,000. Marie used the radium in her research. Again in 1929, during another visit to the United States, the women gave her a similiar gift of the precious metal, the proceeds from which she used to establish a research institute in Warsaw.

Ironically, it was Curie's long exposure to radiation that made her ill. A Swiss doctor, examining her blood tests, diagnosed "pernicious anemia in its extreme form." His report of her death read "aplastic pernicious anemia of rapid, feverish development. The bone marrow did not react, probably because it had been injured by a long accumulation of radiations."

Daughter Irene Joliet-Curie and her husband, Frédéric Joliot (who changed his name by adding Curie) in 1934 discovered a method of producing artificial radioactivity. Another daughter, Eve, became a well-known writer. Her book *Madame Curie*, an acclaimed biography of her mother, was published in twenty-five languages.

A unit in measuring the activity of a radioactive substance is named *curie*. A violently radioactive chemical element was named *curium* (atomic number 96) for Marie and Pierre Cuire by Glenn Seaborg and his colleagues.

CYNIC, ANTISTHENES

The word *cynic* has undergone a complete turnabout in meaning in the last two thousand years. The Cynic school of philosophy was founded by Antisthenes (born about 440 B.C.), a pupil of Socrates. He took as his starting point the doctrine of his great teacher that virtue rather than pleasure is the chief end of life and constitutes true happiness. From this starting point he argued that because continued happiness is not possible if one has wants and desires that are not satisfied, the wise person is one who looks with contempt on all the ordinary pleasures of life, and lives without regard for riches or honors. Antisthenes had few students because the philosophy he taught required too great an asceticism to be pleasing.

Among the most enthusiastic followers of Antisthenes was Diogenes, who carried the principles of the school to extremes, but was probably responsible for making the school so famous.

The sect took its name from the *Cynsarges*, the name of the Greek building, a gymnasium, where the Cynics first met. This gymnasium was outside the walls of Athens. Antisthenes was required to meet his students there because his mother was not an Athenian by birth. Others say the name came from the Greek word for *dog*, referring to the rudeness of the Cynics, and still others say the name came from a white dog because a white dog had carried away a part of the sacrifice the school offered to Hercules. In Greek *Cynosarges* meant "white dog."

Since the essence of the cynic was self-control and independence, it is odd that the present English meaning is almost opposite, for today's cynic is one who believes all men are motivated by vulgar selfishness.

CYRANO DE BERGERAC

Savinien Cyrano de Bergerac (1619–1655), a Gascon, is one of the few men in history who have become famous because of a prodigious nose. (Jimmy Durante more recently parlayed his nose into a successful movie career and nightclub appearances.) Cyrano was constantly being insulted because of his proboscis and had to fight many duels to vindicate it. His duel single-handedly against a hundred enemies while serving as an officer in the Guards has been documented. It is said that Cyrano fought over a thousand duels.

Cyrano's name became a household word in 1897 when a play, *Cyrano de Bergerac*, written by Edmond Rostand, attained remarkable success. The play was founded on Cyrano's adventures and his many romantic exploits, of which the most poignant was his romantic victory over Roxanne. Although Cyrano captured her love through his ardent letters, he did not seek her for himself but for his friend Christian. Cyrano was such a loyal friend that he did not reveal the deception even after Christian's death. Since then many renowned actors, with false nose attached, have enjoyed interpreting Cyrano's life and his activities.

Cyrano did not die as a result of a sword wound, as some would have you believe, but as a result of an injury caused by a falling object in a house where he was a guest. No one knows whether it fell or was thrown.

CYRIL, CYRILLIC ALPHABET

The alphabet used in the Soviet Union and some other Slavic countries is the *cyrillic alphabet*, a modified Greek alphabet. The author of this invention has never been satisfactorily established, but the name *Cyril* has been attached to it, and it is commonly known as the *cyrillic alphabet*.

Saint Cyril (827–869) and Saint Methodius (825–885) were brothers and Greek churchmen. The brothers were born in Solon, a principal city in Macedonia, and their father was a nobleman of imperial Byzantium. Cyril's secular name was Constantine. He received a fine education and became a librarian to Hagia Sophia, a patriarch of the church, but resigned after a short time to enter a monastery where his brother was studying.

Having acquired a knowledge of Slavic, the brothers were sent to teach the gospel to the Slavs in Moravia. Some time later, the neighboring Germans charged them with heresy. Pope Nicholas I recalled them and exonerated them. The brothers then began a translation of the liturgy and the Bible into Slavic. Saint Methodius actually finished the work, even though the name of the alphabet is Saint Cyril's. Constantine adopted the name *Cyril* during his last illness, Cyril being his patron saint.

DAGUERREOTYPE

The man responsible for "permanent photography" was Louis Jacques Mandé Daguerre (1789–1851), born in Cormeilles-en-Parisis, Seine-et-Oise, France. An artist and a pioneer in photography, Daguerre began his adult life in Paris as a theatrical scenery painter. In 1822, he established the Diorama, a theatrical spectacle that exhibited large panoramic paintings on a transparent canvas illuminated on both sides. The Diorama was housed in a circular building with a revolving floor, enabling spectators to stand at one spot and see everything. The Diorama in Paris was so successful that another was built in Regent's Square in London. The newer one was destroyed by fire in 1839, the year the *daguerreotype* came into general use.

Daguerre's *idée fixe* had been to invent a permanent photographic image. He devoted so much of his time experimenting that his wife, complaining of "malodorous vapors" to no avail, wondered whether he was losing his mind. She had one of his colleagues look in on him. After visiting the workroom, the colleague assured her that her fears were unfounded.

Daguerre became friendly with Joseph Niépce, a Frenchman engaged in a similar photographic process and whose photograph was the first to become permanently fixed, made from sunlight using either glass or paper plates. Daguerre and Niépce became working partners until Niépce's death in 1833. In 1839 Daguerre discovered a proper formula for making a permanent picture, his *daguerreotype process*—an impression made on a light-sensitive, silver-coated metallic plate treated with iodine vapor. Exposure time was reduced from about eight hours to fifteen minutes.

Daguerre's fame was meteoric; he received international acclaim. The halls in which Daguerre's invention was exhibited could not accommodate the crowds. People throughout the world were spellbound. Daguerre was honored by the French Legion of Honor and, after selling his invention to the French government, received, together with Niépce's heirs, a pension for life.

The *daguerreotype* had a major fault: it could not be reproduced. This photographic process was gradually replaced by one invented by an Englishman, W. H. Fox Talbot, whose calotype process enabled a print to be replicated many times from just one negative.

How fleeting is fame based on technological improvement! In 1851 the wet-plate process, which also produced multiple images, but with sharper detail, was invented by another Englishman, Frederick Scott Archer, and it superseded the *daguerreotype* in the photographic field.

DAHLIA

The original *dahlia* was discovered in Mexico. It was a stiff, plain-looking flower with eight red rays around a yellow center.

Dahlias now have almost every kind of shape and color. Some are shaped like balls; others have long, flat petals; one variety has double blossoms with long, twisted petals.

Dahlias are native to tropical America but are now grown throughout the United States, in southern Canada, and Europe. Today thousands of varieties have been crossed and cultivated from the single plant.

The person deserving the credit for this popular flower was Baron Alexander von Humboldt, a German naturalist who, in 1789, during a scientific exploration in Mexico, first spotted it. He sent a specimen to Spain, where the flower was named by Professor Cavanilles, of the Madrid Botanic Garden. But the flower was not named Humboldt; instead the honor was given to Anders Dahl (1751–1789), a fellow professor of Cavanilles and a Swedish botanist, a former pupil of Carolus Linnaeus, a Swedish botanist and taxonomist.

DALTONISM

John Dalton (1766–1844) was the consummate scientist. His interests embraced research, theories, and experimentation.

Dalton was not permitted to attend Cambridge or Oxford because those schools were open only to members of the Church of England, and Dalton was born a Quaker. So determined was he to make something of himself that, although primarily self-taught (he had only an elementary-school education), he pursued his interests with complete dedication, eventually becoming president of the Philosophical Society, an honorary office he held until his death.

Dalton's study of gases led to the development of partial pressure, known as Dalton's law. His meteorological surveys laid the groundwork for his atomic theory, for which he was elected to the Royal Society and awarded a medal.

Dalton and his brother were color blind. For this personal reason he devoted research time to this visual defect and was the first to describe the condition in a paper titled *Extraordinary Facts Relating to the Vision of Colours* (1794). Sir David Brewster (1781–1868), the inventor of the kaleidoscope, later introduced the term *color blindness* to denote defective color vision.

With a vision for the future, John Dalton willed his eyes to science to further the study of color blindness. *Daltonism* has become a synonym for color blindness.

DAMOCLES, DAMOCLEAN

The story of the sword of Damocles, told by the Roman orator Cicero, points out that perils and responsibilities often accompany royalty. It also symbolizes the uncertainty of human greatness and life in general. When we say "hanging by a thread" we mean being in imminent danger, a danger that may be described as *damoclean*.

Damocles was a courtier of Dionysius the Elder (430–367), who in the fifth century was the ruler—or tyrant—of the Sicilian city-state Syracuse. Dionysius distrusted him because he knew Damocles was a sycophant. The king grew tired of hearing Damocles extolling the tyrant's wealth, power, virtue, and felicity. Deciding to teach the sycophant the real perils of power, King Dionysius suggested that Damocles try the delights of absolute power for himself, an offer Damocles eagerly accepted.

Dionysius ordered that a huge banquet be prepared, that Damocles be laid on a bed of solid gold, that he be perfumed and massaged, and that his every whim be met by a bevy of the tyrant's servants. Damocles was having a wonderful time, enjoying the feast and all the attention he was getting, until he happened to look up and see that above him was a sharp sword suspended by a single hair. The courtier was so distraught that he immediately lost his appetite and abandoned the feast. The sumptuous repast set before him no longer had appeal.

DAMON AND PYTHIAS

The story behind the tribulation of Pythias at the hands of the tyrant Dionysius the Elder is legendary. Also legendary is the essence of friendship—the comradeship that enables two people to breathe as one—which has been most poignantly depicted by the lives of *Damon* and *Pythias*, Pythagoreans of Syracuse in Sicily.

When Pythias was condemned to death for conspiring against the tyrant, he sought the privilege of returning home to arrange his affairs. To assure Dionysius that Phythias would return, Damon pledged his life as a hostage, an arrangement that the despot accepted. Phythias went home, but his return was delayed. As Damon was being led to the executioner's block, his friend arrived just in time to save him. Dionysius was so deeply impressed by this depth of friendship that he pardoned Pythias and entreated the two to allow him to join their brotherhood.

Damon and Pythias has become a classical reference meaning two inseparable friends. According to the Greek version, the names of these noble figures are *Damon* and *Phintias*. Correctly put, therefore, is the phrase *Phintias and Damon*. In a play written by Richard Edwards in 1564, the title was switched to *Damon and Pythias*, a title that has held through the centuries.

DARWINISM

Charles Robert Darwin (1809–1882) was born in Shrewsbury, England, where he attended school. His grades were far from distinguished. His father was disgusted and reproved him: "You care for nothing but shooting, dogs, and rat catching, and you will be a disgrace to yourself and all your family." Young Darwin was then sent to Edinburgh to study medicine. This he refused to do because he didn't like the subject. Next he was sent to Cambridge to prepare for the ministry, but Darwin ignored his ministerial studies because of his interest in natural history.

In 1831, the Royal Navy's H.M.S. *Beagle* was about to sail on a scientific voyage. Darwin signed on for this five-year trip so that he might have an excellent firsthand opportunity to make geological observations. Darwin's interest in evolution came later, after he had found fossils that sparked an interest in that subject. Darwin wrote about his experiences on the voyage shortly after arriving home, but his revolutionary work *The Origin of Species by Natural Selection* was not published until November 24, 1859. The book sold out immediately and created quite a furor in theological quarters. It represented a blow to religious opinions, because it replaced belief in the divine creation of species by a natural selection of viable variations and implied that man was not unique but similar to other animals, a theory known as *Darwinism*.

Theologians defended themselves by vociferous condemnations of Darwin's theses. But the Church of England has never attacked *Darwinism*—evolution by natural selection—or, as Herbert Spencer called it, "survival of the fittest."

Darwin's most avid defender was the biologist Thomas Henry Huxley, who coined the word *agnostic* and who was known as "Darwin's Bulldog," for he willingly took on anyone who spoke deprecatingly about evolution. He once told Darwin, "Get on with your work, and leave the wrestling to me."

During Darwin's voyage on the *Beagle*, he was bitten by a large bug that causes Chagas's disease. He became a semi-invalid and lived in constant pain. Darwin was buried in Westminster Abbey.

DAVY CROCKETT HAT

Davy Crockett, Davy Crockett
The man who knows no fear
Davy Crockett, Davy Crockett
King of the wild frontier.

Many distinguished fighters and frontiersmen were killed in the famous battle of the Alamo. Among them was David Crockett, popularly known as Davy Crockett. Crockett (1786–1836) was one of the great scouts during the pioneer days of America. He was also a soldier and a United States congressman.

Crockett was born in Limestone, Greene County, Tennessee. He ran away from home on his fourth day at school and didn't return until he was twelve, whereupon his father hired him out to a passing cattle driver. Although Crockett did not learn to read until he was eighteen, he became wise in the ways of wild frontier life. During the Creek War, he became a colonel in the Tennessee militia under Andrew Jackson. He then went into politics, and, accepting a humorous suggestion, ran for Congress—and was elected. He served for two terms, and his natural wit and homespun stories made him a noted character. His motto was "Be sure you're right, and then go ahead."

After his defeat for re-election to Congress—he had opposed President Jackson's banking and Indian policies—he moved to Texas and joined the war for independence from Mexico. Crockett was warmly welcomed, what with his frontier and political background and his fame as an expert marksman. He was killed on March 6, 1836, at the Alamo, as were James Bowie and other defenders.

Crockett was known for his frontier hat, which he wore constantly, a fur hat with a distinctive tailpiece. Crockett's visual attire made him known in Washington, D.C. as the "coonskin congressman."

He is believed to be the author of the witty but unsophisticated books A *Narrative of the Life of David Crockett*, A *Tour of the North and Down East*, and *Exploits and Adventures in Texas*. He may have dictated these books, but they were written with his robust style and homespun humor.

DAVY LAMP, DAVY MEDAL

Sir Humphrey Davy
Abominated gravy.
He lived in the odium
Of having discovered sodium.

This was the first clerihew written by Edmund Bentley. And although there's no record of Sir Humphrey Davy's dislike of gravy, it is true that he discovered sodium. He also is credited with many other important discoveries that have been beneficial for mankind and have been a boon to science. For example, he discovered the exhilarating effect of nitrous oxide, dubbed "laughing gas." He isolated sodium, potassium, and strontium by passing an electric current through fused soda, potash, and strontia. For this achievement alone, Davy was regarded as one of the greatest chemists.

But Davy's remarkable invention, one that saved many lives, was the

Davy lamp, a lamp made for miners. Its safety feature was an enclosed cage of fine-meshed wire that prevented high heat from escaping to ignite explosive gases in the mines. The *Davy lamp* has been replaced by modern mining lamps, but it saved untold numbers of lives during the many years of its use.

Davy (1778–1829) was the son of a poor wood carver in Penzance, Cornwall, England. When twenty-two, he was appointed assistant lecturer for the Royal Institute, London. During the next year, he became a professor of chemistry there; he was knighted by the British king in 1812 and was thereafter invited to visit France, where he was also honored.

Davy was presented by grateful coal mine owners with an expensive silver dining service. He asked that it be melted down to cover expenses for a *Davy medal,* to be "given annually for the most important discovery in chemistry made anywhere in Europe or Anglo-America."

DECIBEL, BEL

"Watson, come here, I want you" was the first sentence ever spoken over a telephone. On March 10, 1876, in a house in Boston, Alexander Graham Bell (1847–1922) uttered those historic words. The message carried, and the telephone was born.

For those wondering why Bell said something so ordinary on such an auspicious occasion, the reason was that Bell had spilled some acid on himself and needed help from his laboratory assistant, Thomas Watson.

Bell was born in Scotland, but became a naturalized citizen of the United States in 1871. His interest was in teaching the deaf (both his mother and his wife were deaf). Bell became a professor of vocal physiology at Boston University, where he continued his work on telephonic communication. He founded *Science,* the official publication of the Association for the Advancement of Science, was president of the National Geographic Society, and a regent of the Smithsonian Institution.

The *decibel,* one-tenth of a *bel* (*bel* is a clipped version of the inventor's name), is the least audible sound to the human ear. For the technically minded, *decibel* is a unit used to compare two power levels on a logarithmic scale. People hear from 0 to 130 decibels. Above that figure, sound becomes painful to the ear. Most conversations take place at about 60 decibels.

As with some other momentous inventions, the question arose: Who was the first to invent the telephone? There were a number of claimants, but after a decade of litigation, Bell emerged the victor and helped organize the giant American Telephone and Telegraph Company, popularly known as AT&T.

DERBY, KENTUCKY DERBY

The famous Derby (pronounced där-bē), an annual horse race at Epsom Down, England, takes place in Surrey, southwest of London. Although races had been held since the reign of James I, successor to Queen Elizabeth, it was Edward Stanley, the twelfth Earl of Derby (1752–1834), an avid amateur sportsman, who offered a prize in 1780 for an annual race of three-year-old colts, later including fillies. Restricting the race to three-year-olds assured that a horse could win only once.

The flip of a coin decided the name *Derby*, since Sir John Hawkewood was also instrumental in introducing the race. Derby won the flip, but Hawkewood's horse won the race, the first of the Derby races.

The running of the Derby was most festive. The day was called "Derby Day," and fashionable house parties that accompanied the event grew more and more lavish throughout the years. People flocked to Epsom Downs, and the entire area was decorated as if for a country fair. To make the event pseudo-official, Parliament adjourned for the day.

The name *Derby* became generic for a horse racing event, and other countries came to call their important race "The Derby." In the United States the most prominent day for the racing of the best horses is called the "Kentucky Derby," and in France, the "French Derby." The word has also become applied to other competitions, as in "soapbox derby."

A dome-shaped hat is called a bowler in England; in America, a *derby*. It is said that a New York retail clerk, when selling this hat, told his customers that the hat was commonly worn in England and always at the *Derby*. Hence the name for this hard hat. Or was the hat named in honor of the earl? Or his horse race? Take your pick, as you would a horse at Epsom Downs.

DERRICK

Anyone who has ever been a sidewalk engineer—an ogler at workers erecting a building—has seen a crane lifting and moving steel beams and other heavy objects. This crane is called a *derrick*.

Today a derrick is used in the construction of something useful to mankind. Many years ago, however, a derrick was used solely for the destruction of mankind; it was a device to hang people. And only the common people at that. Nobility was accorded the courtesy of beheading.

This gruesome word was named after Godfrey Derrick. Whether he actually invented the gallows that bear his name is unclear but as the official executioner for Queen Elizabeth I and James I, his qualifications assured him a place in the dictionary. Derrick (or Derick) was said to have hanged or beheaded at least three thousand persons.

Derrick came to his job in an odd way. According to a story during

Elizabeth's reign, Derrick was convicted of rape while serving under the provost marshal in the expedition to Cadiz headed by the second Earl of Essex, Robert Devereaux. For this crime he was sentenced to death. But the earl pardoned him when he agreed to become the executioner in London. Ironically, when Essex himself, a onetime favorite of the queen, was condemned to death in 1601, Derrick was his executioner. As a nobleman, Essex was not to be subjected to the indignity of hanging. He was entitled to be beheaded, which was Derrick's responsibility. But Derrick botched the job on the block. He hacked three times at Essex's neck before he severed the head. Essex's friends were so incensed that they rushed Derrick to give him the same treatment he had given Essex. Fortunately for Derrick, guards reached him in time to rescue him.

> He rides circuit with the devil,
> and Derrick must be his host,
> And Tyborne the inn at which he
> will light.
> Dekker, *Bellman of London* (1608)

DERRINGER

Henry Deringer (1786–1868) was a successful manufacturer of squirrel rifles in Philadelphia, the city in which he was born. The rifles worked so well that the demand for them became nationwide.

Deringer then turned his talents to the manufacturing of a short-barreled, wide-bore pocket pistol, with a grip shaped like the head of a bird. It was a single-shot, muzzle-loading percussion pistol that could easily be carried by politicians in a vest pocket or, during the Gay Nineties, concealed by chorus girls in their bosom or other handy place in their clothing. The pistols became exceedingly popular as weapons of defense.

The demand for the gun was so great that the competitors tried all kinds of tricks to duplicate it. One manufacturer even changed the name to *derringer* (with two r's) in an effort to avoid infringement of patent and copyright laws. And it was the spelling of this wildcat version that stuck.

DEWEY DECIMAL SYSTEM

One classification system used by libraries was devised by Melvil Dewey (1851–1931), the father of American library science. The number on the spine of a library book identifies its position on a shelf through a system known as the *Dewey Decimal System*, which is now employed by more than 85 percent of libraries in the United States.

Dewey, born in Adams Center, New York, devised his classification apparatus while a student and acting librarian at Amherst College. In

1876, when Dewey was only in his twenties, he completed his method for classifying publications and published his system under the title *Classification and Subject Index for Cataloguing and Arranging the Books and Pamphlets of a Library.*

Subsequently he helped found the American Library Association, the New York Library Association, and the *Library Journal*, for which he served as first editor. In 1883 Dewey became librarian of Columbia College (now Columbia University), where in 1887 he established the country's first professional school of library science.

Dewey's system used numbers from 000 to 999, dividing the general fields of knowledge into nine main classes, all of which can be subdivided out to several decimal places.

A system of classification was devised at the International Institute of Bibliography in Brussels. It extends the Dewey system, on which it is based, by using various symbols as well as Arabic numerals. The Library of Congress letter/number system provides more flexibility, however, for large collections.

In 1889, Dewey introduced another innovation to facilitate the reading of books, the traveling library, now popularly called the "bookmobile." This system has been of particular importance to the rural community where access to public libraries is inconvenient.

DICKENSIAN

Charles Dickens (1812–1870) was one of the most popular English novelists, and the most popular of his lifetime. He became the recognized exponent of the English Victorian character. His conscience became the public voice of England, awakening the people to the plight of the victims of industrial progress. He expressed a simplified worldview in which good and evil are clear-cut opposites, and his characters, like the world they operate in, have a simplicity of motivation and emotion. These characters, described in such detail that they seem larger than life, are certainly more memorable than most "realistic" characters. They were cruel or suffering, comic or repugnant, as only Dickens could delineate. The characters possessed a myriad of odd gestures, speech patterns, and physiognomies. His general style is usually powerful and persuasive in direct narrative and description.

As a social critic, Dickens focused sharply on the iniquities and inequities of his environment. He revealed the masses to the classes.

Because of Dickens's novels, English people have made noticeable progress in many fields, for he faced the stupefying platitudes of anonymous human fates and gave them value, humor, and incident. His overview of the condition of England led him to see the dead weight of conservatism for its own sake, which tended not to preserve but to stifle the essential genius of the people.

His was a lifelong crusade against illiteracy that, once eradicated, would enable the people to educate themselves for self-government through various social organizations. He fought against the vile industrial conditions and the slums. He viewed contemptuously the misuse of the rich men of parliamentary opportunities and their procrastination. Dickens devoted himself through his writings to fight for humanity and justice—and his thoughts were pervasive in influence.

Dickens had an unhappy childhood. He was born in Landport, Portsmouth, England, and his family moved to Chatham and then to London. His father, a happy-go-lucky man, fell deeply into debt. Dickens went to work in a warehouse, blacking bottles. After working for about a year, he was able to go to school for two years. He then spent some time in a lawyer's office, learned shorthand, and became a reporter of debates in the House of Commons. He contributed to the *Old Monthly Magazine* (1833–1835) and to the *Evening Chronicle* sketches of London life, under the pen name *Boz*.

Dickens wrote fourteen novels and many shorter works. *The Tale of Two Cities* alone would have distinguished him as a great author, as would *Great Expectations*, considered by many as his finest work. *The Pickwick Papers of the Pickwick Club*, better known simply as *Pickwick Papers*, a comic episodic novel, was written in monthly issues, beginning in 1836, and made Dickens successful at the age of twenty-four. Pickwickian remarks were esoteric, not to be taken seriously. The *Papers* aroused so much interest that its main character, Sam Weller, became world-famous. A saying or action of loyalty and cockney-like shrewdness is a *Wellerism*.

Characters in Dickens's works have given the English language many eponyms. In *Oliver Twist*, a melodramatic tale of criminal life, Mr. Brownlow saves Oliver Twist from a gang of thieves, and then adopts him. In that novel, Fagin is a receiver of stolen goods, and "You're a Fagin" is still an expression heard on the street. Think also of the miserly curmudgeon Ebenezer Scrooge in a *Christman Carol*; Uriah Heep in *David Copperfield*, epitomizing a sanctimonious hypocrite and full of sharp practices; Little Nell; and Pecksniff, *pecksiffian* meaning characterized by hypocrisy of unctuous insincerity.

In 1842, Dickens traveled to the United States and Canada. From that sojourn came *American Notes* and *Martin Chuzzlewit*, a powerfully satiric novel of selfishness, hypocrisy, and financial speculation. The novel stirred up a good deal of feeling against him in the United States, but when he visited again, in 1867, he was greeted by large audiences. Unfortunately, traveling was hard on Dickens's health. He died at age fifty-eight.

The remarks of G. K. Chesterton are worth repeating: "There can be no question of the importance of Dickens as a human event in history . . . a naked flame of mere natural genius, breaking out in a man without culture, without tradition, without help from historic religions or philosophies or from the great foreign schools; and revealing a light that never was on sea or land, if only in the long fantastic shadows that it threw from common things."

DIESEL

Diesel is a word best know in its application to an internal combustion engine that utilizes compressed air on which a spray of fuel ignites at a virtually constant temperature. This engine injects crude oil, an oil sold by gasoline stations today because many automobiles and even more trucks and buses are driven by diesel engines.

The story behind the invention of the diesel engine is quite a romantic one; in fact, it is a life-and-death story. It begins with the Franco-Prussian War of 1870. Rudolf Diesel (1858–1913) was born in Paris of German parents who fled to England to avoid the war. Wishing to continue the German education of young Rudolf, his father sent him to Augsburg to an uncle who had offered to take care of him until the war ended. And so at the age of twelve, the boy, an identification tag around his neck, set out by train for his uncle's home. The trip took eight bumpy days, with the engine breaking down intermittently.

Rudolf enrolled at the Munich Polytechnical School. While at his studies he often thought of his uncomfortable train ride to Augsburg, and he determined to produce an engine that would be more efficient than those powered by steam or gas. To this end, Diesel, a student of thermodynamics, conducted numerous experiments and succeeded in constructing an engine—but it blew up in his face. Diesel's diary contained this notation: "The birth of an idea is the happy moment in which everything appears possible and reality has not yet entered into the problem." But Diesel's blown-up engine proved to him that fuel could be ignited by air compression rather than electrical ignition, which meant that sparks were unnecessary.

Although he was almost killed, Diesel remained undaunted. He realized that he hadn't used the right fuel. He then experimented with many substances, from alcohol to peanut oil, and finally discovered that a semirefined crude oil appeared to be the solution. The diesel engine was born, an engine that functions more efficiently than any other. It is used to power trucks, locomotives, ships, and electric generators, among other things, and is considered a major source of industrial power.

Diesel's life ended in misfortune. While traveling on a German ship, the *Dresden*, from Belgium to England, Diesel mysteriously disappeared. He had bade goodnight to some colleagues, but after entering his stateroom, he was never seen again. His bed had not been slept in, and the only clues to his untimely end were his spectacles and cap lying near the ship's stern. Ten days later another ship fished a corpse out of the water. It was determined that the corpse was Diesel's. Whether his death was suicide, murder, or an accident has never been resolved.

DIOGENES

The Greek philosopher Diogenes (c 400–325 B.C.) is best remembered for his idiosyncratic behavior. It was he who walked the streets of Athens during daylight hours with a lighted lantern searching for an honest man, an odd act designed to show his contempt for society. He is remembered as the man who lived in a tub, which he trundled about with him so that he would always have a place in which to sleep; hence the name of *Diogenes crab*, a crab that lives in another crab's empty shell. He surrendered one of his few worldly possessions to the trash heap, a wooden bowl, upon seeing a child drinking from cupped hands. Hence the *Diogenes cup*, cupped hands used as a drinking vessel.

Diogenes was one of the most famous members of the Cynic sect, which was founded by Antisthenes, a pupil of Socrates. The Cynics subscribed to the belief that virtue was the highest good and that a virtuous life was a simple life. All excessive pleasure was to be dismissed, and self-control must govern behavior. Diogenes' followers positioned themselves as the watchdogs of morality.

Alexander the Great was a great admirer of Diogenes, so much so that he once said, "If I were not Alexander I would wish to be Diogenes." Diogenes, who was sunbathing at the moment, did not return the compliment. When Alexander inquired, "Is there any way I can serve you?" Diogenes replied, "Yes, you can, Sire, you can step out of my sunlight."

DOBERMAN PINSCHER

The *Doberman pinscher* is a sleek, agile, and powerful dog, of medium-size, with short glistening hair, rather long legs, and a long, lean head. One of the most popular and respected members of the canine family, it was bred by Louis Dobermann, for whom the breed is named. Dobermann lived in Apolda, Thuringia (a region of West Germany), where he was a night watchman and in the late 1800s, the keeper of the dog pound. He was also the tax collector and so had need for a dog that would protect him from the irate, negligent tax payers and the snarling guard dogs. Dobermann undertook the task of breeding a dog to handle his problems. He was admirably successful in a short period of time.

The Doberman pinscher has the lightning reaction of terriers and the intelligence to serve as a guard dog for both the police and the military. It has also been used as a herder for livestock. The dog is generally black or rust in color, is a high jumper, and ranks next to the greyhound as a runner. Because it is extremely alert and fearless, it is used as a guard in commercial establishments.

Some of the dogs used by Dobermann to shape the Dobie (as the dog was frequently called) included the pinscher (a smaller black and tan dog similar in appearance to the modern Doberman), Rottweilers, and Thuringian Shepherds. Other breeds that contributed their genes are black Greyhounds, Great Danes, Weimaraners, and German Shorthaired Pointers.

Today's Doberman pinscher has lost the second "n" in Dobermann and has mellowed in fierceness to become a family member capable of displaying great gentleness and devotion to children.

Pinscher is pseudo-German, perhaps derived from German Pinzgau, an Austrian district noted for its animal-breeding farms.

DOILY

In the late seventeenth century, during the reign of Queen Anne, an ingenious merchant sold a material that appealed to his customers because it was attractive and cheap. The material was used for summertime wear, but another use for the material has continued to this day, even though the material is no longer used for summer clothing. The shopkeeper, whose shop was in the Strand in London, was named Doily, Doiley, Doyley, or Doyly. His given name is unknown, but his product has thrived. His name, anyway, as doily, has memorialized him in the form of an ornamental mat or napkin used on cake dishes and the like. Hostesses placed these doilies under glassware and finger bowls. They were the precursor of today's mats.

During the early days of Doiley's venture, when the material sold for clothing, according to an issue of January 24, 1712, "Doiley raised a fortune by finding out materials for such Stuffs as might at once be cheap and genteel." Dryden mentioned doyley petticoats, and Steele wrote of his doiley suit in No. 102 of the Tatler. But the spelling has become doily.

In Japan the taxicabs have doilies on the back of the passengers' seats. In America there is another use for the word doily. Men's wigs have different names, depending on their size. A doily is designed for the fellow who still has traces of his own hair on the sides and back of his head.

DOLLAR, PILLARS OF HERCULES

The word dollar, the basic monetary unit of the United States, Canada, New Zealand, Australia, and a few smaller countries, has a history that goes back to the sixteenth century. The locale was Bohemia, now a part of the Czech Republic.

In the valley of Joachimasthal was a mint that coined silver money called *Joachimsthalern*. In the early 1500s a rich silver mine was discovered there. The Counts of Shlick, who owned the mine, began to coin the silver in one-ounce pieces, and the coins were known as Schlickenthalers, after the name of the counts. The simplified *thalers* became a more popular name. The Danes called them *dalers*, from which one can see the emergence of the English word *dollar*.

There is a connection between the English and Spanish languages regarding the word *dollar*. The American dollar sign is either a capital S with two vertical lines superimposed on it or the letter S superimposed on the letter U. How the symbol arose has never been fully explained. The most widely accepted belief is that it was taken from the Spanish dollar, commonly know as "a piece of eight" because an 8 was impressed on it. The 8 stands for eight reales (Spanish coins), the value of the dollar. The official name for the old Spanish dollar was *pillar*, from the original name of the Strait of Gibraltar, the *Pillars of Hercules*, the farthest point that seafaring men dared go. Its symbol was an S, for Spain, with two vertical strokes that represented the famous Pillars.

D'ORSAY PUMP, QUAI D'ORSAY

At one time pumps were popular footwear for men. The trouble with pumps was that they tended to gape on the sides. Alfred Gabriel, the Count d'Orsay (1801–1852), decided that a pump with cut-down sides would fit more snugly. It did. He then added a V-shaped top line. Women came to believe that the pump, since it now fit well, would make a comfortable and stylish shoe for them, too.

A son of a distinguished general, Count d'Orsay was perhaps the last of the dandies. He joined the army and served as a bodyguard for Louis XVIII. He was an exceptionally handsome man and an accomplished painter, sculptor, and wit. He was considered the most perfect gentleman of his day.

D'Orsay entered into a strange relationship with the Lord and Countess Blessington. He married the fifteen-year-old daughter of Lord Blessington by a previous marriage. The couple separated almost immediately, and after Lord Blessington died, d'Orsay married Blessington's widow, who had been living in France, and returned to England with her. This peculiar arrangement was mentioned frequently in Lord Byron's correspondence. D'Orsay was appointed Director of Fine Arts in Paris by Louis Napoleon, whom he had befriended in London. But d'Orsay died in poverty before he could enjoy his new position.

The famous *Quai d'Orsay*, the quay along the Seine where the French foreign affairs and other government agencies are located, was named for d'Orsay's distinguished father. It is a counterpart to England's Downing Street, where England's prime minister resides.

DOULTON WARE

Sir Henry Doulton (1820–1897) enjoyed the benefits of a good education. He discovered the art of making glazed earthenware, and he revolutionized the field of sanitation. Previously, drains had been mostly channels of bricks, which absorbed and distributed the deleterious matter they conveyed.

The *Doulton* enterprise became known for its fine porcelains, which were particularly successful in the United States and Canada. Sir Henry turned his full attention from industrial earthenware to the demands of the domestic market. His development of the standard of art in the design and manufacture of pottery made Doulton ware famous throughout the world. In 1901 the company was authorized to market its products as Royal Doulton (the royal mark appeared in 1902). The company, now under the name of Doulton Fine China, was appointed supplier to Queen Elizabeth II in 1968.

Today the firm of Royal Doulton is regarded as one of the leading designers and manufacturers of high quality pottery.

DOUGLAS FIR

The *Douglas fir* is a beautiful evergreen tree that belongs to the pine family. It is very common in northwestern North America and the Rocky Mountains, and is the source of more timber than any other species of tree in America. It grows nearly three hundred feet tall and ten to twelve feet through the trunk, and may live up to 800 years. Only the Sequoia and redwoods of California are taller.

Its discovery came about through a romantic explorer from Scotland, David Douglas (1798–1834), a botanist, who from 1823 to 1825 collected plant specimens in America for the Royal Horticultural Society and gave his name to the *Douglas fir*. Douglas's adventures took him into unexplored wilderness.

Fortunately, he was a young man and could endure the hardships he encountered. He was gardener of Glasgow's Botanical Garden and collected several hundred plants unknown to Europe at that time. Further, he maintained complete journals of his experiences and his finds, which, when ultimately published, became a valuable source of information. Historians and naturalists have been indebted to him.

Douglas's life came to a premature and grisly end. During an extended tour of the Hawaiian Islands, he was killed by a wild bull.

DOWN OR DOWN'S, SYNDROME

Down's syndrome, or *Down syndrome*, is a disorder caused by chromosome abnormalities that develop during germ-cell formation. If the affected ovum or sperm takes part in fertilization, the fetus will exhibit the syndrome. Characteristics include moderate to severe mental deficiency, slow physical development, stocky build, short hands, and flattened facial features.

The syndrome was first described in 1866 by Dr. John Langdon Haydon Down (1828–1896), born in London and for many years a fellow of the Royal College of Physicians. The disorder had been called *mongolism* because of the Asian characteristics of eyes that appear to slant, but Down's name was later given to this disorder. In 1959 a French biologist, Jerome Lejeune, established that the production of a germ cell with an extra chromosome 21 is the most common cause of Down's syndrome. The possibility of this happening is more likely in the firstborn of an older mother, over forty years of age. Chromosome 21 is the smallest human chromosome, but its genes are of great importance not only in Down's syndrome but in cancer and Alzheimer's disease. People suffering from Down's syndrome may, with recent developments in medicine, live to about fifty years of age, but such individuals do not ordinarily become self-supporting. They are, nevertheless, often unusually sociable and affectionate.

DOWNING STREET

No. 10 Downing Street has been the official residence of the prime minister since 1735, when George II gave it to Sir Horace Walpole to serve for that purpose. Downing Street is a street leading off Whitehall and a synonym for the British government. The street is named after Sir George Downing (1623–1684), who was both a parliamentarian and an ambassador, serving under Cromwell and then Charles II.

The son of a Puritan lawyer and the second graduate of Harvard College, he served in the military for a while during the English Civil War and was a member of the Parliament during Cromwell's protectorate.

Downing was a selfish and treacherous person. He switched his politics, in 1660, to support the restoration of the Stuart monarchy. Under Charles II he became the ambassador to Holland, but his diplomatic intransigence caused the Second Dutch War.

In 1671 Downing was sent to Holland for the express purpose of fomenting another war, but his behavior there was so despicable, so abominable, that it infuriated the Dutch, and he had to flee for his life. No excuse, so far as Charles II was concerned! He had Downing imprisoned for deserting his post. After his release from confinement, however, he was given a high financial position, which he held for the rest of his days.

DRACONIAN JUSTICE. DRACONIC

Draco, an Athenian, was an archon, or chief magistrate, who, in the seventh century B.C., drew up a code of laws—the first in writing—noted for its severity. Previously justice was determined by the elders or by blood feuds. But Draco's code was so extreme, so severe, that it punished with death almost every offense known to Athenians, even such slight offenses as laziness, petty thefts, and urinating in public. Demads, an orator who lived three centuries later, said the code was "written, not in ink, but in blood."

According to tradition, Draco was once asked why he punished such petty crimes with death. He replied, "The smallest of them deserve death, and there is no greater punishment I can find for the greater crimes."

In 594 B.C., Solon, then archon, repealed the Draconian code, but the laws pertaining to homicides were retained. Although Draco's statutes have long since been discountenanced, even those concerned with homicide crimes, his code was a step toward codified justice.

Draco moved to Aegina, where he introduced a similar code. It is said that he was smothered to death accidentally by the warm gestures of the people who threw garments on him to express their admiration. That was one homicide Draco had never considered for severe punishment.

Draconian laws refer to any code that is severe and sanguinary; *draconian* remains a synonym for "rigorous and harsh" and is used to describe repressive legal measures.

DR. FELL, FELL TYPES

A loose translation that sounds more like a jingle has immortalized a noted Oxford scholar, Dr. John Fell, who gave his name to the Fell type faces, which he collected for the University Press. The story that set him apart began in a classroom at Christ Church, Oxford, where Dr. Fell was teaching. Fell was an easy teacher to get along with, for he instigated reforms and tolerated debates in his classroom. However, in one instance a wit named Thomas Brown (1663–1704) had a falling out with this likable teacher. Dr. Fell threatened to expel the student unless he translated a Latin epigram from the satiric Latin poet Martial: *"Non amo te, Sabidi, nec possum dicere quare/Hoc tantum possum dicere non amo te,"* which means, roughly, "I do not love thee, Sabidius, nor can I say why; this much I can say: I do not love you." Tom was up to the task. He improvised with the following paraphrase:

> I do not love thee, Dr. Fell;
> The reason why I cannot tell;
> But this I know, and know full well—
> I do not love thee, Dr. Fell.

Dr. Fell good-naturedly received the paraphrase and remitted the punishment. The jingle has thrived, and so has the name of Dr. Fell, but Tom Brown has been completely forgotten, perhaps because the satirical verse on Dr. Fell was the only one he ever wrote that captured the public's imagination.

DUKES, PUT UP YOUR DUKES

Augustus Frederick (1763–1820) became the Duke of York by royal appointment. Although he was the second son of England's George III, he stood little chance of becoming king. As commander-in-chief of the army, he lost the battles he waged. His interests were many and varied, but none centered on military activities. His favorite pastime was pugilism. Did his devotion to matters of the ring lead boxers to name their fists *dukes*?

Phrase sleuths have come up with several other theories, all of which are unrelated and remain what they are, pure conjecture. In Cockney slang, "forks" was associated with fingers, and fingers with "hands," and hands can become "fists." So remembering the duke's interest in fisticuffs, "put up your *fists*" became "put up your *dukes*."

Another ingenious idea refers to the magnitude of the Duke of Wellington's nose: His troops dubbed their fists *duke busters*, which eventually was reduced to *dukes*.

DUN, "DUN HIM"

When it comes to the origin of the word *dun*, most dictionaries play it safe and mark it obscure. They are wise because etymologists have disagreed for years over which of two plausible theories is the right one.

According to some word historians, *dun*, in the sense of importuning debtors for payment, was derived from Anglo-Saxon *dunan*, "to din or clamor." The thinking here is that a bill collector is bound to get into an argument with the debtor, with much resulting noise. Hence *to din* or *dinning*. Samuel Johnson said the word was derived from Saxon *donon*, signifying "to clamor."

The theory with greater support and more logic, however, is that Joseph Dunn, a famous bailiff of the town of Lincoln, England, was such a relentless bill collector that he became a legend. In fact, so many stories were published about him that his name entered the English language as a generic term. The *British Apollo* in 1708 wrote on the word *dun* as follows: "The word *Dun* owes its birth to one Joe Dun. . . . It became a proverb . . . when a man refused to pay his debts, why don't you Dun him? That is, why don't you send Dun to arrest him? It is now as old as since the days of King Henry the Seventh" (who reigned 1485–1509).

It's common today instead of saying "to make him pay up," to say simply, "dun him."

DUNCAN PHYFE STYLE

One enterprising cabinetmaker contributed significantly to the design of early American furniture. This furniture designer was Duncan Phyfe (1768–1854), Scottish born and an emigré to the United States when only fifteen years old. He was apprenticed to a cabinetmaker in Albany, but nine years later moved to Manhattan and opened his own shop. Then he changed his name from Fife to the more glamorous Phyfe.

The style of this master craftsman became known throughout the Western world, a style greatly desired among leading decorators, many of whom considered him the best American furniture maker of his time. *Duncan Phyfe furniture* was admired for its exact proportions, graceful curving lines, and carved brass ornamentation.

Some pieces were reeded or covered with raised molding. Phyfe's style incorporated the best of the designs of Sheraton, Hepplewhite, and Adam Brothers, with original touches here and there. Further, Phyfe invented certain mechanical devices that made some pieces of furniture more serviceable. His dining room tables, for example, were expandable, and his card tables and sewing cabinets were more functional than others. His later designs were influenced by the Empire style.

DUNCE, DUNSMEN, DUNSERS

John Duns Scotus (1265–1308), born in Duns, Scotland, became a Franciscan friar, then flourished at Cambridge, Oxford and the University of Paris. He was respected as an original thinker, willing to address complex theological problems. An arch-conservative in theological matters, Duns Scotus vehemently objected to the changes brought about by the English Reformers of the 16th century, even suggesting that the last seven of the Ten Commandments be abolished because times had changed radically since Moses brought the Commandments down from Mt. Sinai. He believed that only those of the Ten Commandments that concern our duties toward God belong to the natural law in the strict sense. He also became a champion of the doctrine of the Immaculate Conception. The Roman Catholic Church welcomed his theological concepts, and Duns Scotus, who had been known as "Doctor Subtle" because of his skill in arguments on theology and philosophy, was now dubbed the "Marian Doctor."

Duns Scotus's religious school of thought had many followers fulminating in every pulpit they could. But their hair-splitting theories on divinity were rejected when placed under the spotlight of calmer thought. Even after the master had died, "the old barking noise" could be heard everywhere, expounding the master's theological doctrines. But the intransigence against progress of these followers and the revival of Classical learning during the humanist Renaissance of the sixteenth century moved the people to call them the *Dunsmen, Dunsers*, and then *Dunces*. It is ironic that from the name of one of the most learned scholars and philosophers of the later Middle Ages, a person of depth of thought and sharpness of mind, comes a word that suggests dullness of wit and ignorance—*dunce* or *dull-witted*, a blockhead incapable of learning or scholarship.

ECHO, ECHOIC

Echo, daughter of air and earth, at the behest of Zeus, kept up an incessant chatter so that his wife, Hera (the queen of the heavens), would not know that he was involved in trysts with the nymphs. This chatter so distracted Hera that she was thwarted in her efforts to prove her husband's infidelities. But one day Hera learned of Echo's stratagem and punished her by depriving her of the power of speech—except to repeat what others said.

As if that weren't bad enough, Echo, despite her handicap, fell hopelessly in love with Narcissus, the handsome son of a river god, who scorned all who loved him. When he spurned Echo's love, she gradually wasted away, hiding from society in caves until only her bones and voice were left. She had lost all her charm and beauty and could speak only when spoken to and only repeat words she heard.

Nemesis, goddess of vengeance, thought of an appropriate punishment for Narcissus. She made him fall in love with his own reflection in the waters of a fountain, and, since such love cannot be consummated, he finally pined away and turned into a flower. Echo might not have known it, but Narcissus had the same feeling of loneliness and despair that she had.

EDISON, EDISON EFFECT

Thomas Alva Edison (1847–1931) was one of the most productive American inventors. He invented many electrical devices and systems that played an important role in the development of modern, near-universally available electrical power distribution systems. Writing about Edison could fill a volume. When he died, the *New York Times* devoted four and a half pages to his obituary.

Edison was born in Milan, Ohio. He set up a laboratory in his father's basement when he was only ten years old. At age twelve he began selling newspapers and candy on trains. After having served as a roving reporter, he became the night operator for the Western Union Telegraph Company. Later he was commissioned to improve the stock ticker at the Gold Exchange. With the money he earned he set up an industrial research laboratory. What resulted from his efforts thereafter showed his genius. He invented the phonograph, the light bulb, and he perfected motion-picture equipment. And he accidentally discovered the principle of the radio vacuum tube that made radio and television possible, which came to be known as the "Edison effect."

According to his fans, the Wizard of Menlo Park, as Edison was called, could build anything in his West Orange laboratory from "a lady's watch to a locomotive." Edison has been immortalized by the name of a number of towns, by the great respect and gratitude that people had for him, and, although he's long gone, by the people now enjoying the many benefits that came from his inventive mind.

EGGS BENEDICT

Eggs Benedict is a dish of poached eggs and broiled ham placed on an English muffin and topped with hollandaise sauce. The dish is a standard in fine restaurants and is well accepted by gourmet diners. But who originated this delightful combination has never been satisfactorily determined.

One authority credits the invention of this dish to an American banker named E. C. Benedict. Another attributes its creation to one of the country's leading fine restaurants, the legendary Delmonico Restaurant in New York City. According to this story, regular customers Mr. and Mrs. LeGrand Benedict complained to the maître d'hôtel that the menu had nothing new on it. Out of this colloquy came the now internationally famous recipe: *eggs Benedict*.

According to a report of Wilfred Funk on the origin of eggs Benedict, in the year 1894 a certain Samuel Benedict, a man-about-town and a member of New York's cafe society, came into the old Waldorf-Astoria on 34th Street with a wicked hangover. He knew precisely what he wanted for his breakfast. He ordered bacon, buttered toast, two poached eggs, and a hooker of hollandaise sauce. Oscar, famous maître d'hôtel, was impressed with the dish. He substituted ham and a toasted English muffin in place of the bacon and toast, and named the whole affair *eggs Benedict* in honor of the genial rake.

EIFFEL TOWER

The *Eiffel Tower* was erected for the 1889 Paris Universal Exposition. The designer for this latticework iron tower was France's most renowned authority on iron construction, civil engineer Alexandre Gustave Eiffel (1832–1923). Eiffel had organized an iron construction company in 1867 and quickly became France's foremost builder in his field, specializing in bridges. He did not limit his work solely to France. In fact, in 1885 his firm designed the interior steel framework for the Statue of Liberty, presented by France to the United States. Eiffel had also done railway spans for Russia and some South American countries.

When erected, the *Eiffel Tower* was the world's tallest structure, 984 feet high, until completion of the Chrysler Building in New York City in 1930, which took the crown away from the tower by adding sixty feet. One of the tallest buildings in the world today is the New York World Trade Center, which reaches skyward 1,353 feet.

EINSTEIN, EINSTEINIUM

Einsteinium is a radioactive element discovered by Albert Ghiorso and others in the 1952 fallout from the first hydrogen explosion. The element, 99, was made in the laboratory and was named to honor Albert Einstein (1879–1955).

Einstein was born in Ulm, Wünttemburg, Germany. As a young boy, Einstein was regarded as a slow learner. He did not walk until he was three and didn't talk until later. But as a student at the Polytechnic Institute of Zurich, he showed a deep interest in and a remarkable grasp of mathematics. He became a Swiss citizen in 1905 and took employment at the Swiss Patent Office, but continued his work in pure science.

In 1905 he published four original papers so revolutionary that their importance was not immediately recognized. One of the papers announced his theory of relativity, relating mass to energy.

In 1909, he became professor of theoretical physics at the University of Zurich. In 1911 and 1912, he occupied the same position at the German University in Prague. When he accepted the professorship of physics at the University of Berlin in 1914, he once more assumed German citizenship. In the same year he became director of the Kaiser Wilhelm Physical Institute in Berlin.

Einstein in 1916 extended his specific theory of relativity to the general case, and when his prediction was verified in 1919, he became world famous. He received the Nobel Prize for Physics in 1921.

In 1933, while Einstein was visiting England and the United States, the Nazi government of Germany took his property and deprived him of his positions and his citizenship.

In 1940, Einstein became an American citizen. He accepted a position for life as a member of the staff of the newly created Institute for Advanced Study in Princeton, New Jesey, and he lived there until his death.

At the behest of the American scientific community, Einstein sent a letter to President Roosevelt suggesting the need to build an atomic bomb. The letter led to the development of the bomb, which was eventually exploded over Japan by order of President Truman. Einstein was a pacifist and took no part in the manufacture of the bomb, but without his formula $E=mc^2$ (energy equals mass times the square of the speed of light) it could never have been made.

ELDORADO

The Spanish *Eldorado* means the "gilded man." That name was bestowed on the supposed king of the fabulous city of Manoa, believed to be somewhere on the Amazon. In the sixteenth century, many explorers tried to find Manoa, or Eldorado (the names were used interchangeably by the explorers) and one expedition after another set out with high hopes, just to return with nothing but frustration. The rumor that took hold during that time was that Manoa was so rich that the king, after his bath and rubdown with oil, was dusted with gold, and this had been done so often that his skin had become permanently gold.

In 1530, a Spanish conquistador reported that he had visited Eldorado himself in a city called Omagua. Expeditions from Germany, Spain, and England explored the Bogota highlands, but no trace of him was found. The renowned Sir Walter Raleigh searched for Manoa in the Orinoco lowlands, while Spaniards sought Omagua nearby. In this quest, Pizarro crossed the Andes from Quito, de Oreliana sailed down the Napo and the Amazon, and de Questa explored from Bogota. Clearly, no one was certain of the whereabouts of "The Gilded One." None of the explorations was successful.

Because of the greedy persistence of man this name of an imaginary king has been stamped, metaphorically, on any place of great wealth or one affording an opportunity of acquiring wealth easily.

The story of Eldorado is often mentioned in literature, as in Milton's *Paradise Lost* and Voltaire's *Candide*.

ELIZABETHAN AGE

Queen Elizabeth I (1533–1603) was the daughter of Henry VIII and his second wife, Anne Boleyn, who was beheaded for alleged adultery. Elizabeth served as queen of England from 1558 to 1603, a period in which England came to assert itself as a major European power. Her reign is often called the Elizabethan Age. Elizabeth never married, and she came to be known as the Virgin Queen or Good Queen Bess.

Elizabeth had a difficult time as a child and was imprisoned in the Tower of London by her older sister, Queen Mary. In 1558 Mary, a Catholic, died and Elizabeth ascended to the throne. One of her first acts was to confront the religious problem. This she did. She restored Protestantism and reinstated the English *Book of Common Prayer*. Although she was not harsh to Catholics, her peaceable approach was shattered in 1570 by the interdict of Pope Pius V against Elizabeth. The treatment of English Catholics became increasingly severe.

The history of furniture is closely related to the history of human culture. Many pieces of furniture, with distinctive English forms, appeared during Elizabeth's reign. One was the *drawtable*, a large oval dining table made in halves that could be drawn apart. Another, the *court cupboard*, had open shelves for displaying valuable plates and silverware. But the most impressive pieces of furniture were beds, which featured handsome hardware carvings and expensive fabrics.

The last fifteen years of Elizabeth's reign became known as the Golden Age of Literature because of the remarkable accomplishments that occurred in the arts, especially in literature, poetry, and music. This was the age of the incomparable Bard of Avon, William Shakespeare, Edmund Spenser, and Francis Bacon. Her reign was also one of commercial prosperity and progress. Elizabeth herself was a cultured person, outstanding and invincible. She remarked, "There will never be a queen sitting in my seat with more zeal to my country and care to my subjects. And though you have had and may have princes more mighty and wise sitting in this seat, you never had or shall have any that will be more careful and loving."

EPICURE, EPICUREAN, EPICURISM

An *epicure* is a person who cultivates refined tastes, especially in food and wine; *epicurean* pertains to good eating and drinking. These words derive from Epicurus (c. 341–c.270 B.C.), who was probably born on the island of Samos. He spent a few years in the military and then taught at Mytilene and Lampsacus. His philosophy was that pleasure was the natural aim and highest good, but pleasure had to consist of right living to lead to tranqillity of mind and body.

Epicurus went to Athens in 306 B.C. with a group of disciples and began a school that was in reality a way of life. His school, known as Ho Kepos (the garden), fostered atheism, permitted no marriages, children, or participation in public life. His followers became known as the "philosophers of the garden." Epicurus was a moral man, and his standards were just as high for his students, but the public was unconvinced. In a letter to Menoeceus, he wrote: "When we maintain that pleasure is an end, we do not mean the pleasure of profligates and those that consist in sensuality . . . but freedom from pain in the body and from trouble in the mind. For it is not continuous drinkings, nor the satisfaction of lusts . . . but sober reasoning, searching out the motives for all choice and avoidance."

The many detractors of Epicurus maintained that high living and all the sensual gratification that accompanies it was actually his goal; they came to the conclusion that epicurism was merely an excuse for hedonism.

Although the dictionary says that an epicure derives happiness from refined sensual pleasures, many people believe that the word *sexual* should be substituted for *sensual*. Maybe. But this influential Greek philosopher once wrote: "But while every pleasure is in itself good, not all pleasures are to be chosen, since certain pleasures are produced by means which entail annoyances many times greater. . . . Moreover . . . it is not possible to live pleasantly without living wisely and well and righteously."

EPSOM SALTS

Epsom salts is the name for a crystalline salt of magnesium sulfate heptahydrate. Discovered near the town of Epsom, England, about 1618, it is used internally as a laxative and externally as a soaking aid for bruises, sprains, and local inflammation. The "salt" occurs as an evaporation deposit from mineral waters. Epsom salts are now made in America in large quantities as a byproduct of the manufacture of carbon dioxide for soda water. Much of the supply in Europe comes from the Stassfurt salt beds in Saxony, Germany.

According to Fuller's *Worthies*, the mineral spring was discovered by a farmer who noticed that in spite of a drought, his cows refused to drink water from the spring. On analysis, it was found to contain the bitter purgative, sulphur of magnesia.

Epsom Wells developed into a favorite spa. Aubrey, Pepys, Nell Gwyn, and Queen Anne's consort were among its visitors. Shadwell's comedy *Epsom Wells* (1672) portrays the loose life of the spa in those times.

EUPHUISM, GONGORISM

Euphuism is an artificial literary style, popular in the Elizabethan and Jacobean periods. It derived its name from the name of the hero of two prose romances by John Lyly (1554–1606), *Euphues: The Anatomy of Wit* (1579) and his *Euphues and His England* (1580). There is little plot in either romance; the interest lies chiefly in long philosophic discussions and in the elaborate and affected style that gave rise to the term *euphuism*.

This ornate prose style is characterized by alliteration, lengthy similes, extended comparisons, complicated figures, unduly and neat antitheses, and skillfully balanced sentences. The intent of this elaborate elegance was to woo feminine readers by seeming to edify them, while avoiding scholarly solemnity. The abundant use of literary devices, which produced an overall effect of overrefined artificiality, helped free English prose from the heavy latinized style and added fancy and imagination to prose writing. The titles of Lyly's books were appropriately named, for *Euphues* comes from a Greek word meaning "good nature."

Although criticized by some contemporary writers, and ridiculed by Shakespeare, this bombastic style created a fashion that lasted for half a century. It was frequently imitated by contemporaries, including Queen Elizabeth I, Robert Greene, and Thomas Lodge.

The inflated style of John Lyly was a sister style to that of the Spanish poet Luis de Gongora y Argote (1561–1627), one of the great Spanish lyricists. Though Gongora used his florid, cluttered literary style to good advantage, the clumsy attempts by lesser poets to imitate it have given English the word *Gongorism*, words so presented as to create an unreal world.

Gongora was a priest as well as a poet and dramatist. None of his poems were published while he was alive. His name became a synonym for a style purposely obscure and meaningless, ornate and intricate.

FABIAN TACTICS

The tactics of delay and exerting great caution before proceeding were the strategy of the Roman general Quintus Fabius Maximus, who died circa 203 B.C. He was called the Cunctator (delayer), a nickname given because of his wariness. His tactics gave Rome time to recover its strength and take the offensive against the invading Carthaginian army of Hannibal. Fabian's stratagem was to avoid direct conflict. He maneuvered amid the hills, where Hannibal's cavalry was useless, and used hit-and-run tactics that kept Hannibal off guard and eroded his forces.

The strategy of the Cunctator has been followed by other generals in other wars. General George Washington employed this tactic with success against British soldiers in American Revolution.

In 1884 a British socialist association was organized with the name Fabian Society. The society rejected Marxist revolutionary theory; their credo was that "the reorganization of society" could be accomplished "by stealing inches, not by grasping leagues." The intent of the society was to spread socialism, but gradually. Among their prominent members were Graham Wallace, Sidney and Beatrix Potter Webb, H. G. Wells, George Bernard Shaw, and Annie Besant. Today the society is a research institution.

Fabianism, or Fabian tactics, has come to mean a gradual or cautious policy.

FAHRENHEIT

Gabriel Daniel Fahrenheit (1686–1736) invented the thermometer. Fahrenheit was born in Gdansk, Poland, of German parents and was orphaned at fifteen. With little schooling, he wandered around Europe to learn from amateur scientists, finally settling in Amsterdam. Failing at the merchant's career for which his father trained him, he devoted himself to the study of physics and the manufacture of meteorological instruments.

He invented an alcohol thermometer in 1709, and a mercury thermometer in 1714.

Because of his invention, Fahrenheit was so greatly respected by the academic community that, despite his lack of formal education, he was admitted to the British Royal Society in 1736, shortly before his death at age fifty.

Fahrenheit's temperature scale was based on a normal body temperature of 96 degrees, later corrected to 98.6 degrees, the freezing of water at 32 degrees, and the boiling point of water at 212 degrees. "Whether these degrees are high enough for the hottest fevers, I have not examined," he wrote. "I do not think, however, that the degrees named will ever be exceeded in any fever."

FALLOPIAN TUBES

The anatomist who discovered the function of the tubes that carry ova from the ovaries to the uterus, and for whom the tubes were named, was Gabriel Fallopius (1523–1562). The oviducts found in female mammals, including human beings, is a mistranslation of Fallopius's *tubas*, "trumpets," which was his way of describing the horn-shaped muscles. Fallopius's investigation proved that virgins have hymens, and he coined the word *vagina*.

Fallopius was destined for an ecclesiastical career but turned to medicine. He became a professor of anatomy at Ferrara, then at Pisa University, and subsequently at Padua University, where he headed the anatomy department until his death.

Fallopius, it seems, was a one-man medical lexicographer. In addition to "vagina," he created the medical use of words *palate*, *placenta*, *cochlea*, and *clitoris*.

Some scholars point out that, although Fallopius may have coined the anatomical use of *vagina*, that term, meaning sheath or scabbard, was a good classical Latin word 1,500 years before Fallopius.

Fallopius contributed greatly to the early knowledge of the ear. He described the semicircular canals of the inner ear (responsible for maintaining body equilibrium) and named the cochlea (the snail-shaped organ of hearing in the inner ear).

FARAD, FARADAY

Michael Faraday (1791–1867), the son of a blacksmith, had no chance to go to school, for he was born near London into extreme poverty. He was apprenticed to a bookbinder. But Faraday's interests in the physical sciences drove him to high levels; he educated himself by reading and attending lectures. He became a physicist and chemist whose many experiments contributed greatly to the understanding of electromagnetism.

Faraday was ingenious. He collected his notes taken from the chemistry lectures of Sir Humphry Davy, added illustrations, bound them, and sent them off to Davy, together with a request to become an assistant. Davy made Faraday, at age 21, his assistant at the Royal Institution.

Faraday became one of the immortals of science. He discovered the principle of the electric motor and built a primitive model. Two years later he became the first to liquefy chlorine. His next move—one of his greatest—led him to discover electromagnetic induction, the production of electric current by a change in magnetic intensity. He produced the first stainless steel and discovered benzene and butylene.

Faraday was a devoted scientist and a modest man. Although elected to the Royal Institute, he refused its presidency. Previously he had refused to be knighted, just as he had rejected other honors offered him.

But he did succeed Davy as director of chemistry at the Royal Institution in London.

In addition to the *farad*, also named for him is the *faraday*, a quantity of transferred electricity.

FAUST, FAUSTIAN

Dr. Johann Faust (or Faustus) lived in Württemberg and died about 1538. He roamed through Germany and was said to be a vicious magician and astrologer. He achieved some devilish results and became a magnet for many followers who treated him as a living legend for his knowledge of astrology and necromancy. So much sorcery was associated with his name that he became a vital source for stories, ballads, dramas, operas, and epics.

Christopher Marlowe's *The Tragical History of Dr. Faustus* is the traditional story in which the doctor sought to have his every desire satisfied. He entered into an agreement with *Mephistopheles* for world power, honor, and all kinds of pleasures. But when the twelfth hour struck, what followed was a terrifying scene in which the devil claimed Faust's soul for hell.

The most famous of the Faust dramas was written by the German poet Johann Wolfgang Goethe. It has Faust selling his soul not for worldly power and pleasures but for supreme happiness, which he had never been able to find in his former pursuits. Because he ultimately finds this happiness in unselfish service for mankind, he escapes the snares of Mephistopheles.

Many musical compositions embrace the story of human willingness to part with the soul to gain one's desires. Generally, the protagonist winds up in a losing battle and realizes that the bargain requires the surrender of more than anticipated.

The adjective form *Faustian*—characteristic of Faust (a Faustian novel) or that which resembles or befits Faust—has multiple meanings. It may refer to the willingness to sacrifice spiritual "goods" for worldly ones (a Faustian pact with the Devil), or to an insatiable hunger for knowledge or experience. Or it may refer to one constantly troubled and tormented by spiritual dissatisfaction or spiritual striving.

FERMIUM, FERMION

Enrico Fermi (1901–1954), "the father of the atomic bomb," showed such intelligence and quickness of mind that he gained admission, in 1918, to the Scuola Normale in Pisa, a school for the intellectual elite of Italy. He obtained a Ph.D. from the University of Pisa in 1922. After spending some time abroad, he was appointed to a professorship of physics at the University of Rome in 1926. Such a high position was unheard of in Italy for someone only twenty-five years old. But Fermi had published some thirty substantial papers and had the support of O. M. Corbino, Italy's most distinguished physicist at that time. Fermi's reputation attracted the brightest of the younger Italian physicists.

Fermi's period in Rome (1926–1938) turned out to be remarkably productive in both the theoretical and the experimental fields. When Fermi used uranium of atomic weight 92 as the target of slow neutron bombardment, he obtained radioactive substances he could not identify. Fermi was unaware that he was on the edge of a world-shaking discovery, that he had actually split the atom. This development later was to have a profound impact in the field of nuclear energy. He addressed himself to the task of investigating the properties of a large number of newly created radioactive isotopes. For this work, he was awarded the 1938 Nobel Prize for physics. But the growing anti-Semitism alarmed him. He and his Jewish wife departed Italy for the United States, where he undertook the task of creating a controlled self-sustaining nuclear chain reaction at the University of Chicago. He worked on the atomic bomb at Los Alamos, New Mexico, and was present at the first atomic blast in July 1945.

Fermi, together with the members of his family, became an American citizen. He was a professor of physics at Columbia University in 1939 before moving on to the University of Chicago in 1942. The U.S. Atomic Energy Commission gave him a special $25,000 award in 1954 for his work on the bomb.

Fermi's name is applied to several discoveries: to a unit of length in nuclear physics, *fermi*; to a group of subatomic particles, *fermions*; and to the element *fermium* (atomic number 100), named the year after Fermi's death.

FERRIS WHEEL

The architectural planner for the World's Columbian Exposition in Chicago in 1893 was Daniel H. Burnham. He wanted the exposition to have a native focal point so attractive that it would surpass the Eiffel Tower, which had been built for the 1889 Paris Universal Exposition. Many architects submitted plans, but the one accepted came from a civil engineer named George Washington Gale Ferris (1859–1896), who was born in Galesburg, Illinois, and who became a bridge and railroad engineer. His design, and what he ultimately constructed, consisted of a revolving wheel structure, 650 feet in diameter and supported by towers that stood 140 feet high. Between the rims were 36 cars, each capable of carrying 40 riders. Quite naturally, this wheel came to be called a *Ferris wheel*. It was the wonder of the exposition and was such a delight that it was widely copied and used in many carnivals and amusement parks around the country. It is still a wheel of fun.

The Ferris wheel, which had attracted the delighted attention of so many people and gave such pleasure to families at the World's Columbian Exposition in Chicago, was sold and shipped to St. Louis for the 1904 exhibition, after which the structure, which had been built at a cost of $385,000, was sold as scrap. It fetched less than $2,000.

FLORENCE NIGHTINGALE

Florence Nightingale (1820–1910), English nurse and hospital reformer, and generally considered to be the founder of modern nursing, was born in the Italian city of Florence, for which she was named. Her parents were well-to-do, and when she declared her interest in becoming a nurse, a family upheaval occurred. During those days the only women who served as nurses were prostitutes and other women of low repute.

When the Crimean War broke out, Nightingale was the head of a hospital in London. She and thirty-eight other nurses offered their services to the British army. In 1854, she and her associates took over a poorly run hospital at Scutari. Nightingale worked as many as twenty hours a day and became known as the *Lady with the Lamp* because she visited her patients every night, a pattern that is now called "making the rounds." She also set up strict standards of sanitation and care. The results of this nursing care were remarkable: she reduced the death rate from 42 percent to 2 percent.

Nightingale was venerated not only by the soldiers but also by the English public, who gave her a Ł50,000 fund in recognition of her accomplishments. She turned the fund over to St. Thomas's Hospital, in 1860, to found a school for nurses. She was the author of the classic *Notes on Nursing*, and remained the chief authority of the British government on matters pertaining to public, private, and military health. In 1907, she became the first woman to receive the British Order of Merit. Other than this Nightingale refused commendations and honors. A flannel scarf with sleeves for invalids sitting up in bed was named the *Nightingale*. A *Florence Nightingale* is a ministering angel, especially a nurse.

She insisted that she be treated as an ordinary citizen and that she not be buried in Westminster. Her wishes were respected. When she died at age ninety, the *Lady with the Lamp* was buried in the family plot in a small country churchyard in Hampshire. The only people there were the six British soldiers who carried her casket.

FORSYTHIA

The *forsythia* shrub that sprouts handsome brilliant yellow flowers, is a genus of the olive family, and is among the earliest harbingers of spring. It grows as high as nine feet, and has spreading arched branches. It is sometimes called the *golden bell* because its yellow flowers are shaped like tiny, golden bells, which grow in clusters and bloom before the leaves appear. The forsythia is easily grown in almost any garden soil.

William Forsyth (1737–1804), superintendent of the Royal Gardens at Kensington in London during the reign of George III, introduced many beautiful ornamental plants that had never before grown in England. Among the most popular was a plant named in his honor—the *forsythia*. The plant was native to China but was domesticated in Great Britain at the beginning of the nineteenth century. Gardeners have welcomed this plant because it is easy to propagate, needs little attention, and thrives in partial shade.

FOURDRINIER

Paper is often called "the handmaiden of civilization." It is important as a keeper of records because it is the material on which manuscripts, books, magazines, and newspapers are written or printed. The tools of the financial system—money, checks, drafts, notes, stocks—are also made of paper.

Much of the paper used today is made by a *fourdrinier* machine, a name derived from its inventors. The machine, whose length can reach three hundred feet, forms a wet mass of fibers into a sheet. The first part, called the wet end, is made of a wire-cloth belt on which the fibers are allowed to mat into the form of a sheet. The sheet is then dried as it passes over suction boxes, and is then squeezed between heavy press rolls and passed over steam-heated drier cylinders. The paper passes through calendar (a variant form of "cylinder") presses where a smooth surface is put on the sheet. Finally, it is wound into large paper rolls, a continuous sheet of any desired size.

Henry Fourdrinier, with the help of his brother, Sealy, invented the machine and had it patented in 1807. They spent thirty years perfecting it. After all that time, they received a partial grant from the British Parliament that enabled them to recoup their expenses.

The *Fourdrinier*—in principle—has been in operation ever since it was patented. The automatic machine is still used although the Fourdrinier brothers might be hard put to recognize its modern version.

FRANKLIN STOVE

Benjamin Franklin (1706–1790) was one of America's greatest statesmen. He was a diplomat sent to France to seek aid for the colonists, and he helped frame both the Declaration of Independence and the United States Constitution.

Franklin was born in Boston, the tenth son of seventeen children of a soap and candle maker. At twelve, he was apprenticed to his half-brother James, a printer. He worked as a printer in Philadelphia and for a time in London. He published the *Pennsylvania Gazette* and *Poor Richard's Almanack*.

A prolific inventor, Franklin devised the *Franklin stove*, one of America's first practical heating devices. The stove was a portable, coal-burning apparatus with a pipe connecting it to the chimney. By arranging the flues in an efficient way, he could make his sitting room twice as warm with one-fourth as much fuel as he had been using.

He invented the glass harmonica and bifocals and the Franklin lightning kite. But his interest in civic matters proved as profound as his interest in inventions. He organized the first circulating library, helped establish the first fire company, and founded what is now the University of Pennsylvania.

FREUD, FREUDIAN, FREUDIAN SLIP

Sigmund Freud (1856–1939) was born at Freiberg, in Moravia. He studied medicine in Vienna and Paris and then, in 1884, studied under Josepf Breuer, a Viennese physician who introduced him to the cathartic method of treating hysteria, which focused on allowing patients to confront the root element of their abiding fears. It became the essential starting point of psychoanalysis. The two men explored matters affecting psychotherapy, but then Freud developed the importance of "free association" as a method of treatment. His books became the gospel of psychotherapy. Freud, who was Jewish, was condemned by the Nazis. He fled in 1938 to London, where he lived the remaining year of his life. He died an honored and respected man.

Freud's *The Interpretation of Dreams*, published in 1909, met with extreme hostility. With the passage of time, his views became increasingly accepted.

Freudian theories emphasized the importance of the subconscious, infantile sexuality, and the development of sexuality at the onset of neuroses. His interpretation of dreams are a basic technique of psychoanalysis (the word *psychoanalysis* was coined by Freud). Psychoanalysis today is widely accepted as a treatment for the mentally ill or the disturbed person. Freud's influence has led to wider expressions of the human condition in modern art, poetry, and literature, especially those relating to dreams and their apparent connection with repressed desires, thus linking the arts and the sciences.

Freud postulated the existence of three internal forces that govern a person's psychic life: (1) the *id*, the instinctual force of life—unconscious, uncontrollable, and isolated; (2) the *ego*, the executive force that has contact with the real world; (3) the *super-ego*, the governing force, or moral conscience, that seeks to control and direct the ego into socially acceptable patterns of behavior.

Freudian theory, *Freudianism*, is now a major system of psychoanalysis, and its adherents are known as *Freudians*. However, *Freudian* as an adjective has been adopted by common English in ways that are unencumbered by the complexities of Freud's theories. "Freudian" is frequently applied to any motive that seems inaccessible—or at least is not obvious—to that person's conscious mind. The word especially gains currency when the motive is understood to be veiled by sexual repression.

Freud provided numerous examples of slips of the tongue that hint at what he called the secondary process of mental functioning. These "Freudian slips" are technically known as *parapraxis*, and include slips of the pen as well. They are manifestations of the subconscious use of a word or expression similar to that which we intend to use when our mind is half-thinking of something else. It reveals a repressed subconscious thought or desire. A pregnant woman who says she's to see her stockbroker to check on her stork instead of her stock has slipped in the wrong word, one that was in her subconscious. It is just as much a Freudian slip to murmur an old flame's name while embracing your spouse.

FRIDAY, MAN FRIDAY

An executive's *man Friday*—an assistant who can be counted on to be a wholly reliable and competent overseer—gets his appellation from a character in one of the most renowned adventure novels ever.

Robinson Crusoe is a work of fiction based on an almost incredible true story. It started in Scotland where Alexander Selkirk (1676–1721), a shoemaker's son, was born and raised. Young Selkirk was unhappy in Scotland, so he ran away, joining William Dempler's privateering expedition to the South Seas. It sounded romantic, but Selkirk became completely disenchanted. And so in October 1704, he asked the captain to put him ashore. The captain obliged and left him on one of the desolate Juan Fernández islets. But Selkirk thrived for fifty-two months before being rescued by a ship that passed close to the island in 1709.

This adventure, or misadventure, was recognized by Daniel Defoe as an exciting basis for a good novel. And so in 1719 the book titled *The Life and Strange Surprizing Adventures of Robinson Crusoe* was published.

The book gave birth to the character Friday, a man saved by Crusoe from being served for dinner to cannibals. Friday, so named because Crusoe met him on a Friday, became Crusoe's constant companion and served him in every way possible. The term *man Friday* (and, in more recent times, also *gal Friday*) is used to this day to refer to an underling of unswerving loyalty on whom a person can rely. It frequently is used to designate a competent and dependable employee without whom the boss would surely flounder.

Daniel Defoe (1660–1731) was the son of a London butcher, James Foe. The author (who changed his name to Defoe in middle life) welcomed the arrival of William of Orange in 1688 and wrote *The True-Blue Englishman*. An announced nonconformist, Defoe wrote, in 1702, an ironic pamphlet "The Shortest Way with the Dissenters," for which he was imprisoned for about five months. Defoe, who wrote for the *Review* for many years, turned to the writing of novels as he grew older. His most famous were *Robinson Crusoe* and *Moll Flanders* (1722).

FRISBEE

The *Frisbee*, one might imagine, is a child's toy. But adults also enjoy flipping to one another these plastic, saucer-shaped disks that skim through the air. In fact adults began sailing slim plates as an outdoor sport. Because they were not boomerangs, they therefore needed someone to catch the initial flip and sail it back. One historian maintained that the game began on the Yale campus in 1827 when an undergraduate showed his displeasure at being compelled to attend chapel services by hurling the collection plate through an open door. The flipping of plates caught on (collection plates?), and a new pastime was born.

A story that has better credentials cites the drivers of the Frisbie Pie Company of Bridgeport, Connecticut, who, during their lunch breaks, amused themselves by throwing around tin pie plates. With time, this fun activity took hold at Yale University, and then spread to other campuses around the country. The students found it sport to sail these tins, reminiscent of flying saucers, toward one another and then have them hurled back. One way or another, Yale gets the credit for launching the Frisbee toss.

The name of the pie company was later emblazoned onto the saucer, which then became known as *Frisbee*, and the saucers' material changed to plastic. Just about 1950 a certain Fred Morrison introduced on the West Coast a product he called the original "Flyin' Saucer" and hawked his product for seven years. At that time two ingenious entrepreneurs began the manufacture of plastic circular plates and kept the name "Frisbee" to honor the Frisbie Pie Company. By using assembly lines, they were able to produce large quantities of this throwing disk and, in fact, sold more than 100 million of them.

FROEBELISM

Friedrich Wilhelm August Froebel (1782–1852) devised a system of kindergarten teaching (and he was the first to use the word *kindergarten* for such schools) to help children learn naturally. To develop children's abilities, his program included such activities as claymodeling, matplaiting, paper-cutting, and weaving. Froebel's instructional material remained standard equipment for many years. But Froebel was not given a free rein to institute his useful and farsighted system.

Froebel was born at Oberweissbach, Thuringia, Germany, the son of a Lutheran pastor. His mother died in his infancy, and his life with his father was unpleasant. But things took a turn for the better when he was made the charge of a kindly uncle who took a personal interest in him.

After spending some time as a forester's apprentice and an architectural student at Frankfurt-am-Main, he found his calling when he was invited to teach in a school in Frankfort administered by a follower of Johann H. Pestalozzi (1746–1827). In 1806, Froebel became a tutor to the three sons of Baron von Holtzhausen, from which experience he derived a firm conviction of the vital need for both father and mother to participate in the education of children. Froebel's next important move was to the village of Griesheim, where he opened his own school which he described as the "Universal German Educational Institution." After his marriage in 1818, he moved his school to neighboring Keilhau, and it soon expanded into a flourishing institution.

Froebel worked unstintingly at the school, and there published his notable book *The Education of Man* (1826), an amalgam of idealism, romanticism, and mysticism. But in 1828 his school became suspect to the authorities as a "nest of demagogues." Froebel was removed from direct control and left the school.

In Blankenburg, Germany, Froebel's method of teaching preschool children took root, and several kindergartens were founded. But his unorthodox methods aroused suspicion, culminating, in 1851, in a ban of kindergartens as subversive by the Prussian minister of education. Froebel died the next year.

Froebel's method of teaching and his kindergarten system have gained recognition and have had a profound effect upon educational methods in many countries. Some of his ideas anticipated and inspired nineteenth- and twentieth-century educators, among them John Dewey. The ban against the kindergartens was removed in Germany, and today the kindergarten is a universal educational institution.

Froebelism is based on the premise that man is essentially active and creative rather than merely receptive. Froebel's belief in self-activity and play in child education resulted in the introduction of a series of learning apparatus (toys) devised to stimulate learning.

FUCHSIA, FUCHSIN

The *fuchsia* is an ornamental, chiefly tropical shrub widely cultivated for its showy and drooping purplish, reddish, or white flowers. It is a genus of the evening primrose family, with more than seventy species native to tropical America and several to New Zealand and Tahiti. The flowers are bell-shaped, with stamens extending beyond the petals. They come into life in small clusters or singly, and mature into berries.

Fuchsias are grown as potted plants or in hanging baskets in temperate regions and as shrubs and trees in warmer regions. They do better in warm, humid climates, and they cease to flower when the length of daylight is less than twelve hours.

These plants were first introduced into Europe by the German physician and botanist Leonhard Fuchs (1501–1566), a professor of medicine at the University of Tübingen. His famous work *De historia stirpium* discussed medicinal plants and became a standard text. In 1703, many years after Fuchs's death, the plant was named *fuchsia* by the French botanist Charles Plumier.

Fuchsin or *fuchsine* is a purplish-red aniline dye.

GALLUP POLL

The man who lent his name to the famous poll-taking organization was George Horace Gallup (1901–1984). He was born in Jefferson, Iowa, and attended school in his native state, graduating from Iowa State University. He then became professor of journalism at Iowa and later taught at Drake and Northwestern universities.

Gallup began his studies of sampling methods by checking items in newspapers and magazines. His method set a standard for the field. After spending some time in market research, he began experimenting in 1933 with public opinion polls, and in 1935 he conceived the idea for national poll-taking. In 1936 he correctly predicted the outcome of that year's presidential election and acquired national fame. During the previous year Gallup had founded at Princeton, New Jersey, the American Institute of Public Opinion "to measure and report public opinion on political and social issues of the day without regard to the rightness or wisdom of the views expressed." His method for measuring the public viewpoint was to have trained interviewers question a small but carefully selected cross section of the population. Previously straw polls were the method employed to predict political results. The Gallup poll was the first "scientific" sampling of public opinion.

The Gallup organization spread throughout the Western world. Its polls have been used in many countries to forecast popular opinion in politics and in other fields, particularly cinema.

This quasi-scientific method is not the same as one involving physical science. In the presidential election of 1948, Gallup predicted a stunning defeat for Harry Truman. Both Gallup and Thomas Dewey ate crow. As did, famously, the *Chicago Daily Tribune*.

GALVANIZE

Nontechnically speaking, a person shocked or spurred into action is said to be *galvanized*. Technically, when a metal such as iron or steel is given a protective coating of zinc, it too is *galvanized*. To learn how the word *galvanize*, with its two disparate senses, originated, you must start with a story concerning the cooking of frogs. There are several versions of this story, but all are basically similar. Let us consider Wilder Penfield's version as reported in *Anecdotes*, edited by Clifton Fadiman:

> One evening in the late eighteenth century, an Italian woman stood in her kitchen watching the frogs' legs which she was preparing for the evening meal. "Look at those muscles moving. . . . They always seem to come alive when I hang them on a wire."
>
> Her husband, Luigi Galvani, looked. . . . The cut end of the frog's nerve was in contact with a copper wire, and electric current produced by the contact was passing along the nerve to the muscle. As a result the muscle was twitching and contracting. . . .

He had discovered the key to electricity, and to nerve conduction, and to muscle action. Here was the basis of all animal movement, reflex and voluntary, in frog and man.

Luigi Galvani (1737–1798), born in Bologna, was a physiologist and a lecturer on anatomy at the University of Bologna. He pioneered the branch of physiology relating to electricity, called electrophysiology. Those who studied the strange phenomenon that Galvani reported agreed that the frog's muscles did show signs of vitality. Galvani postulated the theory of *animal electricity*.

However, Galvani's theory was exploded by a fellow Italian, Count Alessandro Volta (after whom the word *volt* was named). He discovered that the twitching of the frog's legs was the result of contact of two unlike metals that produced an electric current. Galvani's scalpel had touched the brass conductor of a nearby electrical machine.

Volta's finding set off a furor in the academic world. Scientists split into two sides—adherents of Galvani's theory and of Volta's. At times the debates were acrimonious. Galvani was castigated as "the frog's dancing master." The disputes created a serious pressure on the shy Galvani. To avoid any further conflict and to conduct other experiments, Galvani departed for the Mediterranean. While he was away, Napoleon conquered Bologna, among other cities, and demanded an oath of fealty to himself from the members of the university faculty. Galvani refused to take the oath and was summarily dismissed. Sometime later the authorities relented and sought to reinstate him, but Galvani refused the offer. In that same year, he died.

Galvani contributed his name to the English language in the word *galvanize* in the technical and nontechnical senses, enriching both science and language.

GARDENIA

An American physician of Scottish descent, Alexander Garden (1730–1791) successfully practiced medicine in Clarkston, South Carolina. However, his devotion to his hobby—botany—accounted for much of his daily interests. He corresponded regularly with European naturalists, including Linnaeus, who honored him by naming the *gardenia*, a waxy white and heavily fragrant flower, after him, even though Dr. Garden had not discovered the flower. The renowned botanist and scholar Richard Warner had introduced it into Europe in 1790 after his journey to the Cape of Good Hope. In any event, the gardenia has ever since been a popular corsage flower.

Although Garden's granddaughter was named *Gardenia*, the good doctor never saw her because his son, Gardenia's father, joined the Revolutionary forces in their struggle against the British. Dr. Garden, completely devoted to the Crown, could not accept his son's disloyalty. After the colonists' success, Dr. Garden left America in 1783 for Britain, where he died in 1791. Legend has is that his grave was covered with gardenias.

According to Willard R. Espy, after the gardenia was named for Dr. Garden, a local botanist, a Dr. Lewis Mottet, was so enraged that he announced that he too had discovered a flower. "And I, too, have named it," he said. "I've named it the *lucia*, after Lucy, my cook." But the *lucia* has never been heard of again, and neither was Lucy.

The gardenia, according to William Morris, isn't any sort of garden flower, as its name might suggest. It's a shrub originally native to china.

GARIBALDI SHIRT, GARIBALDI FISH

The great Italian patriot Giuseppe Garibaldi (1807–1882) was born at Nice, which then belonged to France but subsequently became part of the kingdom of Sardinia, and then part of France again in 1860. Following in his father's footsteps, Garibaldi went to sea at age fifteen. His first patriotic venture was an unsuccessful insurrection at Genoa with Giuseppe Mazzini, a famous revolutionary, to promote Italian liberty. After some years as a guerrilla fighter in South America, he returned to Italy and became involved in warfare of different sorts, but he was then exiled and left for the United States.

In 1854 he was allowed to return to Italy. Garibaldi organized what amounted to a private army and led his famous "Red shirts" against Sicily and Naples, capturing both from Francis II, the last ruler of the two Sicilies. That victory led to Italian unification, and for several months, Garibaldi ruled as dictator of half of Italy. But he voluntarily surrendered his control to form the kingdom of Italy under King Victor Emmanuel II.

President Abraham Lincoln offered Garibaldi a Civil War command, which he refused, but he did make a triumphant tour of Britain, where he was hailed as the "hero of two worlds." After a few more war experiences, he was elected to the French National Assembly but was refused a seat by the other deputies. In 1874 he was elected to the Parliament in Italy, and he retired from public life in 1876.

Garibaldi believed in racial equality and female emancipation and championed the abolition of capital punishment. He was a great liberal, a statesman far ahead of his time. His honesty and good nature made him a favorite with the common people.

The uniform of red shirts was a matter of chance, according to legend. When Garibaldi was raising an army in Montevideo in 1843, a number of red woolen shirts came on the market as a result of trade difficulties caused by the war with Argentina. The government of Uruguay bought them up cheaply and gave them to Garibaldi for his men. When the Italian Legion came over to Italy, they marched in wearing their red shirts.

A woman's loose, high-necked blouse with full sleeves, resembling those that Garibaldi's followers wore, and a brilliant orange fish (*Hypsypopa rubicundus*) found along the Southern California coast, were named for him. Mount Garibaldi, a peak in southern British Columbia, now a popular year-round recreational district, was named by Captain George H. Richads, circa 1860, for the Italian patriot.

GAT, GATLING GUN

Richard Jordan Gatling (1818–1903) was born in Hertford County, North Carolina. He was a physician by education but an inventor by inclination. Because the South had few technical resources, he moved to Indiana, where he devoted all his time to the business of inventing. He invented a practical screw propeller for steamboats, a grain-sowing machine, a hemp-breaking machine, a steam plow, and a wheat drill.

Gatling then became interested in weaponry and invented a crank-operated machine gun, consisting of a cluster of barrels, usually ten, which he patented in 1862. It was mounted on wheels, and the gunner controlled the rate of fire, up to 150 rounds per minute, by turning a hand crank. The gun was accepted by the Union forces, but too late to see much service. Nevertheless, the Confederate leaders were devastated when they learned that the gun had an effective firing range of two thousand yards.

If Colonel Custer had had more confidence in the Gatling guns, he would not have left them behind (which historians say was deliberate), and the massacre of his men at the Battle of Little Big Horn (Custer's last stand) might never have occurred. In any event, Gatling has become immortalized, not because of the Gatling gun, which has long been allocated to the junk heap, but because that gun has given birth to a slang term for a gun, a term that is widely used and immediately understood—the *gat*.

GAUSS'S METHOD, DEGAUSS

Karl Friedrich Gauss (1777–1855), German mathematician and scientist, was one of the three greatest mathematicians of who ever lived, the others being Archimedes and Newton. (Of course, Gauss lived about a century before Albert Einstein.) Gauss's outstanding work includes the discovery of the method of least squares, the discovery of non-Euclidean geometry, and important contributions to the theory of numbers.

At the age of three this mathematical genius called attention to some errors in his father's insurance fund bookkeeping. At ten he was able to sum up, independently, complex arithmetical series. At school he showed little of his precocious talent until age nine. The master set forth a series of numbers in arithmetical progression in what appeared to be a complicated problem. Although Gauss had never been taught the method for solving this problem, he turned in his slate within seconds. At the end of the period there was a pile of slates on top of Gauss's, all with incorrect answers. The master was stunned to see that Gauss had the correct answer. When he was not yet twenty-one years of age, and still a student at Göttingen, he established proof of the fundamental theorem of algebra, which had baffled mathematicians since Euclid's day.

Gauss was not sure whether his major interest was philology or mathematics. He chose the latter in 1796 when he discovered how to construct a regular polygon of seventeen sides, using only a compass and a straightedge. By 1824 he had concluded that it was possible to develop geometry based on the denial of the postulate. Gauss developed the theory of elliptical functions.

Gauss's greatest treatise, a book on the theory of numbers titled *Disquisitiones arithmeticae*, established his reputation in 1801.

On January 1, 1801, Giuseppe Piazzi discovered the asteroid Ceres. After a short time, it was lost in the sun's rays. Recalling his method of least squares, Gauss computed the orbit of Ceres. At the end of the year, the asteroid was clearly seen in the position he had predicted. *Gauss's method* of computing orbits is still in use today.

Gauss originated the *Gauss curvature*, the reciprocal of the product of the two principal radii of curvature of a surface at any of its points, and also the *Gauss curve*, a probability curve. He originated the *Gaussian distribution*, a theoretical frequency distribution used in statistics that is bell-shaped, symmetrical, and of infinite extent. The *Gauss meter* indicates the strength of a magnetic field at any point directly in gauss.

Because of his brilliant mind, science can now wrestle successfully with the mathematical theory of electricity. Gauss was also responsible for studies of magnetism and electricity, and the measurement unit of magnetic induction. A magnetic unit in electricity is named for him.

The German magnetic mines used during World War II took a heavy toll on British shipping. The magnetism of an approaching ship detonated the mines lying on the bottom of the sea. A countermeasure—neutralizing the ship's magnetic field—was created and was called *degaussing*.

GEIGER COUNTER

Hans Wilhelm Geiger (1882–1945) introduced the first successful counter of individual alpha rays through an instrument known as the *Geiger counter*. Geiger was born at Neustadt-an-der-Hardt, Germany. His father was a prominent rabbi and one of the leaders of Reformed Judaism. The son did not follow in his father's footsteps, but instead elected to pursue the study of science. He attended the universities at Munich and Erlangen, and obtained a doctorate in 1906 for work on electrical discharges in gases. He then took up a position at the University of Manchester, where he worked with Ernest Rutherford from 1907 to 1912.

With Rutherford's assistance, Geiger developed an instrument for detecting alpha particles, which became the basis of the modern Geiger counter. He then returned to Germany, where he held important university positions for the rest of his days.

In association with Wilhelm Müller, Geiger produced what is now known as the *Geiger-Müller counter*, a gas-filled counting tube combined with an electronic device capable of reading and measuring the rate of radioactive substances. Ionizing particles penetrate the tube and pulsate the gas; hence the clicking sound.

The *Geiger counter*, as it is generally called, is used for prospecting and for locating nuclear radiation. But more important, it is used by physicians to locate malignancies, and in that role has saved many lives.

GERRYMANDER

Gerrymandering is the practice of dividing a city, state, or country into voting districts in an unfair way to enable the party in power to retain its control. This word entered the English language in 1812 to describe the redistricting of Massachusetts by its governor, Elbridge Gerry. Through that maneuver Gerry's party won fewer popular votes than the opposition, but because of the gerrymandering won almost three times as many seats.

Elbridge Gerry (1744–1814) served as vice president of the United States under James Madison for a year and a half before he became ill and died. The Madison-Gerry ticket, although successful, lost the state of Massachusetts by a wide margin, proof that the people had not forgiven Gerry for juggling their districts.

Gerry was born into a wealthy mercantile family at Marblehead, Massachusetts, and graduated from Harvard University in 1762. He was a signer of the Declaration of Independence, a delegate to the United States Constitutional Convention, and a member of the House of Representatives for four years. In 1797, he was sent to France, together with John Marshall and Charles Cotesworth Pinckney, to discuss the sensitive problems of French privateering. Talleyrand refused to see them and confronted them with Messrs. X, Y, Z, as reports called them. When the French representatives demanded money, Marshall and Pinckney packed their bags and sailed for home, but Gerry remained until President John Adams ordered him back.

Gilbert Stuart, the celebrated artist, while visiting the offices of the Boston *Sentinel*, saw on a wall a map of the new district, which bore the shape of a serpent. He proceeded to add a head, wings, and claws, and remarked to Benjamin Russell, the editor, "That will do for a salamander!" "Better say gerrymander," growled Russell, and so the name given this political reptile insinuated itself into the English language.

GILBERTIAN, GILBERTIANISM

Sir William Schwenck Gilbert (1836–1911), born in Harrow Weald, Middlesex, England, was a playwright and humorist whose plays burlesqued contemporary behavior.

As a young man, Gilbert was left a legacy that enabled him to study law, and in 1863 he was admitted to the bar. Before then Gilbert had been a writer.

In 1870 Gilbert met Arthur Seymour Sullivan, later Sir Arthur (1842–1900), and they formed a partnership in which Gilbert would write the words and Sullivan the librettos of their comic operettas. The partnership lasted for twenty-five years, but relations between the partners were always strained because Sullivan aimed for something higher than comic opera. Despite some personality clashes over the years, the partnership of Gilbert and Sullivan evolved into a commercial success unparalleled in the history of music.

Gilbert finally became estranged because Sullivan had not supported him in an argument over contractual arrangements with the impresario Richard D'Oyley Carte, who had produced many of the Gilbert and Sullivan comic operas, beginning with *Trial by Jury*, and had built the Savoy Theater specially for their productions.

The names of their operettas are known throughout the world. Possibly the most outstanding are *H. M. S. Pinafore* (1878), *The Pirates of Penzance* (1879), *The Mikado* (1885), *The Yeomen of the Guard* (1888), and *The Gondoliers* (1889). Of these, perhaps *The Mikado* furnishes the best example of *Gilbertianism*, a term applied to anything light-hearted and fanciful or humorously topsy-turvy.

Gilbert died from heart failure while trying to rescue a woman in a pond on his country estate.

GILDEROY'S KITE

Gilderoy is not a fictitious name. It was a nickname of a noted robber and cattle stealer of Perthshire, England. The nickname *Gilderoy* came from "gillie roy," a red-haired lad, a sobriquet that fit because Gilderoy had flaming red hair.

Gilderoy was said to have committed some incredible crimes. He picked the pocket of Cardinal Richelieu, and, to make matters worse, did so in the presence of the king. England's Lord Protector Oliver Cromwell fared no better: Gilderoy picked his pockets, too.

Clearly, Gilderoy had very deft fingers. But he made a strategic blunder.

According to reports, Gilderoy and his associates got into trouble and came before a judge who gave them a rough time. He sentenced them to a term longer than usual. When the hooligans were finally released, they retaliated by hanging the judge. For that misadventure, Gilderoy and his five gang members were tried, found guilty, and sentenced to death.

The presiding judge was a hanging judge who took no chances on becoming a hanged judge. He sentenced Patrick MacGregor (Gilderoy's real name) to be hanged higher than the others. The legal axiom then was, the greater the crime, the higher the gallows. Gilderoy's gibbet from ground to pinnacle was thirty feet high. Thousands came to Gallowlee, near Edinburgh, to see Gilderoy hanging in the breeze. His corpse, moving to and fro with the wind, remained on exhibition for weeks. No kite or body had ever been hung higher than Gilderoy's. The year was 1636.

The phrase "to be hung higher than Gilderoy's kite" means to be punished more severely than the very worst criminal.

> Of Gilderoy sae fraid they were,
> They bound him mickle strong,
> Tull Edenburrow they led him thair,
> And on a gallows hung;
> They hung him high aboon the rest,
> He was sae trim a boy . . .
> Percy's *Reliques*

GLADSTONE, GLADSTONE BAG

William Ewart Gladstone (1809–1898), born in Liverpool, England, spent his entire adult life in government service, serving as prime minister four times. He was undoubtedly the greatest British statesman of the nineteenth century. He was eighty-two when he assumed the office of prime minister for the fourth time and was known as the *Grand Old Man* or the *GOM* of Great Britain. The English language has accepted that appellation for any distinguished person whose age befits the description.

Although Gladstone's political life speaks for itself (he was an avid, but unsuccessful, supporter of Home Rule for Ireland), his name lives on in several forms: as a four-wheeled carriage and as cheaper wines because of his reduction of the duty on wine in his 1860 budget. Willard R. Espy, a GOM in the history of English words, puts it this way: "If in an English pub you hear a customer order a gladstone . . . he is requesting a cheap claret."

But what the great Victorian's name is best known for is the *Gladstone bag*, a leather portmanteau made in various sizes, with a wide mouth folding at the top to close with a central clip.

If one cannot afford a Gladstone, a cheap version is the *duffel bag*, which was named for a town near Antwerp, Belgium. This large cloth bag for carrying personal belongings has, like the Gladstone, a big mouth, but is made of canvas or duck.

GOLDWYNISM

Samuel Goldwyn (1882–1974) was one of the greatest pioneer film makers in America and one of Hollywood's most prominent producers. Born in Warsaw, Poland (his name was Samuel Goldfish), he immigrated to the United States as a teenager with only twenty dollars in his pocket. In a small town in New York state, Goldwyn worked in a glove factory. In 1910, he started producing movies with Cecil B. DeMille and his brother-in-law Jesse Lasky. Their initial release was *Squaw Man* (1913). The company merged with Adolph Zukor's *Famous Players*, and then Goldwyn established his own company, Samuel Goldwyn Productions, incorporated as Metro-Goldwyn-Mayer in 1924. Thereafter he worked as an independent producer.

Goldwyn was the first to engage famous writers, such as Ben Hecht, Sinclair Lewis, and Lillian Hellman, to write screenplays. Among his outstanding cinematic features were *Wuthering Heights, Dodsworth, The Little Foxes, The Best Years of Our Lives*, and *Porgy and Bess*. His stable of stars included Pola Negri, Will Rogers, Bebe Daniels, Vilma Banky, and Ronald Coleman. Other luminaries whose careers began with Goldwyn were Gary Cooper, David Niven, Lucille Ball, and Susan Hayward.

Whether Goldwyn twisted his speech purposely for its effect, or whether the gaffes resulted from ignorance, has never been satisfactorily answered. Of course it could be that some of his publicists concocted the quips. These eponymous *Goldwynisms* kept Goldwyn's name in the news. It tickled everyone's fancy to hear him say, "A verbal contract isn't worth the paper it's written on," "Anyone who goes to see a psychiatrist ought to have his head examined," "If Roosevelt were alive he'd turn in his grave," "We have passed a lot of water since this" (a mangling of "A lot of water has passed under the bridge"), "In two words, im-possible," or his wry retort to associates (one often repeated), "Include me out."

Goldwynisms has thus come to refer to Goldwyn's comical misuse of the English language. For example, anyone who says "His brother has his mix all talked up" may be an adherent of malapropism or goldwynism or both.

GOLIATH

The story of David and his battle with the giant *Goliath* has given hope to many people who are determined to face what seem to be insuperable odds. Goliath was a Philistine hero of gigantic size. In *I Samuel* 17:4, Goliath is described as being "six cubits and a span" (about 9 feet or 2.7 meters) tall. Goliath challenged the Hebrews under King Saul to single combat to determine the fate of their respective nations. For forty days no one took up the challenge, until the boy David obtained permission from Saul to fight the Philistine.

The enormous Goliath and the stripling David met and faced each other. The giant waved his sword above his head, as though making a sign of defiance. David had in his hand a small slingshot and a little stone. David reeled back, hurled the stone at the giant, hitting him squarely on the forehead, and slew him. And then with Goliath's own sword, David cut off his head. The frightened Philistines were thus routed.

From the biblical story, a *goliath*, in everyday language, is regarded as a giant. The name *david* is sometimes applied to small, seemingly powerless individuals or groups that confront someone or something much larger than they. The submarines of the Confederacy, in the Civil War, were called davids because they attacked the goliaths of the Union Army.

Today an extremely large business organization may be described as a "goliath" in its sphere of operation. And an individual who performs outstandingly in any field, physical or cerebral, may be called a "goliath."

GORDIAN KNOT

According to Greek legend, in the ancient country of Phrygia, a peasant named Gordius was chosen to be king over the Phrygian people because an oracle had said that their troubles would end if they chose as king the first man who approached the Temple of Zeus driving a wagon. Gordius happened to be that man. To show his gratitude for the honor, he dedicated his wagon to Zeus and tied the ox yoke with a knot so cleverly formed that nobody could untie it. Gradually the legend arose that whoever could untie the knot would become ruler of all Asia.

The Gordian knot stumped all comers. And then Alexander the Great heard about this puzzling situation. He went to the temple, where the legend was repeated. "Well, then," said the conqueror, "it is thus I perform the task," and so saying, he withdrew his sword from its scabbard and slashed through the knot, cutting it in two.

A. T. Pierson in 1891 did not give Alexander credit for his hastiness. "Alexander cut the Gordian knot," quipped Pierson, "which he had not the skill, patience, or strength to untie."

To resolve an intricate problem or task with a single decisive step is expressed by the phrase *to cut the Gordian knot*.

GOTHIC

The Goths were Germanic barbarian tribes that devastated Europe during the third to fifth centuries. They overthrew Rome and established kingdoms in Italy, France, and Spain.

The Renaissance Italians considered the Middle Ages to have been crude and barbaric and the Goths were the best-known barbarians; ergo, the style of the pointed arch was *Gothic*, meaning barbaric. That the Goths had lost their identity centuries before did not matter: Their name implied uncultured, uncivilized, and destructive.

A revival of Gothic architecture was started in the eighteenth century.

Although certain basic designs were characteristic of Gothic, the churches of England, France, and Italy differed. Gothic employs a visual script to reflect the importance of the figures. Numbers are important, too; the number three is associated with the Trinity; four refers to earthly things. The refinements of Gothic architecture and the majesty gained by the edifices adorned with Gothic art have universal appeal. They are not judged to be crude and barbaric, but beautiful and graceful.

One of the most acclaimed examples of Gothic architecture in the world is Notre Dame Cathedral in Paris.

GRAHAM CRACKERS

The man responsible for the Graham cracker was first a temperance leader and then a nutritionist. His puritanical zeal was to eliminate the evils of demon rum, which he maintained increased the evils of the sexual appetite. Sylvester Graham (1794–1851), a graduate of Amherst and an ordained Presbyterian minister, went on the lecture circuit to cure those suffering from what he saw as these evils. He expounded the premise that human beings should eat food the way God grew it, "untouched even by salt and pepper, which would cause insanity." He then accented the need to avoid sinful eating habits such as eating meats and fats, because they aroused the libido. A cardinal point was to substitute baked unsifted wheat flour for white bread. He recommended coarser flour because refined white flour removed vitamins and minerals.

Graham was considered something of a crackpot. He was driven off many platforms by irate bakers, butchers, and others. And mobs of believers and disbelievers had pitched battles. The war against white bread heated up. James Russell Lowell wrote, "I am becoming more and more inclined to Grahamism every day." Such distinguished people joined Graham's crusade as Joseph Smith, the founder of the Mormon church, suffragette Amelia Jenks Bloomer, Bronson Alcott, father of the author of *Little Women*, William Lloyd Garrison, and Horace Greeley.

But after it was all said and done, meat and alcohol won the day. Though Graham could not deliver a knockout punch, he did leave for the American public a tasty coméstible—the *graham cracker*.

GRANGERIZE

The words *grangerize* (to add illustrations to a book) and *grangerism* (the practice of the same) are eponymous from the name of an English vicar who, in 1769, published a six-volume tome titled *Biographical History of England from Egbert the Great to the Revolution, Consisting of Characters Dispersed in Different Classes, and Adapted to a Methodical Catalogue of Engraved British Heads.*

That man was James Granger (1723–1776), whose church was in Shiplake, Oxon, England. He had collected some fourteen thousand engraved portraits cut from books to serve as illustrations in his book. In addition, his book contained a number of blank pages for illustrations, prints, newspaper cuttings, or anything else he might filch later.

Granger suggested in his preface that he was "showing the utility of a collection of engraved portraits." A fad called *grangerizing* developed to collect and paste portraits in appropriate places. This craze led to the mutilation of many books by those in search of engraved portraits. Granger, of course, was the chief mutilating culprit. But because his books sold at auctions for high prices, his success inspired others to keep culling illustrations from any source they could. Fortunately the practice has died down.

Although Granger had a pleasant personality and was admired in his parish, Dr. Johnson disagreed with his liberal views and said of him, "The dog is a Whig. I do not much like to see a Whig in any dress, but I hate to see a Whig in a parson's gown."

The most famous sermon that Granger delivered is said to be "Nature and Extent of Industry," later published as a book, with the wry dedication: "To the inhabitants of the parish of Shiplake who neglect the service of the church, and spend the Sabbath in the worst kind of idleness, this plain sermon, which they never heard, and will probably never read, is inscribed by their sincere well wisher and faithful minister, J. G."

While delivering the sacrament one day in 1776, Granger had an apoplectic fit of such severity that he died.

To *grangerize* in current usage is to mutilate (as in a book or periodical).

GREAT SCOTT!

Many exclamatory expressions have evolved with time, but no one knows where or when most of them arose. In the case of "Great Scott," however, there are some leads that word detectives have followed, but in most instances with questionable results.

The best lead, and one that is subscribed to by a number of wordsmiths, attributes the expression to General Winfield Scott (1786–1866). Nevertheless, the expression did not emanate from him; it was about him. Scott was probably one of America's most brilliant generals; his armies were victorious in many battles in many wars. His men affectionately called him "old Fuss and Feathers" because of his love for colorful military ceremonies and uniforms. Those who were politically opposed to Scott jeeringly called him "Great Scott," denigrating his swagger and "put-on-airs" attitude. Those in the opposite camp exploited the expression as pointing to his dignity and poise. And so there were pros and cons. The pros could boast of Scott's nomination for the presidency of the United States. The contras could say, "True, but he lost the election."

"Great Scott" is still an exclamation of surprise, wonder, admiration, or indignation. Although it seems to have originated in America in the late 1860s, some believe that the term is a euphemism for "Great God!"—a play on the German *GrußGott*.

GREGORIAN CALENDAR

The *Gregorian calendar*, a modification of the Julian, was introduced in 1582 by Pope Gregory XIII. This calendar, called the "New Style" at the time, is now used worldwide. The Julian calendar had prescribed an extra day every fourth year, the idea being that every fourth year should be a leap year to "catch up" the fractions. The calendar calculated the year at some eleven minutes longer than the astronomical year, the time it took the earth to travel around the sun. Pope Gregory corrected the old calendar and adjusted the leap year calculations.

The critical year was 1582, the year that Pope Gregory ordered the calendars to be adjusted to more realistic dates. October 5 of that year was changed to October 15. (Imagine the problems that people had during those lost ten days, what with birthdays, anniversaries, and whatever else was scheduled to occur during that period.) Britain adopted the Gregorian calendar in 1752 when it was ordered that Wednesday, September 2, should be followed by Thursday, September 14. Russia got around to adopting this calendar as well, but not until 1918.

Gregory XIII, born Ugo Buoncompagni at Bologna in 1502, became pope in 1572, changed the calendar in 1582, and died on April 10, 1585.

GRESHAM'S LAW

Gresham's law is based on the theory that if two currencies of the same nominal value but different intrinsic value are in circulation at the same time, the currency with the lower value will eventually drive out of circulation the money with the higher intrinsic value because people will hoard the good money.

The simplest way of enunciating this principle is to say, "Bad money drives out good." The law stems from the fact that money has a value both as money and as a commodity in the open market. The former value is set arbitrarily by law, and is relatively fixed; the latter is determined by supply and demand and varies from time to time. "Good" money has a higher value as a commodity than as money and will disappear from circulation.

The best example of the operation of the law occurs under a bimetallic system, such as the one adopted by the United States in 1792. Congress authorized a $10 gold eagle containing 247.50 grains and a silver dollar of 371.25 grains. At the mint, gold was worth $19.39 an ounce and silver $1.29 an ounce. By 1799, gold was worth $20.30 an ounce in foreign markets. The eagle therefore disappeared from circulation because holders could get almost $1 more an ounce in the market than at the mint.

Henry D. Macleod, a Scottish economist, in 1857, attributed this law to Sir Thomas Gresham (1519–1579), even though Gresham had never stated it and possibly never understood it. In any event, Gresham promulgated it in 1558 to Queen Elizabeth. History has established that the same principle had been enunciated by Nicole Oresme about 1360 and more clearly by Nicolaus Copernicus in 1526.

Gresham was a successful merchant and the founder of the Royal Exchange. He must have known something about money, for he was the financial adviser to four successive English sovereigns. Although Gresham may never have understood the "law," *Gresham's law* has, despite all the criticism addressed to him, survived, under his name, as an accepted economic principle.

The expression *to sup with Sir Thomas Gresham* commemorates Gresham because he built the Royal Exchange, which had a public resting place (called a common lounge) for the homeless and for those who had no money to buy a meal. Therefore, *to sup with Sir Thomas Gresham* meant to go dinnerless.

GRINGO

Many theories have been expounded on the origin of *gringo*. The word has been a contemptuous label for any foreigner by Spaniards who vociferously complained that all foreign accents and dialects sounded like *griego*, or Greek. It was the Mexican way of saying that foreign languages sounded like gibberish, as in "It's Greek to me." *Griego*, slightly altered, became *gringo*, and it was applied not only to the language but also to the speaker, who became *the gringo*.

A more romantic story, but one not fully attested, is that during the Mexican War the troops of General Winfield and General Zachary sang as they marched, as soldiers are apt to do, and their favorite song was repeated so often that the Mexican natives thought that from its first two words they had picked up an expression in English: *gringo*. The opening lines of the song by Robert Burns were

> *Green grow* the Rashes O
> The happiest hours that ere I spent
> Were spent among the lasses O.

One authority claimed that *green coat* was the basis for the term. But some say that it referred to Major Samuel Ringgold, a brilliant strategist who was mortally wounded in the battle of Palo Alto in 1846. It was said that Ringgold's name was so mispronounced that it sounded like *gringo*.

None of these theories have a foundation in fact, because the word had long antedated the Mexican War. According to the *Diccionarío Ca-*

tellano of P. Esteban de Terreros Pando, published in 1787, *gringo* was an established word. The dictionary, in Spanish, contained the following: "In Malaga, they call *Gringoes* those foreigners who have a certain type of accent which keeps them from speaking Spanish easily and naturally; and in Madrid they give the same name, and for the same reason, particularly to the Irish."

GROG, GROGGY

Grog is rough liquor, but in today's language it means any liquor. Although it is no longer a popular beverage, it was at one time the chief drink of British sailors. In fact, grog was issued daily to both crew and officers and became a general name for hard liquor. The name of the beverage that sailors drank did not come from a distillery but from a nickname they bestowed on their chief officer.

Edward Vernon (1684–1757) was commander-in-chief in the West Indies with the naval title of admiral. He was tough, irascible, and a stickler for the rules of discipline. He became concerned by the lack of sobriety of his men and accordingly established a rule that the daily portion of alcoholic beverage be diluted with water. This watered-down substitute made him unpopular with his crew, as one might readily imagine. The sailors dubbed the beverage *grog* after the admiral's nickname, which was "Old Grog." He received that moniker because he habitually wore a *grogram* coat, which is made of a coarse silk fabric.

Anyone who has drunk too much of any intoxicant is likely to be unsteady on his feet. He is disoriented—*groggy*. And so is a prizefighter who appears wobbly. He's said to be punch-drunk, but not because he has drunk too much punch or grog. Even a person as sober as a judge, if dazed or giddy, feels groggy.

GUIDO'S SCALE, ARETINIAN SYLLABLES

About 995 A.D. Guido d'Arezzo, also known as Guido Aretinus, became a Benedictine monk and taught at monasteries in Italy and France. He went twice to Rome to instruct Pope John XIX (reign 1024–1032) and the papal court in his antiphonary.

A musicologist, he originated the *Guido scale* or *Aretinian syllables*. The scale consisted of six syllables—*ut, re, mi, fa, sol, la*—which could be applied to the first six notes of the diatonic scale, starting at any pitch desired. Guido then added a low G, which he called *gamma* after the Greek letter. It later became known as *gamma-ut*.

Gamma was later named "G," as in G-clef; *ut* was renamed *do*, as in *do, re, mi*; and *gamut*, after the final *ti* was added to the scale, entered the English language as a generalized word designating the complete range or extent of anything—notes, prices, choices. "To run the gamut" is to run through the entire series of musical notes, a full display of figures, or a whole range of colors. It is the alphabetical A-to-Z of any subject: "Defense counsel *ran the gamut* of emotions in pleading for clemency—he laughed, he begged, he harangued, he cried."

Guido named the notes in a curious fashion. They came from the first syllables of lines of an ancient Latin hymn to St. John:

Ut queant laxis
*re*sonare fibris.
*Mi*ra gestorum
*fa*muli tuorum,
*Sol*ve polluti
*la*bii reatum
Sancte Iohannes

GUILLOTINE, LOUISETTE

The niceties of putting a person to death became an important topic of discussion during the French Revolution, a time when the frequency and number of persons put to death made the topic not only current but crucial. The two methods of capital punishment were hanging, the usual form of execution for the riffraff, and decapitation, a privilege offered to nobility. Many people considered both forms barbaric. With hanging, some victims did not die immediately but would writhe in pain on the gibbet. With decapitation, nervous hands sometimes missed the crucial spot, and more than one blow became necessary.

Dr. Joseph Ignace Guillotin (1738–1814), a physician during the French Revolution, proposed in a speech on October 10, 1789, to the Constituent Assembly, of which he was a member, a more humanitarian instrument for inflicting capital punishment by decapitation. The device he recommended consisted of a large blade that fell between two upright posts, striking the back of the neck of the victim. Dr. Guillotin informed the amazed assembly: "I can whisk off your head in a twinkling, and you feel no pain." The execution device, with its oblique blade, was adopted but misnamed.

This death-dealing device was not invented by Dr. Guillotin. It was designed by Dr. Antoine Louis, secretary of the College of Surgeons, and built by Tobias Schmidt, a German mechanic, who even supplied a bag to hold the severed head. But similar instruments of death had been used previously in other countries. Italy in the thirteenth century had a decapitator called *mannaia*. Edinburgh had such a device called *maiden*. Reports indicate that a similar beheading machine was used in the Yorkshire town of Halifax.

Although the French device was originally called *Louisette*, the name *guillotine* was more often used. Dr. Guillotin took exception to the name and tried to change it, but the name stuck. After the good doctor's death, however, his family changed the family name legally.

GUPPY, GUPPY SUBMARINE

R. J. Lechmere Guppy (1836–1916), president of the Scientific Association of Trinidad, lends his name to a little tropical fish he discovered that has been the delight of children and adults alike ever since. In 1868 he presented specimens to the British Museum, which put them on display. Almost immediately, the guppy, which was named *Gerardinus guppy* after him but later renamed *Poecilis reticulate*, became a favorite for public and home aquariums throughout the world, and still are one of the best-known and most popular small tropical fish.

The male guppy is seldom longer than two inches, about one-half the length of the female. But unlike the female, the male is very brilliantly spotted and streaked with rainbow colors. The female is a slow-moving, grayish-green fish.

The guppy is native to Venezuela, Trinidad, and neighboring regions. They have been imported to other areas because they are mosquito-larvae eaters, and so help reduce the incidence of malaria.

In World War II a small submarine was developed that was twice as fast as the older styles and more maneuverable. Appropriately, these midget submarines were called *guppies*. But in this instance the name was an acronym for "greater underwater propulsion power."

GUY

On November 5, 1605, a plot to blow up the House of Parliament in London was uncovered. The conspirators, opposed to the anti-Catholic laws imposed by James I, had stored thirty-six barrels of gunpowder in cellars beneath the building, enough to blow it sky-high. On that date the king was to open and address Parliament. When the plotters burrowed through the walls of the cellar, Guy Fawkes, a Roman Catholic convert, was caught in the act, and the other conspirators were rounded up.

The affair was named the Gunpowder Plot, and Fawkes was tried and hanged on January 31, 1606. On every November 5 grotesque effigies of Guy Fawkes were carried through the streets and burned to mark the anniversary of the failed plot. From these odd-looking effigies came the word *guy*. And, understandably, it has a pejorative sense in England.

In America a *guy* is simply a boy or a man. The term is usually dressed up or down to make it complimentary ("a nice guy," "a regular guy") or insulting ("a wise guy," "a tough guy").

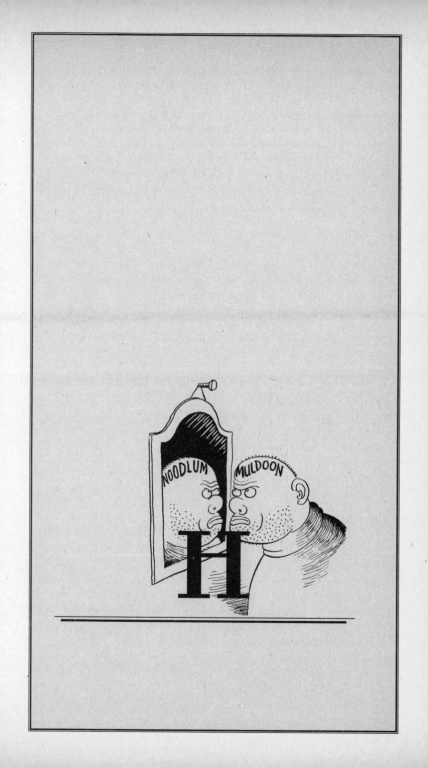

HAM ACTOR

The origin of this derisory term has not been satisfactorily established. In fact, so many paths have been suggested to this word's provenance that it is burdensome to follow them all. Perhaps the best lead is found in the advice Hamlet offers to actors—not to "saw the air too much with your hand" and not "to strut and bellow." Sounds familiar? Ham actors are known to overact and to strive mightily to call attention to themselves. And so it might be that from *Hamlet*, Shakespeare's greatest tragedy, comes the solution: The advice given by Hamlet plus the first syllable of his name may have combined to produce the appellation *ham actor*. Farfetched, but worth considering.

Another possible derivation is from the practice, in the nineteenth century, of using ham fat to remove theatrical makeup. The actor was called a *hamfatter*, and the appellation became the title, during the heyday of minstrels, of a Negro minstrel song, "The Ham-Fat Man."

The Midwest has its candidate, Hamish McCullough (1835–1885), who toured with his own troupe of players regularly in Midwestern States. Hamish's company was called "Ham's actors" (Ham was McCullough's nickname), and the acting of his players was reported to deserve that questionable commendation.

HANSOM CAB

The *hansom cab* was a low-slung closed carriage on two wheels. The driver's seat was in the rear high enough to allow the reins to pass over the roof of the cab and down to the horse in front, which meant that the two passengers it carried had an unobstructed view as well as privacy. The cab was known for its maneuverability and safety features. It became the most popular cab in London from the moment it made its appearance in 1834; in fact, it became a popular cab all over the world. Disraeli referred to it as "the gondola of London."

The cab was the invention of Joseph Aloysius Hansom (1803–1882), a woodworker's son born in York, England. He became a successful architect and designed many important buildings and churches, including the town hall of Birmingham. His original patent for the cab was called the "Patent Safety Cab," which he sold, but with disastrous financial results. Although no one is certain of the amount he received, it is reported to have been about 300 pounds, a pittance considering the tremendous value for something so much in demand.

Hansom cabs are gone now, except in some parks, such as Central Park in New York City, where lovers can have a few moments of privacy while being taken for a jaunt.

HENRY, HENRY INDUCTANCE

Joseph Henry (1797–1878) was an American physicist who made fundamental discoveries related to electromagnetism. His experiments played a large part in the development of the telegraph, telephone, radio, and dynamo.

Henry was born at Albany, New York, and dropped out of school at age thirteen to become a watchmaker's apprentice. Fortunately for the scientific world, he resumed his education three years later, and began experimenting while teaching at Albany Academy. His first important work was the development of the electromagnet. In 1831 Henry demonstrated a telegraph. Samuel Morse used many of Henry's ideas in the telegraph, which he patented six years later. Henry also found a way to produce electric current by moving a magnet through a coil of wire. He arrived independently at this discovery of induced current, but did not publish his work until after Michael Faraday announced the same findings. Faraday received the credit for the discovery, but the unit of electric inductance is now called a *henry*. Henry taught at Princeton University from 1832 to 1846, at which time he became the first secretary, then a director, of the Smithsonian Institution.

Through Henry's meteorological work, a weather-reporting system was created. Henry became the first weather forecaster to initiate scientific weather reporting, a practice that led to the creation of the U.S. Weather Bureau. He also was a primary organizer of the National Academy of Science and its second president.

HERCULEAN TASKS

Hercules, a Greek mythological hero, was the son of Zeus and Alcmene, a mortal woman. Hera, Zeus's wife, was wrathful because of his infidelity and wanted to dispose of his bastard offspring. She tried to kill Hercules in his cradle, but was foiled. She then sent serpents to do him in, but Hercules, strong even then, strangled them.

In his manhood, Hercules was brawny and muscular, but was no match for Hera, who afflicted him with madness. In a fit of insanity he slew his wife and children. To punish him for this grievous act, Apollo sentenced him to serve penance for twelve years under the Argive king, Eurystheus, who imposed upon him twelve tasks of great difficulty and danger.

The first task was the killing of the monster lion Nemea. Hercules strangled it with his bare hands. The second was the killing of a nine-headed beast called Hydra. Every time a head was cut off, two appeared. He burned off all the heads except one, which could not be killed. This one he buried under a rock and dipped his arrow into the Hyda's blood to poison it. The third was the capturing of an Arcadian stag with golden horns and feet of brass. Hercules caught it after a long weary chase, drove it into a snow drift, and then carried it home on his shoulders. The fourth was the capturing of the wild bear of Erymanthus. This he did with his bare hands. The fifth was the cleaning of the stables of King Augeas of Elis. The stables housed three thousand oxen and hadn't been cleaned for thirty years. Hercules turned two rivers into the stables and cleaned them in a day. The sixth was the destruction of the birds of Stympphalus. They had brass claws and ate human flesh. After frightening them with Athena'a rattle, which was filled with dried dragons' eyes, he shot them with poisoned arrows. The seventh was the capture of the mad bull of Crete. Hercules overcame it and carried it away on his shoulders. The eight was the capture of the wild horses of Diomedes. These horses ate human flesh. Hercules caught them and fed them the flesh of Diomedes, whom he had killed. Then he carried the horses on his back to Eurysteus. The ninth labor was obtaining the girdle (sash) of Hippolyta, Queen of the Amazons. Hercules fought and defeated the Amazons, killed Hippolyta, and took her girdle. The tenth was the capture of the ox of Geryon, a creature with three bodies. Hercules killed the giant Eurytion who was guarding the ox, destroyed the giant's two-headed dog, and then drove the ox home. The eleventh labor was the theft of the apples of Hesperides. Hercules asked Atlas to get them. Atlas agreed and placed the world on Hercules's shoulders. Hercules said he would carry the world forever but he would first need a pad for his shoulders. Atlas agreed to hold the world while Hercules fetched a pad. After Atlas took the world back, Hercules simply made off with the apples. The twelfth labor was to bring Cerberus, the watchdog of the lower world, up to earth. With Pluto's permission, Hercules carried the dog to Eurystheus, although Cerberus bit a big piece out of his back. The king was so terrified of the dog that he hid himself in a large jar.

A *Herculean task* implies a prodigious task, possibly a seemingly impossible one.

HIPPOCRATIC OATH

Not much is known about the life of Hippocrates (c. 460–c. 375 B.C.), who was given the appellation the "father of medicine." He is believed to have been born on the island of Cos and to have been a member of a famous family of priest-physicians, the Asclepiadae. He was known to be an acute and indefatigable observer. He practiced as both physician and surgeon and is credited with having separated medicine from superstition. His writings, or perhaps the treatises of his followers, known as the *Hippocratic Collection*, are still read.

Although modern science has determined that their interpretation of natural causes for disease was erroneous, Hippocrates's refutation of traditional beliefs that the gods were behind all human ills was a major step forward.

The *Hippocratic oath* is still administered in many schools of medicine, but some portions of it are no longer sworn to. It represents the rules that ought to govern medical ethics. The *Hippocratic oath*, in abridged form, is as follows:

You do solemnly swear, each man by whatever he holds most sacred, that you will be loyal to the profession of medicine and just and generous to its members; that you will lead your lives and practice your art in uprightness and honor, that into what-soever house you shall enter, it shall be for the good of the sick to the utmost of your power, you holding yourselves far aloof from wrong, from corruption, from the tempting of others to vice; that you will exercise your art solely for the cure of your patients and will give no drug, perform no operation, for a crim-inal purpose, even if solicited, far less suggest it; that whatsoever you shall see or hear of the lives of men which is not fitting to be spoken, you will keep inviolably secret. These things you do swear. Let each man bow the head in sign of acquiescence. And now, if you will be true to this, your oath, may prosperity and good repute be ever yours; the opposite if you shall prove your-self forsworn.

HOBSON'S CHOICE

Where to elect there is but one.
'Tis Hobson's choice—take that or none.
Thomas Ward

When, years ago, you went to buy a Ford, and the auto dealer said take any color as long as it's black, you were given *Hobson's choice*. The choice boils down to no choice at all because there is no alternative. A person driven to a single course of action has only a Hobson's choice.

The phrase originated from the practice of Thomas Hobson (1544–1631), a liveryman in seventeenth-century Cambridge, England, whose customers, especially the students from the university, if unrestricted, would always select his fastest horses and ride them to exhaustion. He knew, as he put it, that "scholars ride hard." Knowing that the welfare of the horses would be best served if they were used in rotation, he established a rule that his customers could not select a horse of their own choosing but had to hire the one he placed nearest the stable door, which was the horse that had had the most rest. The customer could accept the offer or reject it—that is, ride off or walk.

Hobson was a well-known character in his day. He amassed a fortune during his lifetime, owned a half-dozen manor houses, and left sufficient funds to maintain a public aqueduct and fountain in the Cambridge marketplace. The poet John Milton knew Hobson as a young man, and wrote a humorous epitaph upon his death, which included the lines:

Ease was his chief disease; and to judge right,
He died for heaviness that his cart went light;
His leisure told him that his time was come,
And lack of load made his life burdensome.

Melton's epitaph for Hobson.

HOMERIC

Some people maintain that the *Homeric writings* were the work of many
men. But historians interested in that point have concluded that the
Iliad and the *Odyssey* were poems from the poet Homer, a blind Greek
who wandered from city to city in the ninth century B.C. reciting his
epic poems. The episodes from his epic poems and the words he has
contributed to the English language remain as monuments of a magnificent mind that knew no boundaries.

Homeric means imposing, magnificent, or, in another sense, mighty,
colossal, monumental, titanic. The scale and sweep of Homeric narrative
is mighty and full of grandeur. His characters are larger-than-life: Achilles, the brave and dangerous young man who dies so young; Odysseus,
the man of experience whose triumph is survival; Penelope, Odysseus's
faithful wife, who stealthily unravels the threads of her tapestry every
night lest she be forced to take a suitor. All of these characters demonstrate the extraordinary powers of the human spirit.

Homer in the Odyssey speaks of the deeds of the gods and men as
the subject of epic poetry. Much of the Homeric poems is concerned
with the gods, and the action hinges on their intervention.

Many of today's expressions have come from Homer's works. Hector,
a hero in the *Iliad*, refers to a bully or to a blustering, swaggering fellow.
Trojans, as recorded in Vergil's *Aeneid* and Homer's *Iliad*, were hard-
working, determined, industrious people. Hence: "He worked like a Trojan." A person who shows pluck, determination, and energy has Trojan
characteristics. And Homer was the first to say, "Out of sight, out of
mind." The Achilles heel and the Achilles tendon are in current usage;
the Achilles heel is a person's vulnerable spot, and the Achilles tendon
is the tendon running from the heel bone to the calf muscle of the leg.
That "Homer sometimes nods" is an expression that means that even
the wisest and most gifted of men, like Homer, make mistakes. The
expression first appeared in Horace's *De Arte Poetica*: "Sometimes even
good old Homer nods."

The English language is indebted to Homer for the word *stentorian*,
from Stentor, a Greek herald during the Trojan War. His voice was "as
loud as that of fifty men together." And when a man is characterized as
a *Nestor*, he is being referred to as an old man with the wisdom of the
ancient Nestor, the Homeric hero who fought in the Trojan War with
the Greeks. It is reputed that he lived so long that he ruled three generations of men.

Alexander the Great showed his high regard for Homer by carrying an edition of Homer on his campaigns. He always placed it under his pillow at night with his sword.

Many of the great minds of the world have been compared to Homer; he is a standard to measure men by. Plato has been called the Homer of philosophers, Milton the English Homer, and Ossian the Gaelic Homer. Byron called Fielding the prose Homer of human nature, and Dryden said that Shakespeare was the Homer of our dramatic poets.

HOODLUM, HOOD

A *hoodlum* is a young street ruffian, especially one belonging to a gang. He—and hoodlums are only *he*—is a thug, a gangster, completely reprehensible. The word is a varied eponymous form of the real name of the leader of a gang of toughs who plagued California during the last part of the nineteenth century, harassing Chinese laborers especially.

But there are other theories of the origin of *Hoodlum*. John Bartlett reports, without attestation, that in 1871 a San Francisco newspaper reporter was assigned to cover gang leader Muldoon's felonious activities, an assignment that undoubtedly put the reporter's safety in jeopardy. The ingenious reporter dreamed up an unusual means for guarding against reprisal from Muldoon and his gang—he spelled Muldoon's name backwards. He reported the criminality of a person named "Noodlum." The newspaper's compositor read the initial "N" as an "H." And so an illegitimate word from an illegitimate parent was born. And the word *hoodlum* thrived, became a a part of the English language, and found a resting place in every dictionary. Today small-time and big-time crooks as well are known as hoodlums or, shortened, *hoods*.

H. L. Mencken reported that *hoodlum*, first recorded in the San Francisco area about 1870, may have come from a Bavarian dialect term, *hodalump*, of precisely the same meaning—a small-time gangster. At that time the Germans constituted a large part of the comunity, and many of them were Bavarians.

The word *hoodwink* has unrelated origins—criminal activity in the sixteenth century gave birth to this word. Thieves practiced a form of early-bird mugging. They would pull the hood, or cowl, down over the eyes of the intended victim, thus blinding him and making him an easy prey to be robbed. The poor devil who was targeted was said to be *hoodwinked*.

HOOKER

How the word *hooker* came to mean "prostitute" has never been satisfactorily established. Willard R. Espy says that the word *harlot* is descended from Old German *Hari*, "army," and *Lot*, "loiterer," a camp follower. But *hooker*, some believe, evolved because British ships used to sail to the Hook of Holland. Ladies of the night, and perhaps of the day, too, lay in wait (or, as Espy put it, "stood in wait, and lay afterward") to please their customers. Some authorities subscribe to the belief that a *hooker* was so called because she hooked her curved parasol handle into the arm of male passersby.

John Ciardi says the word arose as a bit of British slang. *London Labour and London Poor*, published in four volumes (1851–1862) in London by Henry Mayhew, who also published the magazine *Punch*, reported this statement: "We hooks a white collar (a clergyman) now and then," and from another, "I've hooked many a man by showing an ankle on a wet day." Was this an analogy to hooking a fish? Or did the word come from a notorious New York City waterfront neighborhood called "Hook," where vice was known to be rampant?

The belief that describing a lady of pleasure as a *hooker* arose because of "Fighting Joe," a Union general who put the red-light district in Washington off limits, is considered by most wordsmiths to be a case of folk etymology. The general's name was Joseph Hooker, but that is as far as the connection goes. Furthermore, William Morris confirmed that "hooker" appeared in print at least once before the Civil War, in 1859. Morris decided to write to his friend Bruce Catton, one of the nation's foremost authorities on the Civil War. Morris noted that General Hooker's reputation was not of the highest and quoted Charles Francis Adams, Jr., as calling him a "man of blemished character . . . whose headquarters was a place to which no self-respecting man liked to go, and no decent woman could go—a combination of barroom and brothel."

Here is Catton's comment:

> That business about Joe Hooker and the soiled doves of Civil War Washington pops up every so often. I agree with you that the term "hooker" did not originate during the Civil War, but it certainly became popular then. During these war years, Washington developed a large and segregated district—the word "segregated" had a different meaning as used then—somewhere south of Constitution Avenue. This became known as Hooker's Division in tribute to the proclivities of General Hooker and the name has stuck ever since.

HOOLIGANISM

Ernest Weekly, in his *Romance of Words* (1912), says the original Hooligans were a spirited Irish family of that name whose activities enlivened the drab monotony of life in Southwark, England, about fourteen years earlier. Clarence Rook's memoir, *The Hooligan Nights* (1899), notes, "There was, but a few years ago, a man called Patrick Hooligan, who walked to and fro among his fellow men, robbing them and occasionally bashing them. . . . It is . . . certain that he lived in Irish Court, that he was employed as a chucker-out (a bouncer) at various resorts in the neighborhood. Moreover, he could do more than his share of tea-leafing (stealing) . . . being handy with his fingers. . . . Finally, one day he had a difference with a constable, put his light out . . . He was . . . given a lifer. But he had not been in gaol long before he had to go into the hospital, where he died. . . . The man must have had a forceful personality . . . a fascination, which elevated him into a type. It was doubtless the combination of skill and strength, a certain exuberance of lawlessness, an utter absence of scruple in his dealings, which marked him out as a leader among men. . . . He left a great tradition . . . He established a cult."

Hooliganism is rowdy behavior. The word became a favorite term to describe misbehavior in some foreign countries, particularly Russia. It is said that a czar, on visiting England, picked up the word and took it back with him duty-free.

HOUDINI

The master magician, the great illusionist, the stellar escape artist Harry Houdini (1874–1926), was born Ehrich Weiss in Budapest, Hungary. When he came to America and became an American citizen, he adopted his stage name, after Jean Eugène Robert Houdin (1805–1871), who had been considered the foremost French magician.

Houdini became world-famous in 1900 after a performance in London at which he demonstrated an unusual talent of freeing himself from "impossible traps," such as handcuffs, locks, and straitjackets, even when suspended in the air or submerged in water. No lock could hold him, not even that of the condemned cell at the Washington jail.

In October 1926, some students were invited by Houdini to his dressing room. Houdini sat on his couch to check his mail at which time a J. Gordon Whitehead, an amateur boxer, asked whether it was true that Houdini could withstand any body blow not below the belt or on his face. When Houdini agreed, Whitehead, while Houdini was rising from the couch, struck him three times on the stomach. Houdini had not tensed his muscles. He fell back on his couch, subsequently developing gangrene in his appendix and then peritonitis. In the 1920s that latter affliction was a virtual sentence of death.

The cultlike adoration, almost worship, of necromancers followed him to his grave. Because he once said that if anyone can break the shackles of death, he can, his devotees hold an annual séance at his gravesite in the Machpelah Cemetery, in Glendale, Long Island.

The Houdini Room in the Library of Congress houses the extensive library that Houdini donated.

To "pull a Houdini" is to make an amazing escape, and a *Houdini* is anyone with seemingly magical powers in any field.

HUSKY

A man called *husky* is being compared to a dog, and a sled dog at that. But because this dog, stocky and muscular, symbolizes great strength, an informal sense has evolved for *husky*, meaning big and burly. Harriet

Beecher Stowe used that designation for a stocky and muscular man in a story published in 1869. Describing a man as husky is not meant to be disparaging.

But to return to the sled dog: It is a breed developed in Siberia. Experts believe that the name derives from that of the Eskimo group Chukchi. This dog is so strong that it is capable of pulling a load for sixty miles in one day. Although not related to the wolf family, the Husky howls like a wolf, eats raw fish, and sleeps on snow. North Canadian Indians called this dog *uskimi*, which meant Eskimo. The explorers thought they were hearing "huskemaus," but they called the dogs *Eski*, a shortening of *Eskimo*. Eventually they corrupted the contraction *Eski* by fronting it with an *h*, and from it *Husky* emerged—and stayed.

A *husky throat* is a dry one, characterized by a voice that has lost its timbre. Unrelated is the activity of *husking* corn.

HYACINTH

A *hyacinth* is a varicolored fragrant plant with a terminal cluster of flowers. This harbinger of spring takes its name from a legendary handsome Greek youth. But in the beauty of this lovely flower lies a tragic story.

The son of Amyclae, a Spartan king, was a youth named Hyacinthus. He was so handsome that he was beloved by both Apollo (god of the sun) and Zephyrus (god of the west wind). Hyacinthus returned the love of Apollo, whereupon Zephyrus became insanely jealous. One day while Apollo was engaged in a game of throwing with Hyacinthus, Zephyrus, far from the gentle soul he was reputed to be—a soft, warm breeze called a *zephyr* was named after him—caused a discus tossed by Apollo to strike the lad's head. Hyacinthus died, and from his blood sprang the flower that bears his name—the *hyacinth*, a delicate flower with breathtaking spikes of white, pink, yellow, or purple flowers. On the petals appeared a legendary exclamation of grief: *ai ai*.

The Greek word *huakinthos* became the Latin word *hyacinthus*, entering the English language as *hyacinth*. Horticulturists believe that the original flower was a lily, gladiolus, or iris. It is now taken to mean any of the *hyacinthus* group of bulbous herbs of the lily family.

I

IRIS, IRIDESCENCE, IRIDIUM

Iris was a pretty young girl who had the misfortune of being seen by the lustful Zeus. His jealous wife, Hera, turned Iris into a rainbow, and she became the goddess of the rainbow and the messenger of the gods. Whenever she had to convey a message to someone on earth, she took a convenient stairway down from heaven—a rainbow. Her name was derived from the Greek word for rainbow, and a sister word, *iridescence*, is a play of colors producing rainbow effects.

Besides being poetically associated with the popular plant with large, beautifully colored flowers and with the rainbow, the name in English, is given to the colored membrane surrounding the pupil of the eye. The amount of pigment contained in the iris determines eye color. When there is very little pigment, the eye appears blue; with increased pigment, the shade becomes deep brown to black.

Fleur de lis stands for "flower of the lily" in French (*lis* means lily). *Fleur de lis* is also the name of a design supposed to represent the white iris. The design became the emblem of the kings of France in the 1100s. Charles V changed the pattern to three golden fleur-de-lis on a blue field.

The term *irid* is used also in *iridium*, one of the densest terrestrial substances. It is a metallic element of the platinum group that, when combined with other elements, forms a substance with the various colors of the rainbow.

JACOB'S LADDER

A prophetic dream by the patriarch Jacob of a ladder ascending to heaven has given us the term *Jacob's ladder*. "And he dreamed that there was a ladder set up on the earth, and the top of it reached to heaven, and behold, the angels of God were ascending and descending on it" (Genesis 28:12-13).

Jacob was the son of Isaac and Rebecca, and the father of twelve sons who became the heads of the twelve tribes of Israel. His name means "heel grabber" because he gripped the heel of Esau, his twin brother, as Jacob left his mother's body. Jacob was blessed with a new name, *Israel*, and is thus the eponymous ancestor of the Jewish state of Israel.

In mundane activities, a *Jacob's ladder* is a useful device to ascend from a smaller ship to a larger one or to descend from a larger ship to a smaller one. The ladder is made of rope or cable with wooden or metal rungs. Harbor pilots use such a ladder to come aboard.

A steep winding road, a twisting path up a mountain, or a flight of steps up a cliff are sometimes called *Jacob's ladder*. The name is also used for an herb or small plant with a flower-and-leaf formation resembling a ladder.

JACQUARD

Jacquard is the name of an elaborate woven design found in tablecloth damask, bedspreads, and brocades. The weave gets its name from the *Jacquard loom*, on which flower designs or even pictures of men and women can be woven. The name *jacquard* is also used for a type of knitting that requires a machine somewhat like the Jacquard loom to make changes in color or design.

The invention of the *Jacquard loom* by Joseph Marie Jacquard (1752–1834), born in Lyons, France, simplified weaving, but it also cost thousands of silk workers their jobs. There was much turmoil, and Jacquard on one occasion was seized by an angry mob and barely escaped with his life. The problem subsided when Napoleon purchased the loom and declared it to be the property of the French state. The purchase hastened the lowering of silk prices, which, in turn, greatly improved the market for silk, and thus helped the reemployment of workers in that industry. In 1819 Jacquard was awarded a gold medal and the Cross of the Legion of Honour. The use of his loom spread to England in the 1820s and from there virtually worldwide.

The loom was so constructed that each warp thread could be raised or lowered. It thus became the first practical machine to weave intricate patterns. It was operated and controlled by punched cards, forerunners of those used with the modern computer.

Jacquard is a fabric woven by the jacquard method.

JANUARY, JANUS, JANITOR

Janus was appointed to his job as god of gates and doors because he had two faces, one looking backward and the other forward. It was said that he knew the past and foresaw the future—an attribute that can be represented by a door because it looks two ways.

The Romans had some doubts about the trustworthiness of Janus. His temple in the Roman Forum had two doors which were closed when Rome was at peace but open during wartime. The open doors meant that the god had gone out to assist the warriors. During peacetime, the doors were closed to make certain that this god, the safeguard of the city, would not escape. Clearly the Romans took no chances with Janus. When at peace, they would slam the doors shut in both his faces.

Ovid tells the story of the nymph of Carna, who beguiled her suitors by inducing them to go into a cave with the promise that she would follow shortly after and let them make love to her; she then promptly ran away. But when she tried this trick on Janus, he saw her departing with his second, backward-looking face, whereupon she granted him her favors, and he in return gave her the power to chase away nocturnal vampires, a power she used to save their son Proca.

From Janus came the word *janitor*, meaning doorkeeper. The responsibility of the janitor eventually extended to the entire building. Janus also gives us *January*, the name of the first month in the year.

JEKYLL-HYDE PERSONALITY

The term *Jekyll and Hyde* is most often used to designate a two-faced person who alternates between a charming personality and one that is extremely unpleasant. The phrase is taken from a classic tale by Robert Louis Stevenson (1850–1894), *The Strange Case of Dr. Jekyll and Mr. Hyde* (1886).

In the story, Dr. Jekyll was a physician who enjoyed a good reputation. He discovered a potion that would change him into an evil dwarf named Mr. Hyde. After experimenting with the drug several times, Jekyll found it difficult to reconvert. He was becoming more Hyde than Jekyll. With time Hyde committed a murder and was tried for it. His lawyer revealed the gruesome secret of Jekyll's life, whereupon Hyde committed suicide.

Psychologists might term *Jekyll/Hyde* a split personality. Stevenson had probed deeply into the so-called split personality. He had been taught from his youth that man consisted of evil, wild urges kept in control only by dint of great effort, ever threatening to break out in "the duality of man's nature." It is said that Stevenson fashioned his story after a case involving William Brodie (1741–1788), a respected citizen of Edinburgh who at night joined a masked gang of toughs, robbing and terrorizing the very same persons he championed during the day. Brodie was caught and hanged.

Dr. Jekyll and Mr. Hyde has caught the imagination of many dramatists and screen writers. In the last few decades, there have been at least three movies dealing with the story of Dr. Jekyll, each one approaching the character from a different psychological angle.

John Barrymore portrayed Jekyll/Hyde without makeup in 1920; Fredric March won an Oscar in 1932 for his sensitive portrayal of that split personality; and Spencer Tracy presented another version just nine years later.

JEZEBEL, JEZEBELIAN, JEHU

The adjective form *Jezebélian* characterizes a woman who is wicked and shameless. Jezebel was a Phoenician princess who became the wife of Ahab, king of Israel, and attempted to convert Ahab to worship Baal, the god of the Phoenicians, above Jehovah. Jezebel was not a character to be admired. She arranged for the wholesale slaughter of the Lord's prophets. Indeed, she was known as "the wanton woman of the painted face." But the rebel general Jehu, a politically ambitious follower of the Lord, destroyed the Baal devotees, and proclaimed himself king of Israel.

Jezebel put on makeup ("painted her face," *Kings II*, ix, 30) and was then trampled by horses and eaten by dogs—a quite vengeful ending to ". . . the whoredom of Jezebel and her witchcraft" (Kings II, ix, 22).

Today, a woman who flaunts her bold spirits and loose morals may be called a *Jezebel*.

Jehu, King of Israel (845–816), was renowned for driving his chariot at high speeds. According to the Bible, when he went to war, he rode in a chariot which he drove furiously.

Any fast, reckless driver today may be called *a Jehu*, but formerly a *Jehu* was a coachman who drove at a rattling pace.

JINGO, JINGOISM

> We don't want to fight,
> But by jingo! if we do
> We've got the ships, we've got the men
> And got the money, too.

A *jingo* is a rabid patriot who favors an aggressive foreign policy for his country. *Jingoism* is to Britain what *chauvinism* is to France. Originally *by jingo* was employed merely as a mild oath. There have been many conjectures of the genesis of the phrase, including "by Jesus" and "by Jainko," the supreme god of the Basques. In the seventeenth century, *jingo* was a common expression of conjurers, but they never revealed the meaning. The *Oxford English Dictionary* states that *jingo* was originally "a piece of conjurer's gibberish." It was the only English term derived from the Basques tongue.

With the advent of the Russo-Turkish War of 1877–1878, *jingo* came to be applied to superpatriots itching for war at the slightest provocation. There was much excitement in England just before the British Mediterranean squadron was sent to Gallipoli to frustrate Russia's designs on Constantinople. In 1878 the "Great MacDermott" sang a popular music hall ditty, written by G. W. Hunt, which took the music halls by storm. The Russophobes became known as *jingoes*, and a noisy war-mongering policy has been labeled *jingoism*.

JOE MILLER

A *Joe Miller* is a stale joke. If you tell your friends the jokes you heard as a youngster, they're probably *Joe Millers*. Poor Joe Miller. No one would like his name to serve as an eponym for a stale jest. Comedians who tell warmed over, well-known jokes are said to have taken them from *Joe Miller's Joke Book*.

Joe Miller (1684–1738) was a popular English comic actor during the early 1700s. He performed at the Drury Lane Theater in London, but his parts were minor. Although his dialogue did not call for many jests, the audience took delight in quoting the witty remarks he made.

A year after Joe Miller's death, a certain Joe Mottley, without permission from anyone, compiled a book titled *Joe Miller's Jest-Book, or The Wit's Vade Mecum*. The book contained only three jests ever spoken by Miller; the rest consisted of poor puns and dull witticisms. Other publishers jumped on the comic bandwagon, and soon there was a flood of joke books that bore the name *Joe Miller*. Readers responded the way audiences did to the same joke time after time: "That's a Joe Miller." The name became a synonym for any timeworn joke.

Joe Miller's memory is being unfairly tarnished when his name is associated with a hackneyed jest taken from this old book. Joe, of course, never saw the book. Furthermore, Joe was unschooled; he could neither read nor write.

JUGGERNAUT

Juggernaut is an English version of the Hindustani name *Jaganath*. It was the eponym given to Krishna, chief Hindu deity and Lord of the World. In Hindu belief *Juggernaut* is the name of a great idol to the god Vishnu. During the summer worship festival, his image is mounted on an enormous decorated cart and then pulled by hundreds of pilgrims from its temple at Puri, in Orissa, over the sand to another sanctuary. The cart is 35 feet square and 45 feet high and has sixteen wheels, each seven feet in diameter. The journey takes several days. The belief that pilgrims purposely hurl themselves under the wheels of the cart on the last day of the journey to ensure their admittance into heaven is without foundation.

People crushed needlessly or ruthlessly by customs or institutions are said to be sacrificing themselves to some sweeping force they cannot stop. They are victims, because a *juggernaut* cannot be stopped, and it will destroy anything that stands in its path. It is a moving force like a locomotive or a football fullback.

JUMBO

Some animals have given their names to synonyms that are just as descriptive as words derived from an eponym. One that comes to mind quickly, and one that is used frequently, is *Jumbo*. It is, in the words of P. T. Barnum, who introduced the elephant bearing this name, "the universal synonym for stupendous things."

Barnum was a showman who didn't hesitate to exaggerate if it helped his business. Jumbo had been captured by a hunting party in Africa in 1869. The natives were amazed at its tremendous size and therefore dubbed the animal *jumbo*, which in Swahili means "chief." The beast weighed six and a half tons and stood ten feet, nine inches at the shoulders. Jumbo lived at the London Zoo for seventeen years. His daily rations consisted of 200 pounds of hay, five pails of water, and a quart of whiskey.

In 1882 Jumbo had a change of residence. The London Zoo was experiencing financial problems, and to ease the burden, the zoo sold Jumbo to Phineas Taylor Barnum (1810–1891). The English public was incensed, and even Queen Victoria added her voice in an effort to retain this "national treasure." But Barnum won out and brought Jumbo to the United States. The transport took fifteen days, and Jumbo survived aboard the ship by drinking enormous quantities of beer. On Jumbo's arrival in America, Barnum proceeded in his modest style to inform Americans how fortunate they were to have Jumbo on their land. His advertisement read: Jumbo the Only Mastondon on Earth . . . The Gentle and Historic Lord of Beasts . . . The Towering Monarch of his Mighty Race . . . The Prodigious Pet of both England and America . . . Steadily Growing in Tremendous Height and Weight . . . Jumbo, the Universal Synonym for Stupendous things. . . .

Jumbo was a star attraction, and his name did become a household word for anything of large size, such as a "jumbo package," or the oversized jets, such as the Boeing 747 and the DC 10. In 1885 Jumbo was accidentally struck down and killed by a railway engine in an Ontario railroad yard. It is said that Barnum wept, but whether because he had lost a moneymaking resource or because of sentiment, we'll never know. But we do know that many Americans wept for the loss of an animal they loved.

KID MCCOY, REAL MCCOY

Something bona fide, the genuine article, the real thing is sometimes spoken of as the *Real McCoy*. It could be said to be Simon Pure, which likewise means the genuine or real thing. But the story behind the Real McCoy has a stronger punch. It should be borne in mind that so many theories concerning the origin of the *Real McCoy* have been advanced that, if all were recorded, they would fill pages. H. L. Mencken, who included at least a half-dozen in his writings, observed ironically that "the origin of this term has been much debated and is still unsettled."

Eric Partridge said he was certain the term referred to the excellent whiskey that A. and M. McKay of Glasgow, exporters of Scotch, sent to the United States. McCoy was a slang term for good whiskey at the turn of the century, and Partridge's theory in *From Sanskrit to Brazil* (1950) stated that *the Real McKay* was later "transformed to the real McCoy, first under the impact of the hero worship that, in the late 1890s, accrued to boxer Kid McCoy and then accrued, at least in New York State, to bootlegger Bill McCoy."

A rival distillery of the McKay clan used the name "clear McCoy," and their product was considered superior to American brands.

The most popular story concerning the origin of *the real McCoy* is one that involves a pugilist named Norman Selby, whose fighting name was Kid McCoy. That Selby was the Real McCoy was supposed to have been established in an American saloon. Kid McCoy became involved in a brawl with another barroom patron who refused to believe that he was talking with the great fighter, saying, "You are a fake." The Kid, angered, slugged the doubter on the jaw, who, while rubbing his jaw from his seat in the sawdust, exclaimed, "You're the Real McCoy, all right."

Norman Selby, born in 1873 in Indiana to parents who were farmers, ran away from home and began fighting under the name Kid McCoy in 1891. Six years later, the Kid fought the world's welterweight champion, Tommy Ryan, and slugged him to defeat. The Kid now had the crown and continued a successful ring career until he fought Gentleman Jim Corbett and, as they say, bit the canvas. It was widely believed that the fight was fixed, and the Kid's reputation was therefore irreparably damaged.

Selby was married ten times, three times to the same woman. In 1924 he was convicted of a manslaughter charge in the death of his married lover. After serving a prison sentence of nine years, he worked for the Henry Ford Company in a security capacity for its gardens. In 1940, Selby decided that he had had his last fight—with life. He committed suicide.

KLIEG LIGHT

As the film industry was getting started, so was another industry most useful to both stage and the early motion pictures. It was the *klieg light*, a light invented by the Kleigl brothers, John H. (1869–1959) and Anton T. (1872–1927), born in Bad Kissingen, Germany. Their invention was a carbon-arc lamp that gave forth such an intense light that it became indispensable to the movie industry.

The light was so powerful that a person in its glare would find his or her eyes watering. Because these incandescent lights were high in ultraviolet rays, they could cause a form of conjunctivitis. The condition became known as *kliegeyes*. It therefore became necessary for those exposed to the light to protect their eyes by wearing dark glasses. The dark glasses came to identify cinematic characters, even those "hopefuls" merely aspiring to stardom, so that the "shades" became an important and permanent part of their dress. Not only did the glasses give the stars a certain amount of anonymity, but they also made the wearer look somewhat glamorous because the eyes were hidden from view.

The lamp was called the *klieg light* because the brothers' name was hard to pronounce.

KNICKERS, KNICKERBOCKER

Knickerbocker is a Dutch family name that evolved from the occupation of a *knicker baker*, a man who baked slabs of clay for building bricks known as *knickers*. The surname *knickerbaker* in time was adjusted to *knickerbocker*. But knickers as a short breeches garment can be credited to Washington Irving—not that he was a clothing stylist, but because his two-volume guide was illustrated with these breeches. Irving wrote a humorous but pompous story of the early life of New York, as told by one of the early settlers. He chose the pseudonym Diedrich Knickerbocker. The book, titled *A History of New York from the Beginning of the World to the End of the Dutch Dynasty*, was published in 1809.

Although this delightful work became better known by its shorter title, *Knickerbocker's History of New York*, the short breeches, fitting loosely and gathered at the knee, developed a fashion hold after illustrations by the great comic artist George Cruikshank appeared in a later edition in the 1850s. These breeches were first called *knickerbockers*, but the name was later shortened to *knickers*. They became popular as knee pants for young boys, for cyclists, and for outdoor men who play golf, and even for silk bloomers for women. And so knickers were born.

LACONIC

Laconia, that ancient Greek country of which Lacedaemon or Sparta was the capital, was the land of the Spartans. Sparta was also known as Laconia, and Spartans as Laconians. These people were noted for their parsimonious speech. The name of their country, Laconia, has given English the adjective *laconic*, which means brief, concise, pithy.

On one occasion Philip of Macedon threatened to invade their land. He announced: "If I enter Laconia, I will level it to the ground." The response he received was a single word: "If." That's laconic at its best. An equally famous classic example of a laconic message is: "Veni, vidi, vici"—Caesar's concise report ("I came, I saw, I conquered"). Sir Charles Napier, British soldier and administrator, served in India. In 1842, Napier seized Sind and noted that he had no right to do so. His dispatch of the news of his conquest was one Latin word: "Peccavi" ("I have sinned"). The historical accuracy of this pun has not been substantiated.

A lady sitting next to President Coolidge tried to coax him into talking with her. "I made a bet, Mr. Coolidge, that I could get more than two words out of you." Said Coolidge, "You lose." On a more contemporary note, General McAuliffe's reply to the German demand during World War II that he surrender was a single word: "Nuts!"

LAVALIERE

Louis XIV, the Sun King, was married to the Austrian Marie-Thérèse, for whom he cared little because she reputedly had hair between her breasts. Louis XIV fancied Henrietta, the wife of his brother, Philip of Orléans. So that the queen would be thrown off the trail, Louis took Henrietta's maid of honor as his mistress. She was known as the *maîtresse en titre*, a semiofficial position since a certain Agnes Sorel, known as "the Queen of Beauty" in the thirteenth century.

The lovely Louise Françoise de la Baume Le Blanc was only sixteen years of age. Though brought into this royal comedy as a blind, she and the king soon fell in love. Unfortunately the love story ended unhappily. Although Louise bore the king three children, the insatiable Louis lost his heart to Madame Montespan. But at the end of his affair with Louise in 1667, Louis made her the Duchesse de la Vallière, granting her the estate of Vaujours. Louise entered a convent at age thirty and remained there until she died in 1710 at age seventy-six.

Louise was exceedingly well-liked in Europe while she was the king's favorite, because she was beautiful and introduced glamorous fashions. A badge of distinction, so to speak, was a large bow she wore around her neck called a *lavallière* in her honor. The word *lavaliere* has passed into the English language to represent a chain around the neck from which dangles a pendant.

LEOTARDS

A *leotard* is a tight-fitting elastic garment that worn by ballet dancers, and covers the entire torso. The romantic story behind this garment deals with its use by daredevil circus aerialists and goes back more than a hundred years.

Jules Léotard (1842–1870), born in Toulouse, France, was an aerialist almost from birth, according to his *Memoirs*. This small volume stated that his parents could control his crying only by hanging him upside down from a trapeze.

When Léotard grew to manhood, he became the star attraction in Paris's *Cirque Napoleon*, at which he introduced his exciting innovation: the flying trapeze. Such acrobatics had never been seen before, and the audience was amazed. Then he gave them reason for more amazement: Performing on a taut wire high above the ground, he performed an aerial somersault, the first of its kind.

Léotard's name persists, however, not because he was Europe's most famous and colorful acrobatic circus performer, but because in an 1859 circus act in Paris, he wore an audacious one-piece, skin-tight bodysuit that revealed every curve and rippling muscle in his body. This garb, designed by this great performer, has borne the name *leotard* ever since.

Though the leotard has been well-received the advice he offered men in his *Memoirs* was not. "Do you want to be adored by the ladies?" he wrote. "A trapeze is not required, but instead of draping yourself in unflattering clothes, invented by ladies and which give us the air of ridiculous manikins, put on a more natural garb, *which does not hide your best features*" (italics supplied). And what garb was meant? Of course the *leotard*.

LESBIAN, LESBIANISM, SAPPHISM

Lesbianism is the practice of homosexuality by females. Nevertheless, the word *homosexual* refers to one who engages in sexual acts with a person of the same sex, whether man or woman. But males engaged in love-making with males have only one designation—*homosexuals*.

On the island of Lesbos in the Aegean Sea during the earlier half of the sixth century lived the Greek poet Sappho. She became the leader of a group of women whose behavior was characterized by strong homosexual feelings. Hence from the name given this manifestation we have *sapphism*, an eponymous derivative from her name, and *lesbianism*, an eponymous derivative from her birthplace.

Sappho (620–565 B.C.) was born at Mytilene or Eresus on the island of Lesbos. According to Ovid, the outstanding Roman poet, Sappho's father died when she was only six years old. It is believed that she married and had a daughter (some say a son). In any event, Sappho, the most famous female poet of her time, wrote her poems on Lesbos and gathered women there to teach them the art of poetry. Whether her followers engaged in sexual love has never been proved any more than that her followers of today are interested in poetry.

Sappho's passionate lyrics, especially the poem in which she pleaded with Aphrodite to help her arouse ardor in a certain woman, have given fodder to those convinced of her homosexuality. But only fragments of her vibrant poems have survived, some in mere scraps.

LEVI'S, JEANS

Levi Strauss (1829–1902) emigrated from Bavaria and became a dry goods salesman in New York City. During the California Gold Rush, Levi, then twenty-four, headed West with a load of canvas that he intended to make into tents for the prospectors. But in San Francisco, where he landed from his clipper ship, he learned that the greatest need of the men was for pants. And so he used his canvas to make pants. When his canvas ran out, he switched to denim, adding blue coloring. He then founded the Levi Strauss Company to manufacture these sturdy, close-fitting pants. Called *Levi's* by the miners, they were an immediate success because the strain points were reinforced with copper rivets, making them especially useful to miners and others who filled their pockets with ore samples.

The generic term for these denim pants, *blue jeans*, actually came after the specific brand. Though the pants themselves have a distinctly American origin, the word *jeans* derives from Italy.

The manufacture of denims (*denim* comes from the phrase *serge de Nîmes*, after the city of Nimes) into garments, primarily pants, took place in Italian Genoa, which in Middle English was *jine* or *Gene* from the French *Gênes*. Hence the ubiquitous uniform of today is called in English *jeans* or blue jeans. *Levis* has also become a synonym for jeans or denims.

The Levi Strauss clothing company today is one of the world's largest clothing company dealers, with sales exceeding $2 billion annually.

LILLIPUTIAN

Jonathan Swift (1667–1745) was a great English satirist. His most celebrated work, and the one for which he is best known, is *Gulliver's Travels*. It includes an account of the travels of one Captain Lemuel Gulliver to Lilliput, a country whose inhabitants were no more than six inches tall. Ultimately, Gulliver traveled to the country of Brobdingnag, inhabited by giants. They were "like steeple spires, and they covered ten yards with every step." To those people, Gulliver looked lilliputian, "not so big as a round little worm plucked from the lazy finger of a maid." Although *lilliputian* for "tiny" and *brobdingnagian* for "gigantic" have been admitted into the English language, the latter word has had little acceptance, perhaps because it's so difficult to pronounce. Today *lilliputian*, from Swift's fiercely brilliant political satire, is an adjective applied to any diminutive person or object.

Jonathan Swift was born in Dublin, Ireland, the son of wealthy English parents. His father died before he was born, and he was raised by a miserly uncle. Swift was so bright that at the age of five he could read almost any chapter in the Bible. After attending Trinity College in Dublin, Swift left for England and obtained a position as secretary to Sir William Temple, which enabled him to study and write. It was at Temple's home that he met Esther Johnson, whom he called Hester and whom he encouraged to live nearby. Swift immortalized Hester in his famous *Journal to Stella*, one of the greatest diaries in the records of English literature. Swift was involved with another woman, Ester Vanhomrigh, whom he called Vanessa. Vanessa followed Swift to Ireland, learned about Hester, and sent her a biting, denunciatory letter. Shortly thereafter Vanessa died. In 1742, Swift became mentally ill and died three years later.

LIMELIGHT, DRUMMOND LIGHT

Thomas Drummond (1797–1840) invented the first "limelight" in 1816 and it later became essential theatrical equipment. The so-called *Drummond light* emitted a powerful beam that could be concentrated on one part of the stage. The person in its glare was said to be in the *limelight*, a pithy way of saying that someone is in the full glare of public attention or notoriety or, to borrow a theatrical term, is "center stage."

This vivid light is a combination of oxygen and hydrogen on a surface of lime or, more simply, calcium oxide, which has a brilliant luminosity when incandescent.

Drummond invented his light for lighthouses. Sometime after Drummond's death, the limelight came to be used extensively in theaters and remained their main source for prominent lighting for many years.

LINNAEAN CLASSIFICATION

Carolus Linnaeus (1707–1778), the most famous of all naturalists, was born Carl von Linné, but subsequently adopted the Latin form of his Swedish name. The son of a clergyman, Linnaeus became an avid botanist at a very early age; his nickname was "the little botanist." He studied at Lund and Uppsala, eventually becoming a professor of botany at Uppsala in 1741. He took time out to become a physician and a professor of medicine. But he returned to his first love and wrote many books on the subject: *Systema nature* (1735), *Fundaments botanica* (1736), *Genera plantarum* (1737), *Flora lapponica* (1737), *Philosophia botanica* (1751), *Species plantarum* (1753), and others. His books marked the beginning of taxonomy, a system of scientific nomenclature of plants and animals. His *Species plantarum* set the stage for a system he devised, the *Linnaean system*, which divided the kingdom of animals, vegetables, and minerals into classes, orders, genera, species, and varieties. He was the first to label man *homo sapiens*, "wise or sapient."

LISTER, LISTERINE

To have one's name become a household word seems to be a mark of success for some people and a goal worth striving for. But to others, it is anathema. In the nineteenth century, an English physician, the founder of antiseptic surgery, a brilliantly famous man, had his name pre-empted by a manufacturer of a commercial product.

Dr. Joseph Lister (1827–1912), whose treatment of wounds by anti-sepsis revolutionized modern surgery, was born at Upton, Essex, and earned his medical degree at age twenty-five at University College, London. He served as professor of surgery at Glasgow University (1860–1869), Edinburgh University (1869–1877), and at King's College (1871–1894). He was made a baronet, elevated to the peerage, and became surgeon to Queen Victoria. He was the first physician to be made a British peer. He was also the founder of the Lister Institute of Preventive Medicine in London.

Lister learned from Pasteur's theory that fermentation was caused by bacteria, a theory that led him to conclude that pus was also due to bacteria. He determined that germs were carried by surgical instruments as well as by the hands of the attendants. He then proceeded to intro-duce the use of antiseptic solution on hands, instruments, and bandages.

In 1881, a mouthwash was marketed by an American company under the trademark *Listerine*. It was an obvious attempt to trade on the dis-tinguished surgeon's name. According to H. L. Mencken, as reported in *The American Language*, Dr. Lister was quite unhappy about the com-mercialization of his name, but his efforts to disassociate it from the product were fruitless. In any event, the product became exceedingly popular, and the name so generic that the name *listerine* might now apply to any antiseptic mouthwash.

Lister was once summoned to remove a fishbone from the throat of a rich lord. The surgeon was successful, and the patient, overcome with gratitude, asked what was owed him. Lister replied, "My lord, suppose we settle for half of what you would be willing to pay if the bone were still lodged in your throat."

LOBSTER NEWBURG

Charles Wenberg was a prosperous shipping magnate in the nineteenth century, according to one story. Some say he was merely a captain on a West Indies ship. Regardless, he gave a recipe to Lorenzo Delmonico, the New York restaurateur famed for his opulent salon, for a dish that would be an epicure's dream. The recipe called for heavy cream, sherry, egg yoke, cayenne, and loads and loads of lobster meat, an astoundingly rich concoction. Lorenzo saw the merit in this rich concoction and told his chef to follow it carefully.

The dish turned out to be a gastronomic delight. The wealthy patrons of Delmonico literally ate it up. So successful was the dish and so pleased was the chef that he named the dish in honor of Wenberg, *Lobster Wenberg*. Some time after this celebratory event, Wenberg, in the Delmonico dining room, drank too much, talked too loud, and picked a fight with another diner. Wenberg was ejected, and so was his name from the menu. The very next day the menu at Delmonico read: *Lobster Newburg*. What a penalty! The chef reversed the "w" and the "n," so that the Wen became New, and for good measure, altered the spelling to New*burg*. Thus, Wenberg's combativeness cost him a place in the hierarchy of eponyms.

LOGANBERRY

The loganberry is shaped like a blackberry, has the color of a raspberry, and is thought to have the flavor of both. However, its sharp taste is not to everyone's liking. The man who raised this berry was James Harvey Logan (1841–1928), a lawyer and an amateur horticulturist.

Born in Indiana, Logan migrated to Missouri and became a schoolteacher. To change the direction of his life, Logan took on a job of driving an ox team for the Overland Telegraph Company. Arriving at the West Coast, Logan changed direction again by studying law. He settled in Santa Cruz, California, passed the bar examinations, and was elected a district attorney. He then was elected to the Superior Court, which he served from 1880 to 1892, when he retired.

Logan was through with law but not with life. His abiding interest was in horticulture. To this end, he began to experiment with fruit and vegetables. The berry that bears his name had its birth in 1881 (he was still a judge) when he planted a row of wild California blackberries between a row of Texas early blackberries. After he planted the second generation seedlings, he discovered the product was two distinct fruits— one, a blackberry having a different taste, and two, a berry that resembled a raspberry but with a delightful flavor of its own and quite distinctive from the others. And so Logan became the berry's father, but he never fully disclosed his horticultural methods.

LUCULLAN, LUCULLAN FEAST

Lucius Licinius Lucullus (c. 117–57 B.C.) had a career of accomplishments as a Roman general and statesman. He put the fleet of Mithridates to flight and enjoyed other military successes. When he governed the province of Africa, he served as consul, but Pompey relieved him of his duties. Lucullus had amassed such a tremendous fortune that he could retire in Rome to live a life of luxury and splendor in an extremely elegant style. And so he did.

Legend has it that after Lucullus had ordered an elaborate dinner, he was reminded that he was having no guests that night. Unconcerned, he then made the statement that has come down through the centuries, *"Lucullus sups with Lucullus."* According to Brewer, that statement can be said only by a glutton who eats alone.

The cost of his many banquets cannot be measured in terms of today's market. One can say only that they were sumptuous and fit for a gourmet's palette. His parties were attended by noted artists, writers, and philosophers of the day.

Any extravagant meal, any elegant banquet of unmatched luxury, may rightly be termed a *Lucullan feast*.

LUDDITE, LUDDITE RIOTS

Technical improvements may develop at the expense of dislocated lives. That sociological problem confronted Ned Ludd of Leicestershire, England, a half-witted laborer who proceeded to take the matter in hand by smashing two knitting machines. Although not much is known about him, his name has survived to describe those who destroy labor-saving devices or machinery acquired by their employers. In the years 1811 to 1816, machine-breaking riots occurred in the manufacturing districts of Nottinghamshire, Cheshire, and Yorkshire. The textile workers blamed the new machinery for their unemployment and distress. They were branded as *Luddites*, after their legendary leader.

Lord Byron's *The Song of the Luddites*, published in 1830 but written fourteen years earlier, challenged repressive legislation in the House of Lords. The *Luddite* movement is the background of Charlotte Bronte's *Shirley* (1849).

Today *Luddites* are still those who fear the development of machinery that would eliminate the need for their employment. Some may take a strong stand against plants where war implements are being manufactured that would cause human destructions. It is also a term used to describe those who fear or are confused by technology.

LYNCH, LYNCH LAW

Lynch law is mob law, condemnation without due process as required by the Constitution. The victim of a "trial" by a vigilante committee was usually given summary execution.

Word historians have been perturbed by the history of this word because many have claimed the source of the eponymous word *lynch*. One that sounds ridiculous involved a young man named Walt, who killed his friend, Gomez, because he thought Gomez was courting his girlfriend. He later learned that all the friend was doing was teaching Spanish to the girlfriend's father. Walt voluntarily confessed to the police. His father, James Lynch Fitzstephen, of Galway, was both mayor and chief magistrate, and presided over Walt's trial. The defendant pleaded guilty and was sentenced to be executed. But because Walt was so well-liked in the community, no one would carry out the sentence. Walt's father had no alternative but to hang his son himself. This he did from a window of their house.

According to another account, perhaps equally apocryphal, in North Carolina, at Lynch Creek, a bizarre form of trial and execution was held on the corpse of a Tory who had already been hanged, the thought being to justify the sentence *post facto*. This was a case of hanging one on a dead man.

Two men with the name Lynch lived in Virginia at about the same time and presided over a vigilance committee: Charles, from 1736 to 1796, and William, from 1742 to 1820. The credit for the word *lynch*—or the discredit for it—has been given to each of these men by their respective followers seeking the dubious honor of being the first *lyncher*.

Charles was a planter, a justice of the peace, and a colonel in the militia. William was a member of a vigilance committee in Pittsylvania, Virginia. The weight of the evidence, according to some lexicographers, tilts toward Charles, even though both men engaged in summary executions.

Although William Lynch and cohorts were not the first vigilantes to take the law into their own hands, they were the first to enter into a compact that stated the reasons for their actions and justification for a kangaroo court. Lynch and a group of his neighbors made a declaration of justifiable punishment, which received widespread publicity because of an editorial on lynching written by Edgar Allan Poe in 1836 when he edited the *Southern Literary Messenger*. Poe even quoted their compact:

> Whereas many of the inhabitants of Pittsylvania . . . have sustained great and intolerable losses by a set of lawless men . . . that have hitherto escaped the civil power with impunity . . . we, the subscribers, being determined to put a stop to the iniquitous practices of those unlawful wretches, do enter into the following association . . . upon hearing or having sufficient reason, that any . . . species of villany (has) been committed within our neighborhood we will forthwith . . . repair immediately to the person or persons suspected . . . and if they will not desist from their evil practices, we will inflict such corporeal punishment on him or them as to us shall seem adequate to the crime committed or the damage sustained. . . . In witness whereof we have hereunto set our hands, this 22nd day of September 1780.

MACADAMIZE, TARMAC

What pleasure would you get from a sleek, fast automobile if the road you were driving on was filled with ruts and puddles of water? You couldn't make much time, and what time you did make would be uncomfortable.

The man who saved us from these conditions never saw an automobile because none had been invented during his lifetime. John Loudon McAdam (1756–1836), whose name has a variant spelling of Macadam, was born in Ayr, Scotland, but his care, on the death of his father in 1770, was entrusted to a merchant uncle in New York. McAdam was put to work in his uncle's counting house, and by the time he was twenty-seven, he had acquired a tidy fortune.

When McAdam returned to his native Scotland, he was appalled by the condition of the roads, which were of rubble granite. The lives of horses that trod on them were shortened, and, after a heavy rain, the roads became a morass and were all but impassable.

McAdam conducted road-making experiments at Falmouth and Bristol and conceived the idea of a roadbed consisting of layers of broken stones of nearly uniform size. Placed over a convex roadbed which allowed water to drain off, the stones would then be crushed into position by traffic. Roads so built were said to be *macadamized.*

McAdam's roads were a boon to transportation. He was appointed general surveyor in 1827 for all English highways.

A bituminous binder for roads is called *tarmac.* Airfields have also been called *tarmacs* ("There are two planes on the tarmac"). One can find McAdam's name in *tarmac,* a shortening of *tarmacadam.*

But MacAdam never had the pleasure of seeing his name (or a part of it) used with *tarmac.* It was sixty years after his death, in 1903, that the Wright brothers made their famous flight.

Automobiles jar the stones loose on a macadam road. A more compact surface, such as asphalt, has generally replaced macadam.

MACH 1, MACH NUMBER

When airplanes first started to fly, their speed was measured like that of a moving vehicle on the ground. As air speeds increased, that method became obsolete, and a new method had to be found.

Ernst Mach (1838–1916), an Austrian physicist, philosopher, mathematician, and physiologist, has given his name to the measurement of aircraft speeds. Mach was born in Moravia and held successive university chairs, first at Graz, in mathematics; second, Prague, in physics; and then in Vienna, in the philosophy of inductive sciences.

Mach studied the action of bodies moving at high speeds through gases, and computed their speed in terms of the ratio between their velocity and the speed of sound. This, in air at sea level, is about 764 miles per hour. His experiments were published but remained obscure until the speed of aircraft began to approach the speed of sound. On October 14, 1947, thirty-one years after Mach's death, Captain Charles Yeager broke the sound barrier or, as scientists prefer to call it, "Mach 1."

Mach's investigation into supersonic sound speeds of projectiles led to the present system for measuring speeds faster than sound—the Mach number. A Mach number under 1 (0.50) indicates a subsonic speed, a number over 1 (1.5, 3.2, etc.) indicates a supersonic speed—one faster than the speed of sound. Mach in addition gave his name to the Mach angle, the angle a shock wave makes with the direction of flight.

Mach rejected Newton's idea about absolute space and time, which affected the thinking of Albert Einstein, and which cleared the way to one of the greatest discoveries for mankind—Einstein's theory of relativity.

MACHIAVELLIAN

Niccolò Machiavelli (1469–1527) was born in Florence, Italy, to a distinguished family. He held various posts in the Florentine government and was staunchly opposed to the return of the Medici family to power. When the Medicis resumed their political position, they tortured and imprisoned him. Although they later pardoned him, his public life was ended.

Machiavelli then took up his pen and wrote several excellently styled plays and a short novel, but the treatise *The Prince* has given him the label "the founder of political science." The thesis he propounded was that political subjects, although bound by traditional moral codes, owe allegiance to, and had to respect and accept any obligations imposed upon them by, their rulers; rulers rightfully could maintain their power by any means whatsoever. Bad faith and deception practiced by rulers were not to be questioned. Morally Machiavelli was completely reprehensible, having no sensitivity to ethical considerations. For example, he said, "To be feared gives more security than to be loved"; "A prudent ruler cannot and should not observe faith when such observance is to his disadvantage." He emerged from his cocoon when Pope Leo X commissioned him to write a report on the reform of Florence. But he never again was an important political figure.

His name has given the English language *Machiavellian*, which means characterized by political intrigue, duplicity, unscrupulousness, and brilliant dissembling.

MACINTOSH, MACKINTOSH

Charles Macintosh—or Mackintosh, as it is sometimes spelled—(1766–1843) was an enterprising Scottish chemist who patented a process in 1823 that created a waterproof fabric. A method of cementing two or more layers of cloth together through the solvent action of naphtha on India rubber led to the production not only of a waterproof jacket but also to life preservers, fishing boots and hot-water bottles, among other things.

The Duke of Wellington reportedly was much impressed by this invention, and decided to test it for practical use in the army. He had forty of his soldiers set out on a raft supported by two pontoons of the cloth. The soldiers remained dry, the raft kept floating, Wellington was won over, and the macintosh was given a tremendous boost.

Captain William Perry, on an Arctic exploration, used waterproof covers for all his supplies. He later wrote: "Just before halting at 6 A.M. on the 5th of July 1827, the ice at the margin of the flow broke while the men were handling provisions out of the boats; and we narrowly escaped the loss of a bag of cocoa, which fell overboard, but fortunately . . . this bag, made out of Macintosh's waterproof canvas, did not suffer the slightest injury."

The inventor of the waterproof fabric was not Charles Macintosh, however, but James Syme. He invented the process in 1823 while a student at Edinburgh University. Macintosh, without seeking permission from Syme, obtained a patent on the process and manufactured numerous articles using it.

MAE WEST

Mae West (1892–1980) was an American stage, film, and nightclub comedienne known for sex appeal and saucy, suggestive wit. Her trademarks were her tight gowns, blonde hair, sultry voice, audacious manner, and racy double entendres. Her sly, risqué remark, "Why don't you come up and see me sometime?" took the country by storm and became an oft-repeated come-on.

West was born in Brooklyn, New York, and performed in vaudeville while a child. When only five, she was named "Baby Vamp" at a church social where she perfected her famous seductive walk.

Mae West starred on Broadway in salacious shows, such as *Sex* and *Pleasure Man*. The play *Sex*, which she wrote and directed (1926), made her an instant celebrity because the police charged her with obscenity. In Hollywood she made her film debut in *Night after Night* (1932) with George Raft. In *She Done Him Wrong*, with Cary Grant, she proved she could act. Many more successful films followed.

How her name became associated with the airman's pneumatic life jacket has never been proved. But the common assumption is that some airman noticed that the jacket, when inflated, gave the wearer a generous bosom like Mae's own and the name *Mae West* became fixed as the name of the life jacket.

An army tank with twin turrets was also named after her, but she is best remembered for the life jacket. For this honor, Mae West remarked, "I've been in *Who's Who*, and I know what's what, but it's the first time I ever made the dictionary."

MAGENTA

The color *magenta* was named after the Battle of Magenta (Italy), or rather, after the blood-spattered battlefield.

The Battle of Magenta took place in the region of Lombardy on June 4, 1859. The French and the Piedmontese defeated the Austrians, supposedly liberating Italy. But the liberators could claim only a Pyrrhic victory because so many soldiers were slain on each side that their bodies had to be buried in a common grave. More than seven thousand bodies were interred together.

The battle was fought just before a brilliant red aniline dye derived from coal tar was discovered. The dye was called *magenta* because of its resemblance to the blood that was shed at the battle.

MAGNOLIA

About thirty-five widely distributed species of *Magnolia* exist in North America, Mexico, and in eastern Asia and the Himalayas. They are chiefly small trees, both evergreen and deciduous, with stout, aromatic twigs and branches. The hardiest of the Magnolias are widely planted as ornamental. They are handsome in shape, foliage, and especially in flower. In the South, they reach an astronomical 100 feet.

The name for these beautiful flowering shrubs and trees was an honor bestowed on Pierre Magnol (1638–1715), a professor of botany at Montpelier University in France. Magnol, a Protestant, had a difficult time getting an education in mostly Catholic France. His courses in botany made him prominent, and eventually put him in the good graces of Swedish scientist Carolus Linnaeus, who honored him by naming the beautiful *Magnolia* tree after him because he had originated the classification of plants by families, a scientific innovation.

The tree was introduced into Europe from Japan about 1709, while Magnol was alive, but the tree was not named until after his death.

MALAPROPISM

This word entered the English language through the name of a character in *The Rivals* (1775), a play written by Englishman Richard Brinsley Sheridan (1751–1816). The play introduced Mrs. Malaprop, an endearing late-middle-age woman given to confusing similar-sounding words, with hilarious results. The word she used, although sounding somewhat like the the word intended, had a completely different meaning. For example, she described someone "as headstrong as an allegory (*alligator*) on the banks of the Nile."

Mrs. Malaprop delivered her lines with such aplomb that her audience responded to her blunders with delight. Among her linguistic blunders: "I would by no means want a daughter of mine to be a progeny (*prodigy*) of learning;" "Don't attempt to extirpate (*exculpate*) yourself from this matter;" "He is the very pineapple (pinnacle) of politeness." Such mixups as "supercilious (*superficial*) knowledge," "contagious (*contiguous*) countries," and "to illiterate (*obliterate*) him from your mind" had audiences roaring with laughter. Today, any grotesque misapplication of a word, especially by one resembling it, is a *malapropism*.

Sheridan wrote all his major comedies when he was in his twenties. He then forsook his writings for politics and, as a member of Parliament, was an outstanding talented orator, comparable to England's most distinguished orators, Edmund Burke and Prime Minister William Pitt.

MALPIGHIAN

Marcello Malpighi (1628–1694), an Italian physician, anatomist, and physiologist, was a great scientist who is not well-known outside the field of medicine. Born at Crevalore, near Bologna, the eldest of eight children, he was orphaned at twenty-one, and most of the family responsibilities fell on his shoulders.

Malpighi later decided to study medicine. In 1653, he received his medical degree from the University of Bologna, and within three years was named a professor. But Malpighi decided to move on and soon accepted a professorship at the University of Pisa, where, together with G. A. Borelli, he discovered the spiral character of heart muscles. When Malpighi retired from academic life, he was called to Rome as the personal physician of Pope Innocent XII.

Malpighi also studied the circulation of blood, and he was one of the first people to use a microscope to study animal and vegetable structures. He was the first to discover that capillaries form the connecting links between arteries and veins, the first to make an anatomical study of the brain, and the first to indicate the nature of the papillae on the tongue. He was responsible for knowledge pertaining to the mucous layer of skin, now called the *Malpighian layer*, and the *Malpighian capsules* of the kidney and the spleen. He also worked on the anatomy of the silkworm. The tube-shaped gland in insects and related animals that secrete urine into the alimentary canal is called the *Malipighian tube*.

Although an excellent draftsman, Malpighi was a poor writer. But he did leave in writing some studies that have further commemorated him as an outstanding scientist. Stedman's *Concise Medical Dictionary* describes Malpighi as the founder of microscopic anatomy.

MALTHUSIAN, MALTHUSIANISM

Malthus became widely known for his *Essay on the Principles of Population*, published in 1798. The main theory of his book is that population tends to increase faster than the means to feed it. This is called the *Malthusian Doctrine*. Malthus did not claim to be the originator of this idea, but his systematic exposition drew attention to the population problem.

Malthus's theories as a whole are referred to as *Malthusianism*. Supporters of Malthus or his theories are known as *Malthusians*.

Charles Darwin read Malthus's works and noted the phrase "struggle for existence." This thought stimulated Darwin to find the key to biological evolution in the face of natural selection, for it suggested the relationship between progress and the survival of the fittest.

MANHATTAN

Schoolchildren are familiar with the purchase of *Manhattan* from the Manhattes Indians for twenty-four dollars worth of kettles, axes, and cloth. *Manhattan* is one of five boroughs of New York City, but is the hub of the island. Its population is greater than that of some small countries. And it has been, and is, the "melting pot" of the country, with its racial, religious, and ethnic mix.

The *Manhattan cocktail*, a mixture of whiskey, vermouth, and bitters, was introduced at New York's Manhattan Club in 1874 at a banquet given by Winston Churchill's mother, Jennie Jerome. The club was named for the borough, and the borough for the Indians who had lived there. And then there is *Manhattan clam chowder*, with tomatoes swimming in it, unlike the milky clam soup from New England. And the name *Manhattan project*, undertaken to build the atomic bomb, has become a part of history.

MANSARD

A *mansard* roof, instead of forming an inverted V, has rafters that are broken up and the lower slope is almost perpendicular, the upper more nearly flat; thus it has a double slope on each side. The roof allows for high rooms and useful space within the building.

The lower slope of the roof, fitted with dormer windows, forms an additional story to the house. In the seventeenth century, Parisian householders were taxed according to the number of stories they had "under roof." This design enabled the house owner to have an added story, unseen, without paying an increase in taxes.

The roof was named for the French architect Nicolas François Mansart (1598–1666), who is credited with having designed it. Another French architect, Pierre Lescot, employed a similar roof plan on the Louvre many years before Mansard was born.

Mansart's designs epitomizes French Renaissance classicism. Some of Mansart's monumental works include the churches of Sainte-Marie de Chaillot and Visitation de Sainte-Marie, the Hôtel de la Villière in Paris, and several châteaux. Victorian architects adopted the mansard roof about two centuries later, and in America many houses have a mansard roof.

In 1636, Louis XIII appointed Mansart the royal architect. He was asked by the newly appointed Surintendant des Bâtements to provide a design for the east facade of the Palais du Louvre. When Mansart refused to agree to any alterations of his plans, he was replaced by Roman architects headed by the famous Giovanni Lorenzo Bernini (1598–1680).

Mansart's grand nephew by marriage, Jules Hardouin Mansart (1645–1708), designed the magnificent Hall of Mirrors at the palace of Versailles, the Hôtel des Invalides (Napoleon's final resting place), and the Place Vendôme.

MARATHON

A *marathon* is any kind of activity that goes on at great length or any test of endurance. In fact, the American language, under the misconception that *-thon* means endurance or long distance, has acquired many words simply by attaching that ending. Now there are *talkathons*, *telethons*, *danceathons*, and *walkathons*. No one has as yet come up with *workathon*. The word *marathon*, along with its step-sisters, goes back to ancient times. A *marathon* was not a race; it was the name of a narrow valley in Greece, where in 490 B.C. the Athenians, with a numerically inferior force, overcame and defeated the Persians. The Persians were so penned in that they were unable to use their cavalry, and the Athenians proceeded to slaughter all 6,400 of them. The Greeks lost only 192.

Miltiades, the Athenian general, fearing that the Athenians might surrender to a Persian attack by sea in ignorance of the victory at Marathon, dispatched Pheidippides, his fastest runner, to bring home the news of the victory. Sometime earlier Pheidippides had run to Sparta and back to seek help against the Persians, and, without sufficient rest, raced some twenty-six miles to Athens and gasped out the news: "Rejoice—we conquer," and fell dead.

When the Olympic games were revived for the first time in 1896, a modern "marathon" was staged, covering 26 miles and 385 yards, to commemorate the famous run from Marathon to Athens. Appropriately, the victor was a Greek.

MARCONIGRAM, MARCONIGRAPH

The great electrical engineer and inventor Marchese Guglielmo Marconi (1874–1937) gave the world wireless telegraphy, a form of communication of extreme usefulness. He was born of Italian-Irish parentage at

Bologna and was educated privately. He exhibited an interest in electrical communication at an early age, and commenced experiments with telegraphic communication through space by means of electromagnetic waves. After the government of Italy refused his offer of the invention, he went to England and had it patented. He succeeded in establishing communication across the English Channel, and three years later he bridged the Atlantic, receiving signals at St. John's, Newfoundland, from a sending station in Cornwall, England, thus proving that the curvature of the earth was no obstacle to further communications.

After demonstrating the value of telegraphic communication in warfare, Marconi turned his attention to developing the magnetic detector, the horizontal direction antenna, and the time-spark system for generating continuous waves. Many honors were bestowed on him, and in 1909 he shared the Nobel Prize for physics with Karl Ferdinand Braun.

The English language is indebted to Marconi for the *marconigram*, a message transmitted by wireless telegraphy, and for the verb form *marconigraphed*.

MARMALADE

Marmalade is a bitter, jellylike preserve, once made from quinces but now primarily from oranges, including some of their peel. This word has thrived in folk stories, even though there is no direct line between the preserve and its ancestor.

A story repeated for centuries says that when Mary Queen of Scots (1542–1587) was out of sorts, the only food that could tempt her was a conserve of oranges, for which she had an inordinate fondness. Hence the name of this jam after the queen's indisposition: *Marie malade* ("sick Mary"), which, with time, became *marmalade*. Willard R. Espy reports that in a London *Times* tournament dealing with the British trusty breakfast companion *marmalade*, the question was, who invented it? There were many zany answers, but the one with the greatest appeal was that it took a canny Scot to see value in the peel that others threw away. In Margaret Irwin's *The Gay Galliard, The Love Story of Mary Queen of Scots* appeared this etymological gem: "*Marie est malade*, he had muttered again and again as he racked his brain to invent something for her; and 'Mariemalade' they had called it ever since."

Marmalade is a word that has come to us through antiquity. In Grecian times it was called *melimelon*, "sweet apple," and the Romans called it *melimelum*. *Marmalade*, by whatever name, traveled to Portugal, where the Portuguese named it *marmelada*, meaning quince conserve, from *marmelo*, meaning quince. *Marmalade* continued its travels to England, where, as early as 1524, this notation appeared in Henry VIII's *Letters*: "one box of marmalade . . . presented by Hull of Exeter." British housewives have, for many centuries, made *marmalade* with oranges.

MARTINET

Jean Martinet (?–1672) was a lieutenant colonel of Louis XIV's regiment of foot and inspector general of infantry. He was an autocratic drill master, known for sharp military efficiency and his insistence that his orders be carried out exactly to the last detail. He drove his men to their limits, demanding maximum effort, and accepted nothing less than instant obedience and a polished performance. His men were taught to ask no questions. The king was so impressed by Martinet's regimental organization that he required all noblemen to command a platoon in Martinet's regiment before purchasing their own command in an infantry regiment.

Because of Martinet's disciplined training program, France was the first to have a professional national army on the continent. Previously, French soldiers, as well as those from other lands, were a hodgepodge of free-lance mercenaries. Martinet insisted that his men obey standardized methods of drill. He taught them how to advance when under fire, and he introduced the bayonet as a combat weapon. But the demands made upon the soldiers—order, precision, rigid drill—did not endear Martinet to them.

During the siege of Duisberg in 1672, Martinet was killed by a shot from French artillery while leading an assault. Whether the shot was fired accidentally or intentionally has never been established.

MASOCHISM, MASOCHIST

The word *masochism* comes to us courtesy of Chevalier Leopold von Sacher-Masoch (1836–1895), Austrian novelist. Sacher-Masoch did not invent masochism, but it was a recurring theme in his novels and he can certainly be credited with bringing the concept into the open. He wrote *The Legacy of Cain*, which he had begun in 1870 and finished in 1877, and *False Ermine*, published in 1873. His heroines were large, domineering, Brunnhilde-type women dressed in furs and wielding nail-studded whips on their "slaves," timid men. His best-known and most widely read book was *Venus im Pelz* (*Venus in Furs*), published around 1890, which explicitly described the pleasure received from the infliction of pain through a nail-studded whip and the sexual gratification that ensued, and the need for the partner to wear furs to stimulate the masochistic sufferer, the central character in the book. Sacher-Masoch gained widespread notoriety, and he was much sought after as a lecturer.

Sacher-Masoch's father was a respected chief of police in Graz, in southern Austria, and Sacher-Masoch's education was solid. He received a doctorate in law at the age of nineteen and became a lecturer at the university. On his twenty-first birthday he celebrated with the publication of his *Rebellion in Ghent under Charles V*, a good accounting of the times, but a book not well-received.

Submission to physical abuse was the central theme of Sacher-Masoch's life and his books. He had numerous lovers and two marriages—all relationships that ended in disaster.

A mistress named Fanny Pistor entered into a contract with Sacher-Masoch, which read in part:

> Herr Leopold Sacher-Masoch gives his word of honor to Frau Pistor to become her slave and to comply unreservedly for six months, with every one of her desires and commands. For her part, Frau Fanny Pistor is not to extract from him performance of any action contrary to honor . . . is also to allow him to devote six hours a day to his professional work, and agrees never to read his correspondence or his literary compositions. . . . Frau Pistor, on her side, promises to wear furs as often as possible, especially when she is in a cruel mood.

He met his first wife under bizarre circumstances. Using a pretext, the woman arranged for a rendezvous under a street lamppost in Graz. She came dressed in furs, and a black veil covered her face. She said her name was Wanda, a name Sacher-Masoch had used in a novel. When later she produced a whip and beat him with it, Sacher-Masoch arranged to marry her. At the private ceremony the groom came dressed in white and the bride in furs. After Wanda left him, several mistresses later, he remarried. This wife did not tolerate her husband's peculiarities very long. After he tried to strangle her, she had him committed to the Charenton Lunatic Asylum, where he spent the rest of his days.

The prominent German neurologist and psychiatrist Richard von Krafft-Ebing studied the career of Sacher-Masoch and named his malady *masochism*.

MASON-DIXON LINE

It is generally understood that the *Mason and Dixon line* divides the North from the South in the Atlantic region of the United States, and it is used as a figure of speech when discussing regional custom and viewpoints of all sorts. Below the Mason-Dixon line is considered the South, and the phrase during the Civil War was used to mean the difference between free and slave states.

The story behind this "line" began during colonial times when the Penns of Pennsylvania and the Calverts of Maryland had a dispute over their land grants. The matter was eventually taken to a London court and, in 1760, a compromise was reached. The compromise consisted simply of letting two English astronomers, acting as surveyors, mark the boundaries of the two grants. The names of these astronomer-surveyors were Charles Mason and Jeremiah Dixon.

Mason and Dixon decided on an ambitious program. They imported from England milestones bearing the arms of the Penns on one side and of the Calverts on the other. The markers were placed every five miles, but the task was just too much for them. By 1767 they had placed the markers—had run the line—244 miles. The survey was completed by others for Maryland in 1773, all the way to its western border. The southern boundary of Pennsylvania was completed six years later. The line was fixed at 39° 43' 26.3° N.

MASON JAR

Ever since the *mason jar* was invented, it has been a household necessity. It provides a perfect means for making home preserves. The jars, made of glass, have wide mouths with a glass or metal screw and are perfect containers.

The jar was invented by John L. Mason, a New Yorker, in 1857 and patented the next year. The jars carried the inscription "Mason's Patent Nov. 30th 1858." Mason had a metalwork shop in New York but began his manufacturing of the jars at a glassworks in New Jersey. It is said that he had so little business sense that he lost most of his patent rights to others, who manufactured and then distributed similar jars. The name *mason jar* became a catchall for all such jars. In dire financial straits, Mason died in 1902 in a New York City house of relief.

MATA HARI

Mata Hari, a Dutch subject, was born Gertrud Margareta Zelle (1876–1917). She was educated in a convent and married a Dutch officer, a cruel, drunken roué, whom she later divorced. In 1903 she went to Paris to become a professional Hindu dancer. She had accompanied her husband when he was stationed in Java and learned some of the temple dances. She was immediately successful, using her Hindu persona "Mata Hari." Her repertoire consisted of erotic dances, including her famous "Dance of the Seven Veils."

The Germans, in the year before World War I, realized her worth in espionage and therefore sent her to a school to be trained as a spy. She was "H21" in their service. The French knew of her activities, but were loath to arrest her because the names of her French lovers would be disclosed and a scandal would ensue. But in February 1917, the French made their move and arrested her. The prosecutor at her trial claimed that her spying had caused the death of at least 50,000 Frenchmen. Mata Hari was convicted and sentenced to be executed. Last-minute efforts by some of her French lovers to forestall the execution failed. On October 15, 1917, at Vincennes, she was executed by a firing squad.

Mata Hari's name has been a synonym for the shadowy, dangerous *femme fatale.*

MAUDLIN

> And now where'er he goes
> Among the Galilean mountains
> Or more unwelcome ways,
> He's followed by two faithful fountains;
> Two walking baths;
> Two weeping motions;
> Portable and compendious oceans.

The English poet Richard Crashaw (1613–1649) wrote this curious poem about Jesus and Magdalene. Mary Magdalene is often portrayed by classical painters with eyes swollen and red from weeping. In an early French form her name was spelled *Madelaine*; in English it was *Magdalene*. Gradually the name was corrupted to *Maudlin*, which has come to stand for stupidly sentimental. To be unguardedly drunk is to be *maudlin drunk*, characteristic of one who goes on a crying jag after overimbibing. Any tearfully or weakly emotional person is *maudlin*, whether drunk or a teetotaler. The word is applied to those who shed tears over little or nothing.

The British pronunciation of *Magdalene* is "maudlin," and the spelling followed the sound. Cambridge University has an institution named *Magdalene College*. Oxford University has its *Magdalen College*. But whether or not the final "e" is used, the names are pronounced the same—"Maudlin."

MAUSER RIFLE

Peter Paul Mauser (1838–1914) was born at Oberndorf am Neckar, Württemberg, Germany. Young Peter Paul had a good beginning to become a gunsmith. His father was a master gunsmith at the government arms factory, and at age twelve, Peter Paul went to work there.

Young Mauser's first invention was a small breech-loading cannon. Together with his brother, William, he produced a bolt-action single shot metallic-cartridge rifle, which was adopted by the Prussian army in 1871. The next Mauser improvement was a repeating model of the 1871 rifle. Then, as smokeless powder appeared, he developed the charger-loading small-bore bolt action rifle, upon which most later infantry arms have been modeled. The dominant characteristic of this rifle is a box magazine holding a staggered column of cartridges loaded from a charger that does not enter the action, with a bolt handle at the rear of the bolt. More than twenty nations have adopted the Mauser rifle. In ordinary speech we use the word rifle for a shoulder weapon, but really a rifle is any gun with a rifled barrel, a barrel with a series of spiral grooves on its inner surface to make the bullet spin rapidly as it leaves the gun.

MAUSOLEUM

Mausolus, a satrap (governor) of Caria, in Asia Minor (now part of Turkey), was a virtually independent ruler of a part of the Persian kingdom. He had dreams of controlling larger territories, especially certain Greek islands that he coveted. To this end he engineered a successful coup, after first persuading Greek allies to turn against Greece.

Probably the most important decision he made was moving his capital to Halicarnassus. It was there that Mausolus planned a grand edifice in which he was to be interred. The best architects were hired to design the monument, and Mausolus himself aided in the construction.

Mausolus died in 353 B.C. His sister, whom he had made his queen, the inconsolably grief-stricken Artemisia, completed the project and joined her husband two years later. The sepulchral monument was so vast and splendid that it came to be counted as one of the Seven Wonders of the Ancient World. It reached more than a hundred feet in height and contained statuary of the entombed Mausolus and Artemisia. An earthquake in 1375 destroyed it, and the stones that were strewn about were used for other buildings. Sir Charles Newton, in 1859, brought back to England parts of the frieze and two huge statues for display in the British Museum.

The Greeks called the structure *mausoleion* after the entombed ruler. The English borrowed the word as *mausoleum*, a name now applied to any large and imposing burial structure.

MAVERICK

Samuel A. Maverick (1803–1870) was a lawyer, a signer of the Texas Declaration of Independence, a prominent citizen of San Antonio, and the owner of 385,000 acres in the state. His name became part of our language after he accepted 400 head of cattle as a settlement of a claim. Maverick had no ranch experience, so he turned over the herd to a hired hand, who allowed the cattle to graze unbranded, according to a letter from W. A. Seidel, Sr. of Knippa Falls, Texas, a friend of a grandson of Maverick, and published in the *Wall Street Journal* in July 1977. The cattle roamed, especially the calves. Neighboring cattlemen took advantage of the situation; they branded the strays with their own brands and then simply added them to their herd. And so, even though Maverick subsequently sold his depleted herd, unbranded cattle came to be known as "mavericks," and such cattle could be claimed by any rancher.

By extension, in general usage today, a *maverick* is an unorthodox individual, a masterless person, who deviates from the customary way of doing things, refusing to be branded, so to speak, thus taking an independent stand. It may apply to anyone who has no particular attachment for a place or a group of people, or, in politics, to a person who does not acknowledge party leadership or whose cause is unsupported by his constituency. He is, to borrow a popular phrase, "swimming upstream."

MAXIM GUN, MAXIM SILENCER

There were three Maxims, all inventors. The elder Maxim, Sir Hiram Stevens (1840–1916), was born near Sangerville, Maine. He moved to England and became a naturalized British citizen. Between the years 1881 and 1884, he invented the first fully automatic machine gun. It operated from the recoil of a cartridge that expelled the empty shell and reloaded the weapon at the same time. As long as the trigger was depressed, the *Maxim gun* kept firing until all ammunition was expended. The gun had a water-cooled barrel and a 250-round belt. Maxim's company was bought by the giant Vickers Armstrong Ltd. in 1896.

Maxim's other inventions received less attention, but they show the ingenuity of an active mind. He invented an automatic fire sprinkler, a gas meter, a delayed-action fuse, a smokeless powder, and an inhaler for bronchitis. He also experimented with internal-combustion engines for automobiles and airplanes. For these accomplishments, Maxim was knighted.

Maxim's brother, Hudson (1853–1927), was born at Orneville, Maine, with the name Isaac Weston Maxim, but he preferred and adopted the name Hudson. Hudson began his career as a book publisher, but turned to explosives, setting up a manufacturing company that he sold to E. I. du Pont in 1897. He is best known for having invented the high explosive *maximite*, one and a half times as powerful as dynamite, for use in artillery shells.

Hiram Percy Maxim (1869–1936), born in Brooklyn, New York, was the son of Hiram. Young Hiram invented the *Maxim silencer* for firearms, designed to make the firing of a weapon practically noiseless. But his silencers found other commercial uses. They have been used to eliminate noises of gasoline engines, compressors, blowers, vacuum pumps, and machines with a high-velocity discharge of steam or air.

MAXWELL'S EQUATIONS, MAXWELL'S LAW

Although the name James Clerk Maxwell is not well-known today, he made remarkable contributions to the electromagnetic theory, known as *Maxwell's Equations* and *Maxwell's Law*. Through his keen knowledge of mathematics he unlocked some of the mysteries of nature. He is credited with having formulated the modern theory of electricity.

Maxwell (1831–1879) was born in Edinburgh, Scotland, and was educated at Edinburgh University and at Trinity College, Cambridge University. He taught natural philosophy at some universities, and later became the first professor of experimental physics at Cambridge.

His studies led him to conclude that electromagnetic waves could be produced. He also determined that light waves are electromagnetic and not mechanical, as had been believed. He published his *Theory of Heat* in 1871 and his great work *Treatise on Electricity and Magnetism* in 1873. Few scientists at that time were able to follow his thinking, but it is now recognized as the foundation of modern electromagnetic theory, and Maxwell as one of the greatest theoretical physicists of all time. His interest in color and vision led him to demonstrate that different colors on a moving top blended together when the top was spun. His mathematical studies of the motion of molecules in gas proved that all molecules do not move at the same speed.

Maxwell is best known for a unit of magnetic flux called the *maxwell*. A *maxwell* is a unit equal to the flux perpendicularly intersecting an area of one square centimeter in a region where the magnetic induction is one gauss.

MAYONNAISE

Word historians agree on the place where the term *mayonnaise* developed but not how it developed at that place. *Mayonnaise* originally was a French dressing, but it has been completely Americanized. It consists of beaten egg yolk, butter or olive oil, lemon juice or vinegar, and seasonings.

Port Mahón in Minorca, at one time *Portus Magonis*, was named after Mago, the younger brother of the Carthaginian general Hannibal, who had planned to devastate Rome in the second Punic War. It became the capital of the Spanish island of Minorca. There's no argument that Port Mahón gave its name to *mayonnaise*.

Some say, however, that this sauce was created in 1762 by the chefs of Richelieu to memorialize the victory of the French over the the British. But others say that Duc de Richelieu himself prepared this dressing. Richelieu was known as a glutton. The dressing came about, it is said, when Richelieu raided the nearest kitchen and tossed what edibles he could find into one pot. And presto—*mayonnaise*.

A more credible story is that chefs created a dressing in Paris in honor of Richelieu's victory at Port Mahón. They named it *Mahonnaise*.

MCCARTHYISM

Joseph Raymond McCarthy (1909–1957) was born in Grand Chute, Wisconsin, graduated from Marquette University, and, after passing the bar examination, was elected a local judge. In 1946 he was elected to the United States Senate, where, after a period of quiet, he began a witch-hunt for communists in American government.

He leveled sweeping charges against the Roosevelt and Truman administrations for "twenty years of treason" and accused them of being soft on communists. He hounded Americans of all stripes, charging them with communist affiliation or sympathy.

Hollywood writers and television personalities were particularly targets; they were reviled and accused of being card-carrying members of the Communist Party. Many people lost their jobs because they refused to incriminate their friends. McCarthy attacked George C. Marshall—Army general former secretary of state, and Nobel peace prize recipient—and charged that the State Department was harboring several hundred communists. He accused the Voice of America and the Army Signal Corps of subversion. He attacked many of Eisenhower's appointees, but his crusade reached a climax in 1954 with a nationally televised investigation of circumstances surrounding the promotion of an allegedly disloyal Army dentist.

In December 1954 the Senate voted 67 to 22 to formally condemn McCarthy for certain of his actions. Thereupon his influence precipitously declined, and, after a long period of illness, he died at Bethesda, Maryland.

The term *McCarthyism*, inspired by McCarthy's activities, denoted violent and unfounded political attack and became eponymous for political witch-hunting.

MEDICEAN

The Medici family ruled Florence from the fifteenth to the eighteenth centuries. The patriarch was Giovanni de' Medici (?–1429), a banker, whose son Cosimo (the Elder, 1389–1464) was famous as a patron of the arts and learning. His grandson Lorenzo the Magnificent (1449–1492) was one of the outstanding figures of the Renaissance.

From Lorenzo (1395–1440), brother of Cosimo the Elder, came the line of Grand Dukes of Tuscany, the first being great-grandson Cosimo (1519–1574), who was regarded by many as the original of Machiavelli's *The Prince*. The Medici family gave three popes to the church: Leo, in whose pontificate the Reformation began; Clement VII, who refused Henry VIII's divorce from Catherine of Aragon; and Leo XI, who was pope for only a few months in 1605.

Medicean has come to mean pertaining to the Medicis, whether it concerns their banking affairs, their martial life, their religious ascendencies, their fostering of the arts, or whatever else they might have been involved in.

MELBA TOAST, PEACH MELBA, CHICKEN TETRAZZINI, SAUCE CARUSO

Many world-famous singers have had gourmet tastes and a gourmand appetite. For example, Luisa Tetrazzini, whose role in *Lucia di Lammermoor* thrilled opera lovers on many continents, was immortalized by a dish called *chicken Tetrazzini*, in which chicken is blanketed in pasta and immersed in a rich, creamy sauce of cheese and mushrooms. Enrico Caruso, considered the greatest tenor of all times, is remembered by *sauce Caruso*, a marinara sauce with sauteed mushrooms and chicken livers.

Possibly the world's greatest lyric soprano was Dame Nellie Melba. Of the two gastronomic inventions that honored Dame Melba, one was the dieter's delight and the other the dieter's ruination.

While staying at the Savoy in London, Melba explained to the waiter that she was dieting and ordered her breakfast toast to be extra thin. The toast she got was not only extra thin but also, by mistake, extra burnt. Nevertheless, Melba found it to be delicious. The maître d', taking advantage of Melba's prominence as one of the great divas of the nineteenth century, placed the dish on the menu and called it *Melba toast*. A subsequent story that made the rounds was that the famous French chef, Auguste Escoffier, honored Melba at the Ritz Carlton in London by a concoction of ice cream and peach halves, topped with a sauce of currants and raspberries, and served in a sculptured swan of ice. The dish was named, of course, *peach Melba*.

Melba, whose real name was Helen Porter Mitchell, was born in Burnley, Victoria, Australia, on May 19, 1861. She studied voice in Melbourne and then in Paris. She made her grand-opera debut in Brussels in 1887 as Gilda in *Rigoletto* under the name Melba, taking her name from the city of Melbourne. She went on to become a world-famous coloratura soprano, the celebrated star of London's Covent Garden, the Paris Opera, La Scala, and New York's Metropolitan. Upon her retirement in 1926, she became president of the Melbourne conservatoire. She died in Sydney, Australia on February 23, 1931.

MENDELEVIUM

Scientists had worked for many years to devise a universal system for classifying the elements, but with limited success. Dimitri Ivanovich Mendeleev, or Mendeleyev (1834–1907), inaugurated a system called the *Periodic Law of the Chemical Elements* which arranged the elements in order of increasing atomic weight so that they could be arranged in tables of vertical columns. Not only were scientists now able to check disputed data about known elements, but this system showed a number of spaces into which no known element would fit. This indicated to Mendeleev that certain elements had not yet been discovered. The system was remarkable in that it was able to predict with great accuracy both the atomic weights and general properties of elements that were later discovered.

Born in Siberia and educated at the University of St. Petersburg, Mendeleev became the director of weights and measures for the czar and introduced the metric system into his country. In 1955, four eminent American scientists—Glenn Seaborg, Bernard Harvey, Gregory Choppin, and S. G. Thompson—discovered an artificially produced radioactive element, 101, and named it *mendelevium* for Dimitri Mendeleev.

Mendelevium is formed in the laboratory by bombarding the element *einsteinium* with alpha particles.

MENDELISM, MENDEL'S LAW

Mendel's law of heredity, called *Mendelism*, was expounded by an Austrian monk in the mid-nineteenth century. Gregor Johann Mendel (1822–1884) was born of peasant stock in the part of the Austro-Hungarian Empire that later became Czechoslovakia. Though he was extremely poor and had a meager education, he was able to attend the University of Vienna through the help of a friendly patron.

Mendel became a substitute teacher at the Brünn Modern School, a title he retained during his fourteen-year tenure. But from the very beginning he worked unceasingly on his theory of the laws of heredity.

Mendel's experiments with peas had shown, that the characteristics of the parents of cross-bred offspring reappear in certain proportions in successive generations according to definite laws. He propounded three laws: the law of segregation; the principle of independent assortment; and the principle of dominance.

About 1900, three men independently did similar experiments and derived the same conclusions: Hugo de Vries of the Netherlands; Carl Correns of Germany; and Erich von Tschermak of Austria. But Mendel had anticipated them by thirty-five years.

Since then *Mendelian genetics* has become a new science, and it has formed the bridge between the other two great generalizations of nineteenth-century biology—cell theory and the theory of evolution.

Mendel's only recognition during his lifetime came in the monastery, and that was his election as abbot at Brünn.

MENTOR

A *mentor* is a guide or trusted friend, a wise and faithful counselor. And that is the way Odysseus considered *Mentor*, as revealed in Homer's epic poem the *Odyssey*.

When Odysseus, the hero of the poem, left home to join the besiegers of Troy, he prepared for a long stay. Hence he entrusted his young son, Telemachus, to the care of Mentor, an old man, and placed Mentor in charge of the household, including his wife, Penelope. However, things got out of hand, going from bad to worse in his house. Penelope's suitors drank up the contents of the wine cellar and butchered the cattle for their own use.

Pallas Athene spotted all these goings-on from Mount Olympus and realized that Odysseus would be without a home upon his return. She asked the father of gods, Zeus, whether she should go down and help out. He agreed, so Athene assumed the shape of *Mentor* and whispered sound advice into the ear of Telemachus. Her advice was rewarded, and to this day a *mentor* is a wise counselor, a tutor or coach.

MERCATOR PROJECTION

The famous Flemish cartographer Gerardus Mercator (1512–1594) was given at birth the name Gerhard, the family name being Kremer (meaning shopkeeper or merchant), but he preferred the Latinized version of his full name. Mercator set up a geographical center at Louvain, was employed by Charles V, and then devoted the rest of his days to map making. His works included several accurate maps and globes, which freed geographers from "the tyranny of Ptolemy." That distinguished Greco-Egyptian mathematician and astronomer had underestimated the earth's size.

Mercator became the father of modern cartography. He revolutionized map making, adjusting for the difference between a flat surface (used for all maps) and the earth's curves, scaling and projecting each point on the map. He then devised the world as a globe rather than a cone, setting up on his cylindrical charts meridians as straight lines perpendicular to the equator and latitudes as straight lines parallel to the equator. This innovation made navigating simpler and safer and came to be known as *Mercator projection*.

Mercator was accused of heresy, and fled to Duisberg, Germany in 1559. He accepted the Chair of Cosmography at the Louvian University and performed most of his important work there. His charts, first used by him in 1568, have been in use ever since.

MERCERIZE

John Mercer (1791–1866) worked in his father's cotton mill in Lancaster, England, and, through a fellow worker, learned to read and write when he was ten years old. John's primary interest, which had been music, changed to the art of dyeing and, because he was a handloom weaver, he worked on and invented devices that wove stripes and checks.

A story that was current in young Mercer's time was that Mercer went to another town to obtain a marriage license, but while browsing at a bookstall came across James Parkinson's *Chemical Pocket-book*. Merely from a reading of this book, Mercer got a job as a chemist to make calico prints at a fabric printshop. Mercer was so talented with fabrics that he was eventually admitted to partnership in the business. After thirty years the partnership was dissolved, freeing Mercer to continue his experiments. In 1850, at the age of fifty-nine, he perfected a process for treating cottons with caustic soda, sulphuric acid, and zinc chloride, which shrinks, strengthens, and gives a permanent silky luster to the fabric. Furthermore, cloth so treated made the fabric more absorbent so that it held dyes more readily.

Mercer's process was not so successful as it might have been, however, because of the shrinkage of the fabric. He had overlooked the treating of the material under tension. Long after his death, a correction was made, and the shrinkage was virtually eliminated. But Mercer's name remained as the inventor of the treatment process. Today we say that cotton goods have been *mercerized*, or that we have bought a spool of *mercerized cotton*.

MESMERISM, MESMERIZE

Franz Anton Mesmer, born in Germany on May 23, 1733, studied for the priesthood, then law. Finally he took up the study of medicine and became a serious student at the University of Vienna. He ultimately became a faculty member there.

Dr. Mesmer was convinced that magnets had curative properties. He believed in it so deeply that he even kept a magnet in a little sack around his neck. Unaware of his own hypnotic powers as a *mesmerist*, he attributed success to the stroking of his patients with a magnet. Throughout his adult life he also believed that a magic fluid, magnetic and invisible, surrounded everything animate and inanimate. This fluid had beneficent effects on human beings. He was convinced of its existence, even though he could not prove it. In later years, however, Mesmer, in an about-face, came to believe that his patients who had recovered had done so, not from his magnet, but from his stroking manipulations. Also he maintained that his hands held a healing power, which he called "animal magnetism."

His claim attracted considerable interest in Paris, where he had moved in 1778. Patients flocked to his healing sessions, and Mesmer did achieve remarkable success, especially with hysterical patients. But when he sought the approval of the medical profession, some doctors denounced him as a faker, a charlatan. His refusal to divulge his secrets to a medical commission militated against acceptance of his theories.

In 1784, a board of commissioners, including Benjamin Franklin, the U.S. commissioner to France, Antoine Lavoisier, and Joseph Guillotin, was appointed by King Louis XVI to investigate Mesmer's claims. The commission concluded that the supposed magnetic fluid could not be perceived by the senses and that its existence could not be inferred from a study of the patients. It branded the theory of animal magnetism a fraud, and stated that "Imagination without magnetism produces convulsions, and magnetism without imagination produces nothing."

Mesmer retired from his medical practice, the report having damaged his reputation, and his prominence declined into obscurity. He died on March 5, 1815, near his German birthplace, at Meersburg, Baden.

Mozart immortalized Mesmer in his *Cosi fan tutte*.

> This magnetic stone
> Should give the traveler pause

Once it was used by Mesmer,
Who was born
In Germany's green fields,
And who won great fame
In France.

A pupil of Mesmer's, Puységur, is credited with the first use of the term *mesmerism* to indicate Mesmer's practice, a form of hypnotism, which is the art of producing trance-sleep.

MESSERSCHMITT

The *Messerschmitt* was the most famous German fighter plane in World War II. Wilhelm (better known as Willy) Messerschmitt (1898–1978) was a German aircraft designer, engineer, and industrialist. He made and flew his own plane at age fifteen. By the time he reached twenty-six, he had formed his own aircraft manufacturing company.

Messerschmitt was best known for the airplanes he produced for the Luftwaffe in World War II. More then 30,000 of his ME-109 single-engine fighter planes were built; these fighters gave the Luftwaffe air supremacy during the early part of the war. Messerschmitt's ME-262 was the first operational combat jet.

After the war, Willy Messerschmitt was examined by an Allied denazification court in 1948. The court found that he had been forced to build aircraft for the German war effort. For the next ten years, Messerschmitt and his company manufactured prefabricated houses and sewing machines. They resumed building airplanes in 1958.

METHUSELAH

The term *methuselah* in general conversation today is taken to mean a very old man, possibly incredibly old. According to the Bible (Genesis 5:27), Methuselah lived 969 years, which makes him the oldest figure in the Bible: "When Enoch had lived sixty-five years, he became the father of Methuselah. Enoch walked with God after the birth of Methuselah three hundred years. . . . When Methuselah had lived a hundred and eighty-seven years, he became the father of Lamech. Methuselah lived after the birth of Lamech seven hundred and eighty-two years, and had other sons and daughters. Thus all the days of Methuselah were nine hundred and sixty-nine years, and he died."

MIDAS TOUCH

In modern usage, the *Midas touch* is a talent at succeeding financially at almost any enterprise. This is not the moral of the story, however. Midas was the king of ancient Phrygia, which is now central Turkey. In one myth, the tutor of Dionysus, Silenus, was brought in drunk to Midas, who recognized him and instead of meting out a punishment, treated him lavishly and took him back to Lydia and restored him to the god. Dionysus was so happy to see Silenus that he offered Midas whatever he wished. The king wished that everything he touched would turn to gold. Midas was at first delighted with the results, but his joy turned to horror when he realized that his food and drink were also being transformed. He finally prayed to lose his gift and was told by the god to wash in the River Pactolus, the sands of which were thenceforth filled with gold dust.

Another story concerns a music contest between Apollo and Pan. When the judge awarded the prize to Apollo, Midas expressed his disagreement. Apollo thereupon gave him the ears of an ass for his folly. Although by wearing a cap, Midas succeeded in hiding his humiliation, he had to show his ears to his barber. This man, although ordered to keep the secret on pain of death, felt unable to keep quiet about it. So he dug a pit in the ground, whispered the news into its depths, and filled the pit in. Unfortunately for Midas, the soil put forth reeds which, when rustled by the breeze, whispered the truth to the whole world: "King Midas has ass's ears."

MNEMONICS

Zeus had many wives, Hera being his number one and his chief nemesis. But he was also married to Mnemosyne, the goddess of memory. Zeus sired with her the nine muses: Calliope, patron of epic poetry; Terpsichore, goddess of choral dance; Clio, presiding over history; Erato, over lyric and amatory poetry; Euterpe, over music; Melpomene, over tragedy; Polyhmnia, over sacred music; Thalia, over comic and bucolic poetry; and Urania, over astronomy.

Mnemosyne came from a distinguished background, the daughter of heaven and earth (Uranus and Gaea). Her godly duty was to protect memory, and through her name has come the word *mnemonics*, the art of improving one's memory. In Greek, *mnemonikos* means mindful. The system *mnemonics* depends on association. A word, a name, a territory—almost anything can be used to stimulate memory. To remember how to distinguish stationery from stationary, for example, one might think of the fact that a *letter* has two *e*'s and no *a*'s. Therefore, the word for the paper on which letters are written is *stationery*.

MOLOTOV COCKTAIL,

The antitank weapon called a *Molotov cocktail* was not named to honor Molotov. Although how it was so dubbed is a matter of dispute, it is believed to have been named by the Finns during the Russo-Finnish War of 1939–1940 as a satirical honor for their antagonist—a cocktail *for* Molotov. In any event it has been used with lethal success by the armies of several countries. The weapon is a simple one. It consists of a bottle filled with inflammable fluid such as gasoline, with a slow fuse such as a rag protruding from the neck. The rag is ignited and the bottle thrown against the side of a tank, where it bursts into flames, spreading the liquid over the surface of the tank. The "cocktail" is very much like a homemade grenade. A cannister of incendiary bombs, launched from a plane as it opens and showers the bombs over a wide area, is called a *Molotov breadbasket*.

Molotov, the alias of the Russian diplomat Vyacheslav Mikhailovich Skriabin (1890–1986), dominated Russian foreign policy under Stalin. He was so indispensable to Stalin that he accompanied him to all the important international conferences. He negotiated the infamous Molotov-Ribbentrop pact, in 1939, otherwise known as the Pact of Steel. After Stalin's death, Molotov fell out of favor with Khrushchev, who labeled him a saboteur of peace, accused him of policy failures, and then bestowed on him the supreme honor of ambassador to Mongolia. He was expelled from the Communist Party in 1964, the very party he helped found. But in a show of compassion, the party reinstated him in 1984, at which time he was ninety-four years of age.

MORGAN HORSE

America has a classic breed of horses, the *Justin Morgan*, which took its name from its owner, Justin Morgan (1747–1789), a Vermont schoolteacher. This horse, a thoroughbred stallion that was probably a blend of Arabian and some other elements, was purchased in Massachusetts and named *Figure*. Morgan trained Figure and the horse won many contests, even against larger thoroughbreds. The owner then decided to change the horse's name to his name, and presto—*Justin Morgan*. It thereafter became the founding sire of a whole breed of horses.

The horse was small, about 800 pounds and fourteen hands high, had a short neck and a delicate head. After the owner's death, the horse was sold many times, but its distinctive breed continued until the strain died out. It became America's favorite saddle and trotting horse, until the Hambletonian strain replaced it as a trotter. But *Justin Morgan* will long be remembered as the only American horse to sire a distinctive breed.

MORRIS CHAIR

The *Morris chair*, an easy chair with a movable back, took its name from William Morris (1834–1896), an Englishman who was thought to be a true Renaissance man. Eric Partridge described him as a "poet, pamphleteer, master craftsman who influenced politicians, printers, architects, and furniture designers." Morris's theory was that objects should be produced as much for their beauty as for their utility. He founded a decorating firm and a factory dedicated to reforming Victorian taste in color and design. His interest in furniture developed after he moved into a London flat and had a hard time finding furnishings to suit his taste. In his spare time, Morris designed a chair for comfort, one with an adjustable back, removable pillows, and straight wooden arms.

Morris established a vogue for handmade objects and was an important designer of glass, jewelry, sculpture, wallpaper, and furniture in modified Gothic styles. But the *Morris chair* overshadowed his other designs.

Morris's scholarly background had no direct connection with his invention of the Morris chair. He was was an eminent English poet and artist and one of the originators of *Oxford and Cambridge Magazine*, which was printed for a year on his expense. He acquired interests in and studied the practical art of dyeing and carpet weaving. His interests took him into typography, and he organized the Kelmscot Press in 1890 in Hammersmith, for which he designed special type and ornamental letters and borders for use in publishing medieval French romances. In addition, he published volumes of his own verse and produced illuminated manuscripts, his work featuring two editions of Edward FitzGerald's *Omar Khayyam*.

MORSE CODE

The Morse code is named for its inventor, Samuel Finley Breese Morse (1791–1872), who was born in Charlestown, Massachusetts, the son of a Calvinist minister. He graduated from Yale and then went to England to study painting and design under Washington Allston and Benjamin West. While still a young man, Morse showed considerable talent and exhibited his artwork at the Royal Academy. After his return to America, he gained a reputation as a portrait painter and won recognition as a sculptor. He founded, in 1826, the National Academy of Design and was its first president. In 1832 he received a professorship at the University of New York. But Morse was more than a painter. He had an inventive mind and developed an intense interest in electricity. Although he taught art, he spent much time studying electricity with professors in other departments of the university.

The idea of the telegraph occurred to Morse during a dinner discussion at sea in 1832. It soon became his main interest. By 1835, he had set up a successful telegraph line in his room. With a grant from Congress of $30,000 Morse built an experimental line from Baltimore to Washington. It was over that line that Morse sent his historic message, "What hath God wrought." The honor of choosing the words was given to Annie Ellsworth, daughter of the commissioner of patents.

Morse was subjected to a great deal of litigation, but he succeeded in patenting his famous code in 1854. First called the *Morse alphabet*, the name was changed to *Morse code*. The demand for the code was international, and Morse became a wealthy man.

MURPHY BED

A bed that can be raised and folded into a wall is called a *Murphy bed*, after its inventor. This once-common folding bed provided more usable daytime living space, and allowed a living room to double as a bedroom. The added space that this bed created, after it swung into a closet, was a real boon during the days of small apartments.

The inventor of this useful piece of furniture was an American, William Lawrence Murphy (1876–1959). The usefulness of this bed disappeared when sofa convertibles came into vogue.

NAPOLEON, NAPOLITAIN

The delectable pastry commonly called a *napoleon* is frequently thought—wrongly—to have been named in honor of Napoleon Bonaparte. To reinforce this belief, a persistent tale circulated that Napoleon carried the pastry in his breast pocket as he went out to conquer Russia. Is that why his hand was always thrust into his coat? This idea is no more than folk etymology.

The flaky, custard cream pastry was first made by Neapolitans, people of Naples, Italy, who called it *Napolitain*. Although the name of the pastry today is generally heard to be napoleon, it nevertheless is a corruption of *Napolitain*.

NAPOLEONIC, WATERLOO

Calling someone *Napoleonic* might refer to Napoleon's short and stocky build, his excessive and greedy loyalty to family, to the desire for power at any cost, or to overweening ambitions. Or it might refer to Napoleon's hair style or his pompous stance with his hand inside his shirt. Napoleon's name is sometime used to denote supremacy in a particular field as in *a Napoleon of finance*.

Although there have been several Napoleons—Napoleon II (1811–1832), who never reigned; Napoleon III (1808–1873) of the Second Empire; and, of course, the incomparable Napoleon I (1769–1821)—Napoleon Bonaparte's reign (1804–1815) is known in French history as the First Empire. Bonaparte's political, military, and personal life consisted of one legend after another. When only seventeen, he proposed marriage to the illegitimate daughter of Louis XV, who turned him down because he had "no future."

One of his great accomplishments that has survived is the *Code Napoleon*, the code of laws prepared under his direction that forms the basis of modern French law and law in the state of Louisiana. Equality, justice, and common sense are its keynotes. But Napoleon is equally well remembered in the barroom by *Napoleon brandy*.

Six years after Napoleon met his Waterloo in 1815, he died of cancer at age fifty-two while imprisoned on the island of St. Helena. (A *Waterloo* is a crushing or decisive defeat.) The devotion of many of his worshipers continues. In 1840, his body was enshrined in Paris in the Invalides, to which the people of the world still make a pilgrimage.

NEMESIS

According to the Greek classics, Nemesis, the daughter of Nox, was the goddess of retributive justice and vengeance. Her divinely appointed task was to maintain the equilibrium between good and evil in the universe. Armed with a sword and scourge, she would ceaselessly seek transgressors of the law and those guilty of impiety and pursue them in her chariot, ready to flay the offenders and to mete out further divine punishment.

Although Nemesis was equally responsible for rewarding the just for their good deeds, good seemed to be in shorter supply than bad, and so Nemesis is usually identified with vengeance. Nemesis has been blamed for the Trojan War. According to some accounts of the legend of Leda and the swan, Zeus (in the form of a swan) raped Nemesis, who gave the impregnated egg to Leda. From the egg was born Helen, whose elopement with Paris, the Trojan prince, ignited the destruction of Troy.

Nowadays, however, a *nemesis* is thought of as a person who is a source of woe or misfortune.

NEWTON, NEWTONIAN

Isaac Newton (1642–1727) was born at Woolsthorpe, Lincolnshire, England, and was educated at Grantham School nearby. He showed a propensity to invent but was considered a poor student. However, at Trinity College, Cambridge University, he showed exceptional ability in mathematics. According to one story, an instructor announced that he would lecture on Johannes Kepler's *Optics*. Newton got a copy of the book, and the next day the instructor was amazed to learn that Newton had mastered the subject.

Within two years after obtaining his degree, Newton discovered mathematical principles and began work on his theory of gravitation, the laws of which he was the first to state. The astronomical system that in the late seventeenth century displaced Copernicanism, and also the theory of gravitation, are known as the Newtonian Philosophy. Newton established the former and discovered the latter. He was responsible for many inventions and discoveries, including a reflecting telescope, integral and differential calculus, the binomial theorem, the method of tangents, and other important mathematical principles. During this period, Newton also began his investigations on the subject of gravitation. *Newtonian* is a concept referring to Newton's work in mathematics and on gravitation (in physics a *newton* is a standard unit of force).

Newton was elected a fellow of the Royal Society in 1672 and in 1703 became its president. He spent some time in Parliament and was appointed warden of the Mint, later becoming master of the Mint. He was a bachelor and was considered a gentle and compassionate person. Although Einstein rejected Newton's explanation of gravitation, but not the facts of its operation, scientists believe that Einstein's work would have been impossible without Newton's discoveries.

Newton's modest personality is well-demonstrated by the following from David Brewster's *Memoirs of the Life Writing and Discoveries of Sir Isaac Newton*: "I do not know what I may appear to the world, but to myself I seem to have been only a boy playing on the sea-shore, and diverting myself in now and then finding a smoother pebble or a prettier shell than ordinary, whilst the great ocean of truth lay all undiscovered before me."

NICOTINE

Warnings about smoking came long after the life of Jean Nicot, the man from whose name the word *nicotine*, a poisonous water-soluble alkaloid, was derived.

Jean Nicot's role in popularizing tobacco began by chance. Nicot (1530–1600) was sent to Portugal in 1559 by Francis II of France to negotiate a marriage between the king's sister, Marguerite of Valois, six years old, and Don Sebastian, the king of Portugal, age five. The negotiations failed, but from this aborted visit came the seeds, literal and figurative, for a worldwide industry of huge proportions.

Nicot was given a gift of strange seeds by Portuguese sailors who had recently returned from America. He cultivated the seedlings with great care and from them grew tobacco leaves, a sample of which he sent to Queen Mother Catherine de Médici, who loved to sniff the "powder." Other prominent persons followed suit. Tobacco became fashionable.

Disputes over tobacco arose from many sources in many lands. James VI of Scotland (later James I of England) voiced bitter and blunt objections. He referred to smoking as "a custom loathsome to the eye, hateful to the nose, harmful to the brain, dangerous to the lungs, and in the black, stinking fumes thereof, nearest resembling the horrible Stygian smoke of the pit that is bottomless." Amurat, a sultan of Turkey, ordered smokers to be shot. The czar punished smokers by having their noses snipped off. The Senate in Berne, Switzerland, added "smoking" to "stealing" and "killing" in the Ten Commandments. The use of tobacco might have been stamped out completely but for the marvel of commerce. The French imposed a state tax of two francs per hundred pounds of tobacco, which brought in about a million francs a year. Tobacco was back in favor.

Nicot was a scholarly person who had hoped to leave a worthwhile legacy—a dictionary of the French language. Ironically, he received no fame for the dictionary he spent so many years compiling and is known instead for *nicotine*, a word that he hadn't even included in his dictionary.

The Swedish botanist Carolus Linnaeus named the genus that includes the common tobacco plant *Nicotiana* in Nicot's honor.

NOSTRADAMUS, NOSTRADAMIC

Michel de Notredame (1503–1566) assumed the Latinized form of his name *Nostradamus*. He was a French doctor and astrologer who published an annual "Almanack" as well as a famous book of prophecies in verse, *Les Centuries* (1555), couched in ambiguous language and open to many interpretations. But some people believed that the prophecies foretold events that eventually occurred.

Nostradamus was born in Provence, France. He practiced as a physician and was known for his medical work during the plague in Lyons. Catherine de Médici invited him to visit her, and Charles IX appointed him his physician-in-ordinary. A prophecy of Nostradamus that had a decided effect on the populace and increased his popularity was the death of Henri II as a result of a wound received at a tournament, just as Nostradamus prophesized.

Although Nostradamus's name is synonymous with soothsayer, it is now used in a contemptuous sense. The saying "as good a prophet as Nostradamus" refers to one who makes a prophecy that is so obscure that the meaning can't be understood. Vague prophecies are referred to as *nostradamic* predictions.

ODYSSEUS, ODYSSEY

Odysseus, in Greek legend, was the king of Ithaca and a leading Greek hero of the Trojan War. He was the son of Laertes and Anticlea; the husband of Penelope, and the father of Telemachus. At first unwilling to go to the Trojan War, he feigned madness by yoking an ass and an ox to a plow and sowing salt. But Palamedes, son of the king of Nauplia, who was seeking recruits for service in the war, placed the infant Telemachus in front of the plow, whereupon Odyssesus proved his sanity by turning aside. At Troy, Odysseus was renowned for his bravery, wisdom, and cunning. His wanderings after the capture of Troy, his return to Ithaca, and his vengeance upon Penelope's suitors, who had taken advantage of his absence, are related in Homer's *Odyssey*.

Odysseus spent seven of his ten years of absence on an island where he was detained by the nymph Calypso, and one year on another island, detained by the enchantress Circe, who transformed his crew into swine to prevent human voyeurism. According to a post-Homeric legend, Odysseus was slain accidentally by Telegonus, his son by Circe.

The epic poem of Homer records the adventure of Odysseus (called Ulysses by the Romans) on his homeward voyage from Troy. Odysseus displayed craftiness on his long voyage to Ithaca, guiding his ship home in spite of Circe and the Cyclops and past the Sirens as well. His voyage, regarded by many as the greatest travelogue of all times, gave birth to the word *odyssey* to mean a long journey or campaign, especially one featuring many changes of fortune, or an extended adventurous wandering.

OEDIPUS COMPLEX

Oedipus complex is the psychoanalytical term for the sexual attraction of a son to his mother, accompanied by manifestations of hostility toward the father.

The name for this psychological pattern in males was taken by Sigmund Freud from the Greek myth of Oedipus because the life of this Theban king seemed to act out in detail the logic of Freud's theory, the repressed desires of the male. Although Oedipus was the subject of many Greek tragedies, his pathetic fate was best dramatized by Sophocles in *Oedipus Rex* and *Oedipus at Colonus*.

Oedipus was the son of Laius, king of Thebes, and of his queen, Jocasta. An oracle warned the parents to beget no children, for the king would perish at the hands of his own son, who would then marry his mother. Having begotten Oedipus while drunkenly out of control of his sexual impulses, the king, trying to circumvent this prophecy of doom, exposed the infant Oedipus on a mountaintop, his feet bound and pierced. He was found by a shepherd and presented to the king of Corinth, who reared him as his own son, giving him the name *Oedipus* because of his swollen feet (*oedipus* in Greek means "swollen feet").

When Oedipus was grown, he was informed by the oracle of the future tragedy of his life. Believing that the Corinthian king was his real father, Oedipus left and resolved never to return to Corinth. On his way to Thebes, his chariot and one coming in an opposite direction could not pass at the same time because the road was too narrow. An argument ensued, and Oedipus killed the stranger—who turned out to be Laius, his natural father.

Oedipus continued on to Thebes, where the celebrated Sphinx, sitting majestically on a rock, kept posing what seemed to be an unanswerable riddle to the Thebans. Whoever failed to solve her riddle, she would kill at once. In desperation, the Thebans offered their kingdom and the hand of Jocasta to anyone who would rid the country of this monster. Oedipus solved the riddle; in innocence married the widowed queen; and became, by her, the father of four children. When Oedipus and his mother discovered that their relationship was incestuous, Jocasta hanged herself, and Oedipus put out his eyes. And thus the prophecy came to pass.

O. HENRY ENDING

William Sydney Porter (1862–1910) was one of the most renowned and intriguing short-story writers in the United States. But his early life was a hard-luck epic filled with trials and tribulations.

Born in Greensboro, North Carolina, Porter was only three when he lost his mother. At fifteen, he left school. Five years later, he migrated to Texas, where he was unsuccessful at various employments. In 1891, he became a bank teller at an Austin bank and was indicted for embezzlement in 1896. Protesting his innocence (the amount was small, and he claimed mismanagement), he fled to Honduras and South America, leaving behind his wife and young son. When Porter learned that his wife was dying, he returned to Texas, was tried and convicted of embezzlement, and served three years in a federal penitentiary. During his incarceration, his son died.

By the time Porter was thirty-five, he had lost everything: His wife and son had died and his association with an Austin humor magazine that he had once edited was gone. While in prison, Porter began writing, using a pseudonym to disguise his identity. On his release, he headed for New York and began a career in journalism. Although troubled by alcoholism, Porter was a prolific writer in the twelve years between his confinement and his death. He wrote 700 stories, publishing *Cabbages and Kings* in 1904, *The Four Million* in 1906, *Voice of the City* in 1908, and *Options* in 1909. His stories, which featured everyday people, were characterized by the use of coincidence and ironic surprise endings. The author's deep emotions penetrated his writings. His "Gift of the Magi" became a classic almost from the time it was written.

Porter had a constant bout with hypoglycemia. He summarized his condition by saying, "I was born eight drinks below par." His last words were an order to a nurse: "Pull up the shades. I don't want to go home in the dark."

OHM, OHM'S LAW

Georg Simon Ohm (1787–1854), was born in Erlangen, Bavaria, Germany, to a family of locksmiths.

Ohm received a doctorate in physics when he was twenty-two and then accepted a position teaching mathematics at the Jesuit college in Cologne. He was not well accepted by his fellow scientists, which caused him to resign. To obtain another teaching assignment, Ohm sent a copy of a book he had written to the monarchs of the various German states. His strategy paid off. The king of Prussia invited him to teach at the Royal Konsistorium in Cologne. His research at that institution led him to discover the basic law of electrical resistance.

The International Electrical Congress voted at its meeting in Chicago in 1893—thirty-nine years after Ohm's death—to adopt his name for a unit of electrical resistance. *Ohm's Law* is set forth as "current equals volts divided by ohms."

O.K., OK

No consensus exists on the derivation of OK. Some say it was an abbreviation used by lumbermen who cut oak trees for furniture. The best-quality oak was "Oak A." Or was it a Choctaw Indian word spelled "Okeh," meaning "it is"? Another theory is that it represented the initials of a railroad clerk, Obadiah Kelly, who stamped OK on parcels for shipment. Then again, bananas without flaws were designated *au quai*—that is, ready to go to the quay for loading. Hence OK.

But the largest following among word authorities is that the genesis of OK can be found in the name of the O.K. Democratic Club, a group that during the presidential campaign of 1840 used the symbol O.K. as its rallying slogan on behalf of Martin Van Buren (1782–1862). Van Buren had adopted the nickname "Old Kinderhook" to refer to his birthplace near Albany and to emphasize his farming background. Van Buren's father was a farmer, and Martin, when a boy, helped with the plow. "Old Kinderhook" became shortened to "O.K.," and the voters were exhorted to "vote right, vote O.K." Van Buren entered the White House for a four-year stay, but his symbol OK became the permanent symbol in the language of the world for "all right." OK has attained such universal acceptance that it vies with Coca-Cola as the best-known term on earth.

OSCAR

Each spring millions of television viewers watch the Academy of Motion Pictures Arts and Sciences's elaborate ceremony at which Oscars (golden trophies) are bestowed on the best performers and other professionals in various categories involved in movie production. The *Oscar* is a ten-inch statuette, weighing seven pounds, bronze on the inside and gold-plated on the outside. It was designed by Cedric Gibbons, a subsequent six-time winner of an Oscar for best art design.

The statuette was first presented in 1927, but it was nameless until 1931. In that year, a new librarian, Mrs. Margaret Herrick, was employed by the Academy. When shown one of the trophies, she noted its resemblance to her uncle. A newspaper reporter sitting nearby overheard the comment, liked it, published it, and thus initiated a permanent name for the prized trophy. Her remark was, "He reminds me of my Uncle Oscar."

Uncle Oscar has been a somewhat shadowy figure. He was supposed to be Oscar Pierce, a wealthy Texan, but that fact has never been satisfactorily established.

OTTOMAN

The *ottoman* is a stuffed or cushioned footstool, sometimes called a hassock. Also called an *ottoman* is a backless couch, which in America never attained the popularity of the footstool.

The namesake that people have been resting their feet on (the footstool) or their entire bodies (the couch) came from Osman I (1288–1320). Europeans sometimes corrupted the name to *Othman* or *Ottoman*, the once-mighty ruler of the Turks and the founder of the *Ottoman Empire*. His descendants ruled the great empire for more than six centuries, until its dissolution in 1919. The *Ottoman Empire* ruled from its capital Constantinople (modern-day Istanbul) vast land areas comprising in southwestern Asia, northeastern Africa, and much of southeastern Europe.

Toward the end of the eighteenth century, there was a surge of interest in Oriental splendors—carpets, pillows, furniture. Shrewd merchants promoted the furniture to feed the imagination of the Eastern potentates. And so backless sofas came into demand, as did the cushioned footstool.

Ottoman takes its name from the feminine form of the French *ottomane*, which in turn comes from the Arabic word for Turkish *Othmani*.

OYSTERS ROCKEFELLER

Oysters Rockefeller is a concoction of oysters topped with a puree of spinach, celery, onion and seasonings, baked on a bed of rock salt, thick enough to keep the oysters in shell from tipping over. The dish was not the brainchild of any Rockefeller, and its name came about through pure fortuity at Antoine's, the renowned New Orleans restaurant. Original words have been lost. This is hearsay: A diner eating the oyster dish commented to the waiter that the flavor was as rich as Rockefeller. And so the dish received its distinguished name from an unknown person who had no idea that the remark would become a culinary verbal monument.

PALLADIUM, PALLADIAN

Pallas Athene, called *Pallas Minerva* in Latin, perhaps is so named from the spear she brandished. In classical legend, the wooden statue of *Pallas*, in the citadel of Troy, which was said to have fallen from heaven, preserved the safety of the city. From this notion has come the general meaning of *palladium*—a safeguard on which anyone or anything can depend. The Trojans knew this legend well. After Odysseus and Diomedes stole the statue, Troy fell.

When William Hyde Wollaston, an English physicist, discovered, in 1803, a rare metallic element associated with platinum and gold, he named it *palladium* for the Grecian goddess and also after the newly discovered asteroid *Pallas*.

The similar-sounding word *Palladian* is derived from the architectural style, based on the classical, introduced by Andrea Palladio (1518–1580). This great architect was given the name Andrea di Pietro Vicenza at birth but was renamed by the scholarly poet Trissimo. Outstanding works of his include the Villa Rotunda at Vicenza and S. Georgio Maggiore in Venice. Palladio was honored with the appellation "the Raphael of architects." His name is still current in *Palladian window*, an architectural unit that he used on grand buildings. It consists of a central window with a round-arch top flanked by two square-topped windows.

The *Palladium* in London derived its name from the mistaken notion that the ancient Palladium, like the great Colosseum, was a place for circuses and fun.

PAMPHLET

The background of the common word *pamphlet* may be entirely amatory. In the twelfth century a Latin poem titled *Pamphilus, seu de Amore* took the staid people of that era by storm. The author of this Latin poem is unknown, but the verses, some three pages in length, became among the best-known of the Middle Ages. This "love-making" poem was so popular that it came to be called simply *Pamphilus*. After the invention of the printing press, the poem appeared in booklet form, and the title, over time, became the one-word *Pamphlet*. Then a *pamphlet* (lower case *p*) came to be defined as a paper-bound or unbound booklet of fewer than a hundred pages. The word *pamphlet*, etymologically, stems from Greek *pamphilos*, meaning "beloved by all."

PANACEA, HYGEIA

The Roman god of medicine, Aesculapius, had seven daughters, among them Panacea and Hygeia, both of whose names have passed into common usage in English.

Panaceas's name means "all-healing." The Greek form of her name was *Panakeia*, from *pan*, meaning all, and *akeisthai*, to heal. Hence the word *panacea* came to mean a cure-all, a universal medicine or remedy.

In the Middle Ages the search for a panacea was one of the self-imposed tasks of the alchemists, which they conducted when they weren't busy transmuting a baser metal into gold. Fable tells of many panaceas, such as the Promethean Unguent, which rendered the body invulnerable; Aladdin's ring; the balsam of Fierabras; and Prince Ahmed's apple, each reputed to be a cure for every disorder known to human beings.

Hygeia, from the Greek *hygies*, means health. The English word *hygiene* can be traced directly to her name. *Hygeia* was endowed with the power to ward off pestilence and to promote health. The preamble of the Hippocratic Oath says: "I swear by Apollo the healer, Asklepios, and Hygeia and Panacea and all the gods and goddesses . . ."

PANIC, PANDEMONIUM, PAN

In the Greek religion, Pan, a god of forests and fields, of flocks and shepherds, came from disputed parentage. He is represented with the torso of a man and the legs, horns, and ears of a goat. Because he dwelt in the woodlands, any weird sound or eerie sigh emanating at night from the mountains or valleys was attributed to him. Pan was a mischievous creature and loved to dart out of underbrush and shout at people just to startle them. A *panic* is caused by overpowering fear. In its theatrical sense, however, *panic* has an opposite connotation—to amuse to the point that the audience is hysterical with laughter.

Sex and music were Pan's chief interests. He was often portrayed playing his panpipes or dancing with nymphs. He set his lustful eye one day on a nymph named Syrinx. But she fled from him to preserve her chastity and was transformed into a bed of reeds. Pan cut the reeds into unequal lengths and fashioned from them his syrinx or panpipe. Pan continued his amorous, lustful pursuits with other nymphs. Although his courtship of Syrinx proved fruitless, the anglicized name of his lovely nymph continues to this day, but in the form of a very ordinary device— a *syringe* (a Syrinx is the vocal organ of birds).

John Milton coined the word *pandemonium* in *Paradise Lost* in 1667. Milton wanted a word to represent a tumultuous disorder. It is used today to describe any wild, unrestrained uproar or any boisterous assembly. Where there is panic there is bound to be pandemonium.

PANDER

The verb *pander* means to cater to, or profit by, the vices of others. But for centuries it meant to act as a go-between in clandestine love affairs.

Pandaro was a character in Boccaccio's *Filostrato*. He was the cousin of Cressida and, living up to his unsavory reputation, acted as go-between in her affair with Troilus. Chaucer took him over in his *Troilus and*

Criseyde as *Pandarus*, changing him from cousin to uncle but retaining his unsavory role. His name came to be used as a generic term for "an arranger of sexual liaisons." In each instance Pandaro or Pandare obtained Cressida's favors for the pleasure of Troilus, son of the king of Troy. But the match did not last long. Cressida deserted her lover for a Greek. Shakespeare through Pandarus intoned: "Since I have such pains to bring you together, let all pitiful goers-between be call'd to the world's end after my name; call them all Pandars."

The sense of *pander* in today's contemporary usage is to appeal to someone's lower tastes or lower nature. It might be said of anyone who gains power and popularity by arousing the emotions and prejudices of people. Such a person might also be called a demagogue.

PANDORA'S BOX

The expression *Pandora's box* may be a good warning to apply to a situation in which it is wise to keep matters under control and under cover, lest a worse situation develop. Or, as it's said on the street, "Don't open up a can of worms."

In Greek mythology, Pandora was the first woman. She was created by Zeus to discredit Prometheus, who had acted as a friend of mortals by bringing them fire. Pandora, which means "all gifts," was fashioned by the smith of the gods, Hephaestus, out of clay, given life and clothes by Athena, granted beauty by Aphrodite so that men would love her, and taught guile and treachery by Hermes. The gods also gave into Pandora's hands a sealed jar containing all the evils that were ever to plague mankind; the only good it contained was Hope, right at the bottom.

Zeus gave Pandora—and her gift—to Epimetheus, Prometheus's brother, who accepted her as his bride. Prometheus had warned his brother never to accept a gift from Zeus, but Epimetheus opened the jar, and out of it flew all the sorrows, diseases, quarrels, and woes that have ever since afflicted human beings. He hastily snapped the lid back on, but it was too late to prevent the torrent of evils escaping into the world. Some accounts say that the spirit Hope also escaped, but others say Hope was trapped inside, unable to alleviate the ills that were now released to bedevil mortals. Some versions say that Pandora opened the jar, and blame her curiosity for the ruin of mankind.

To open a *Pandora's box* is to uncover a source of troublesome problems, or to receive a gift that turns out to be a curse.

PANTALOONS, PANTS

For decades in England no gentleman would dare be seen wearing what were mockingly called *pantaloons*. No less a national hero than the Duke of Wellington was refused admittance to a club because he was wearing long pants rather than the breeches and silken hose expected of a member of royalty or another person of high rank. The *pants* worn in America by almost every man and many women is an abbreviation of *pantaloons*.

The forebear of these articles of dress can be traced to the baggy trousers worn by a character in the Italian *commedia dell'arte*. A physician had been the patron saint of Venice—San Pantaleone. (The literal meaning is "all lion." *Pan* means all, and *leone* is "lion.") *Pantaleone* in the comedies was an elderly buffoon interested only in lechery, but who was usually outwitted by the women. He was always played as an emaciated dotard, wearing spectacles, one-piece, skintight breeches, and stockings that bloomed out above the knees. The passing years has transmogrified this patron saint of Venice into a lovable but simpleminded character in Italian comedy.

With a slight orthographic change to *pantaloon*, his name was then equated with "clown." The word in plural form (*pantaloons*) subsequently entered the English language to describe a particular type of trousers. As fashions changed, *pantaloons* became the name of various types of trousers over the years. In time it was used in the shortened form of *pants* as the designation for trousers in general.

PAP SMEAR

The *Pap* test, a stain-analysis technique for identifying atypical cells and malignancy in cervical-tissue smears, was the invention of George Nicholas Papanicolaou (1883–1962). In the test he devised, a small spatula is inserted into the vagina to remove fluid mixed with urine cells. The fluid is dyed, spread on a glass slide, and examined under a microscope.

Papanicolaou was born in Greece and received a medical degree at Athens and a doctorate in biology at Munich. He immigrated to America in 1914 and became a teacher of medicine. He held a position in pathology at New York Hospital and concurrently taught anatomy at Cornell Medical College. Toward the end of his life he directed the Miami Cancer Institute, which after his death was renamed in his honor.

The medical profession was slow to accept his test, the research for which was begun in the 1920s. It was not until 1942 that a monograph Papanicolaou wrote with Herbert Traut, *Diagnosis of Uterine Cancer by the Vaginal Smear*, changed clinical opinion to his favor by demonstrating the value of early detection.

Today the *Pap smear* is a routine screening test, and is credited with substantially reducing the mortality rate of uterine and cervical cancer.

PARIAH

A *Pariah* for some three thousand years was a member of a lower caste in India called, in Tamil, *Paraiyan*, from Southern India. Pariahs were drum beaters. At certain Hindu festivals, the beating of drums plays an important part. When the British came to India, they employed these lower-caste people as domestics and as servants to whom they assigned other duties. The British corrupted their name to *pariah* with a lower-case *p*. The continental Europeans, thinking that these people were the lowest caste, or even of no caste at all, adopted their mistaken term to mean the equivalent of outcast. Their employers ranked them at the bottom of the social scale. And the sense of that word—an outcast—was imported to England and was adopted into the English language.

PARKINSON'S DISEASE

James Parkinson (1755–1824) was an English surgeon who first described the condition in a paper published in 1817, *An Essay on the Shaking Palsy*. The disease is known as *shaking palsy* or *paralysis agitans*, a literal translation of the Latin.

Parkinson's disease is a progressive disorder of the nervous system characterized by slowness of voluntary movements, muscular rigidity, tremor of resting muscles, a masklike facial expression, stooped posture, and a small-stepped walk without the normal arm swing.

Parkinson was also one of the first to describe the disease of *appendicitis* and to point out that the perforation of the appendix may be a cause of death.

Despite all his medical research, he found time for politics and was elected to the House of Parliament. He fought for universal suffrage and was concerned about health care and the rights of the insane. He became so involved in politics that he was suspected of participating in a proposed plot to assassinate George III in the theater by means of a poisoned dart, the so-called "pop-gun plot." He was examined before the privy council and was found not guilty of complicity.

PARKINSON'S LAW

C. Northcote Parkinson (1909–1993), Raffles Professor of History at the University of Malaya, expounded his satirical "law" in 1955 in the *Economist*. His collection of essays on bureaucratic overload promulgated in book form in 1957 made this historian and economist an unexpected celebrity.

Parkinson's law reads as follows: "Work expands so as to fill the time available for its completion," and the law conversely stated is: "The amount of work completed is in inverse proportion to the number of people employed" and "subordinates multiply at a fixed rate regardless of the amount of work produced." This is somewhat similar to the Law of Diminishing Returns. The law applies equally both to public and to business administrations, its purpose being to call attention to inefficiency in the operation of any bureaucracy, public or private.

PARTHIAN SHOT, PARTING SHOT

A Turkomanic people living southeast of the Caspian Sea and ruled by Scythian nomads, the Parthians were soldiers known to be among the best. Their country was Parthia, and they devoted their lives to becoming expert marksmen and fighters. They rode their horses, fully armored, and their slaves served as infantry. They bested the Roman hordes time and again, beginning with the disastrous defeat of Crassus in 53 B.C. Years later they defeated Mark Antony by repulsing his advance into Persia.

The Parthians were deadly adversaries. They planned their aggressive movements strategically. One of their peculiar maneuvers was to appear to leave the battleground as though in flight, but as the enemy began to rejoice, they turned and discharged their bows. This maneuver has come to be known as the *Parthian shot* or the *parting shot*.

Today any parting or final remark of an insulting nature made on departure and giving one's adversary no time to reply may be called a *Parthian shot*, an allusion to the ancient warriors of Parthia.

PASQUINADE

A *pasquinade* is a witty lampoon or squib, having ridicule for its object, written anonymously, and posted for all to see, or a satire mocking someone that is published in a vehicle of general circulation. Anyone who pins up an unsigned note on the bulletin board, hoping the boss will see it, has posted a *pasquinade*. In 1501 in Rome a mutilated ancient statue was unearthed, restored, and placed near the Piazza Navona. Some say it was a statue of a Roman gladiator named *Pasquino*. Others contend that the statue was named after *Pasquin*, a barber noted for his caustic wit, whose shop was near the field where the statue was found. Whether the statue represented the ancient gladiator or the witty barber, it was called *Pasquino*. It became customary on St. Mark's Day for people to hang on the statue verses of their political, religious, and personal satires. These satires were barbed and often critical of the pope.

From *Pasquino* came the Italian word *pasquinata* and the French *pasquinade*, which entered the English language with no change in spelling.

Unearthed at the opposite end of Rome was another statue, a figure of a recumbent god believed to be Mars. A custom then developed to answer the *pasquinades* by affixing replies to this statue, which was called *Marforio*.

PASTEURIZE

Louis Pasteur (1822–1895), French chemist and microbiologist, decided at an early age to become a painter, but this interest was superseded by a fascination with science. He became a professor of physics at Dijon in 1848, and then a professor of chemistry at Strasbourg, where he met and married the rector's daughter, Mlle. Laurent, who became a devoted fellow worker. At age twenty-two, he accepted the position of dean at Lille.

Pasteur's chief interest during the early stages was in lactic and alcoholic fermentation, that is, discovering a method for checking excessive fermentation and reducing disease in wine, beer, and milk. After much experimentation, he recommended that those liquids be heated to high temperatures and then rapidly cooled, a treatment that frees them from disease-causing bacteria without seriously changing the food value or taste. That formula not only revolutionized the wine and beer industries but also saved the lives of untold numbers of milk drinkers.

Pasteur saved France's silk industry by isolating the bacilli of a disease destroying the silkworm. He then turned his attention to anthrax and chicken cholera with remarkable success, developing the anthrax vaccine. The story behind his study involving hydrophobia is worthy of a four-star movie. He developed a vaccine to immunize dogs against this fatal disease. The vaccine proved itself, but he could not be sure that the same treatment would work for human beings.

The test for its effectiveness came unexpectedly one day when a nine-year-old, Joseph Meister, walked into his laboratory to say he had been bitten by a wild dog. Pasteur realized that without treatment the boy would die. Although he had never experimented with the vaccine on a human being, he decided to inoculate the boy. His colleagues held their breath. Young Meister was given a series of injections—and the vaccine worked.

Pasteur became a sick man as a result of a stroke in 1868. The illness remained with him for the rest of his life, but despite his infirmities, he kept working, serving the Institut Pasteur in Paris in various capacities.

Most people remember Pasteur as the man who developed the process for destroying harmful bacteria in milk, a process called *pasteurization* through which milk is *pasteurized*.

Pasteur saved more lives than can be known. His guiding light was his aphorism, "I would feel that I was stealing if I were to spend a single day without working."

PAVLOV, PAVLOVIAN

Ivan Petrovich Pavlov (1849–1936) was a Russian physiologist who is eponymously remembered because of his attempts to prove that an automatic conditioned reflex can be artificially induced.

Pavlov was born the son of a priest in Ryazan, near Moscow. Although he had planned to follow in his father's footsteps and enter the priesthood, he enrolled instead at St. Petersburg University to study science and physiology, his courses consisting chiefly of chemistry and animal psychology. He also received an M.D. degree from the Medico-

Chirurgical Academy, where he continued to work for virtually the rest of his life.

From 1902 until his death, Pavlov devoted much of his time to research on conditioned reflex. His work had a great impact on behavioural theory. His experiments, which became internationally famous, endeavored to show that the secretion of gastric juices can be stimulated in dogs without food reaching their stomachs. If every time a dog is given food, Pavlov postulated, a bell is rung, eventually the dog's digestive enzymes, controlled by the vagus nerve, will be produced at the sound of the bell. For this work on the physiology of digestion, Pavlov was named a Nobel Prize winner in 1904.

A predictable, conditioned reaction like the reaction of the dog to the sound of the bell is known as a *Pavlovian reaction*. Scientists have come to disagree with Pavlov's basic theory, saying it is an oversimplification of how the brain functions.

PEEPING TOM, LADY GODIVA

There are many versions of the famous ride of *Lady Godiva*. But the one that is most often repeated portrays her as being exceedingly vexed by her husband, Lord Leofric, Lord of Coventry, for imposing exorbitant taxes on his subjects. Although she made persistent pleas to him to reduce the people's burden, he was obdurate and paid no attention to her. But one day, in a sporting mood, he told his wife that he would make a bargain with her: If she would ride through the streets of Coventry without a stitch of clothing, he would concede to her wishes and lower taxes.

To Leofric's astonishment, she accepted the challenge. After asking all the townspeople to stay indoors and close their shutters, Lady Godiva, completely unclad, did indeed mount a white horse and, riding sidesaddle, made the celebrated ride through the town. The townspeople honored her request that they stay indoors with blinds closed—everyone except the town tailor, Tom. While Lady Godiva rode by, he peeped through the shutters and, as legend has it, was struck blind. According to the story, Leofric, after lowering his wife from the horse, then lowered the taxes.

A *Peeping Tom* is a voyeur, a man who sneakily looks at what he has no license to see, peeping at night through other people's windows.

PETER PRINCIPLE

The *Peter principle* states: "In every hierarchy, whether it be government or business, each employee tends to rise to his level of incompetence, every post tends to be filled by an employee incompetent enough to execute his duties." This, in the opinion of the authors, is the principle of bureaucratic organization. It was originally enunciated in the satirical best-selling book *The Peter Principle—Why Things Always Go Wrong,* published in 1969 and written by Dr. Laurence J. Peter and Raymond Hull. Their examples were drawn mostly from the operation of the school system, and they cite as an example the outstanding classroom teacher who has been appointed principal and is hopelessly inept. The promotion essentially demoted her; as a principal she was unable to function well. "All useful work is done by those who have not yet reached their level of incompetence," Peter writes. "The cream rises until it sours."

Peter, a Canadian educator and psychologist, was born in 1919, and devoted all his professional life to the British Columbia education system.

PETREL, STORMY PETREL

Petrels are small dark white-rumped sea birds that, when flying, appear to be patting the water alternately with each foot, as though they were walking on it. This flying habit is particularly noticeable during a stormy period—the birds fly so close to the water with their feet hanging down that it would take a sharp eye to see they were not walking. To older seamen this appearance was reminiscent of St. Peter, who allegedly walked on the Lake of Gennesareth.

The birds have been named *stormy petrels* because they are often seen during stormy weather. Captain Marryat writes in *Poor Jack* that these birds were the souls of drowned and shipwrecked sailors "come to warn us of the approaching storm." The term is used figuratively of any person whose coming portends trouble or who is argumentative.

PHAETON

A *phaeton* is an open four-wheeled carriage drawn by a pair of horses and designed to accommodate two persons plus driver. It was a popular means of transportation during the nineteenth century. It is also the name for an early type of open automobile. The name for these means of transportation was taken from the name *Phaeton*, the son of Helios, god of the sun.

Phaeton as a boy had been taunted by a friend who said that Helios was not his father. To clear up the matter of his paternity, Phaethon journeyed to Helios's palace in the East. Helios was pleased to see him and, to show his fatherly affection, told his son that any wish he had would be granted.

Phaethon thereupon asked that he be permitted to drive the sun chariot for one day. Helios was horrified by that rash request and tried to dissuade his son from it, for he knew how tremendously difficult it was to control the highly spirited steeds who pulled the chariot. But the boy persisted, and Helios reluctantly yielded.

The four horses were yoked to the gleaming chariot, and Phaeton took the reins. His anxious father offered instructions, but once in the sky, Phaethon lost his head, and the horses ran away with him. They at first blazed a gash across the heavens that became the Milky Way. Then they plunged downward and scorched the earth, forming the Sahara Desert and turning the skins of the equatorial people black.

To prevent Phaeton from setting the world on fire, Zeus (Jupiter) hurled a lightning bolt against the charioteer and killed him. Phaeton's blazing corpse fell into the River Eridanus. His sisters, the sea nymphs, who had witnessed his fall, stood on the banks of the river and wept for him. They were turned into weeping poplars, which still line the shores of the river (now the Po).

PHILADELPHIA LAWYER

During the eighteenth century a popular belief held that a *Philadelphia lawyer* was an awesome legal adversary. The reputation of a Philadelphia lawyer carried with it a picture of great talent and the ability to expose the weaknesses of opposition witnesses under cross-examination.

The first recorded use of the phrase *Philadelphia lawyer* was in 1788 in the form "it would puzzle a Philadelphia Lawyer," but it was first heard at the trial of John Peter Zenger, the publisher of the New York *Weekly Journal* (it was what today would be called an "underground" newspaper), who printed a series of articles attacking the provincial government for abuses committed against the people and charging the government with personal corruption. Zenger was arrested in 1734 and indicted for seditious libel. He hired Andrew Hamilton, a distinguished Philadelphia lawyer, to come to his defense. Hamilton traveled to New York by a horse-drawn taxicab and, charging no fee, did come to Zenger's defense, devastating the prosecution. He brilliantly defended the beleaguered publisher and obtained a "not guilty" verdict. During the trial, the term *Philadelphia Lawyer* was used both as praise and opprobrium.

The trial, according to one authority, "was instrumental in establishing a precedent for freedom of the press in American law."

PICKLE

The pickle's provenance can be traced to one William Beukelz or Beukel, a fourteen-century Dutch fisherman who was known as the first to "pickle" food. Though Beukel pickled fish, his name, mispronounced slightly, came to apply to pickled cucumbers.

Although most people enjoy biting into a large dill pickle, they don't want to be *in a pickle*, which is an unpleasant situation. And *to be pickled* is to be steeped in brine, but a person who's *pickled* is steeped in something that will not agree with a sobriety test.

The *Oxford English Dictionary* supports the belief that *pickle* can be found in the medieval Dutch word *pekel*. Wordsmiths agree that *pekel* came from *Beukel* and that *pickle* came from *pekel*.

PICKWICKIAN SENSE

Words or epithets, usually of a derogatory or insulting kind, that in certain circumstances are not to be taken as having the same force or implication they ordinarily would have, are said to be *Pickwickian*. The allusion is to the phrase from Samuel Pickwick of Charles Dickens's *Pickwick Papers*. Mr. Pickwick accused Mr. Blotton of "acting in a vile and calumnious manner," whereupon Mr. Blotton retorted by calling Mr. Pickwick "a humbug." When Mr. Blotton was asked whether he meant the word in its usual sense, he replied that he meant it only "in the *Pickwickian sense*." And the same turned out to be true with Mr. Pickwick. The offensive words were not meant to displease, for, in fact, each person had a high regard for the other.

An insulting remark, then, that is not to be taken seriously is a *Pickwickian*.

PINCHBECK

A London watchmaker who took his name from Pinchbeck, Lincolnshire, invented an alloy of five parts copper and one of zinc that resembled gold. The inventor was Christopher Pinchbeck (1670–1732), whose shop was on Fleet Street. He was an ingenious toy maker, particularly of singing birds and clocks that showed the movements of the planets and stars. The alloy was a welcome invention because it enabled jewelers and others to sell a product that was not gold but looked like it. The products compared with something in gold were inexpensive, but they could be made into interesting designs.

Pinchbeck died shortly after his invention became available on the market. The practices of those selling products made with pinchbeck often were deceptive, and so *pinchbeck* became an eponym for false or sham. Anything spurious or counterfeit was labeled *pinchbeck*. The term is also used to describe anything of inferior quality.

PITMAN, GREGG

Shorthand is an old system for quickly recording speeches. Marcus Tullius Tiro invented what has come to be known as the Tironian system. Tiro was a freedman and amanuensis of Cicero. The ampersand (&), a contraction of the Latin *and*, is still sometimes called the *Tironian sign*. In 1837, Isaac Pitman (1813–1897), after studying Samuel Taylor's scheme for shorthand writing, introduced his shorthand system through his publication *Stenographic Soundhand*, which explained a system phonetically based on dots, dashes, strokes, and curves to signify various sounds. The system was not easy to master because it depended on the slope and position of strokes and on shadings, a light shade giving one phonetic sound and a dark one another. But the Pitman system was universally accepted, and the name *Pitman* became synonymous with "shorthand." Isaac's brother, Benn (1822–1910), immigrated to the United States and devoted his time to popularizing the *Pitman system*.

Sir Isaac Pitman (1813–1898) was born in Trowbridge, Wiltshire, England, the son of an English textile manufacturer. He was employed as a Sunday School superintendent, but devoted much of his life to the study and promulgation of phonetics. His love for phonetics never left him. The epitaph he wrote for his wife's grave read: "In memori ov MERI PITMAN, Weif ov Mr. Eizak Pitman, Fonetik Printer, ov this site. Deid 19 Agust 1857 edjed 64 'Preper tu mit thei God' Amos 4, 12."

Although there are a number of shorthand systems in the United States, the most popular one today, and the chief replacement of the *Pitman* system, is the *Gregg* system. Simpler than the Pitman system, it is based on naturally curved strokes of ordinary written script and does not require the shadings of the older system.

John Robert Gregg (1864–1948) was born in Ireland, but his book *The Phonetic Handwriting* was published in England. Gregg migrated to the United States and introduced his simpler system of writing in shorthand. The Gregg system quickly took over as the most popular in America. That's the long and the short of it.

PLATONIC, PLATONIC LOVE

Platonic love, from the Latin *armor Platonicus*, is nonphysical attraction between a man and a woman, sometimes called *platonic friendship*. This notion of friendship is loosely derived from views stated in Plato's *Symposium*, in which he tells of the pure love of Socrates for young men. In 1626 in England, *platonic love*, the love of friendship only, came to be applied only to a love between a man and a woman, and the talk between them was called *platonics*.

Not much is known about the renowned philosopher. Plato (c. 428–347 B.C.) at birth was given the name Aristocles. His name was changed to Plato by his gymnastic teacher, who admired the great width of his shoulders (in Greek, Plato means "wide"). At age twenty, Plato became a student of Socrates. After the death of Socrates, Plato founded the Academy in 387, the first university, which offered courses in philosophy, mathematics, logic, and government. One of Plato's pupils was Aristotle.

Plato died while attending a wedding feast in Athens. Although his age was uncertain, he is believed to have been about eighty. Philosopher Alfred North Whitehead characterized Western philosophy as "a series of footnotes to Plato."

PLIMSOLL LINE

Samuel Plimsoll (1824–1898) was born in Bristol, England. He started out as a brewery clerk, became a manager, and then became a coal dealer. Elected to Parliament (1868) from Derby, Plimsoll cast about for a cause that could inspire him and also make him famous. He hit on an idea that he was sure would satisfy both these goals. Without any nautical experience or maritime association, Plimsoll became publicly concerned with the plight of seamen who were known to sail on derelict ships. Plimsoll haunted the waterfront, questioning seamen, their wives, stevedores, and anyone affiliated with nautical activities. He learned that many of the ships were of poor quality, and were overloaded and undermanned purposely to make them unseaworthy. If a heavily insured ship were to sink, the unscrupulous ship owner would stand to make a handsome profit. Sailors called these overloaded ships "coffin ships."

Plimsoll pursued his cause with a religious zeal. He published *Our Seamen* (1873), which contained heartrending accounts of the risks sailors might face and scathingly attacked everyone connected with the business of sponsoring these hazardous sea vessels. His publication had a profound impression on the seafaring population and pricked the conscience of some members of Parliament.

When Disraeli caved in to vested interests and announced that a government bill to correct shipping faults would be dropped, Plimsoll lost his temper and shouted that his fellow House members were "villains." Plimsoll was made to apologize, but his sensational outburst is said to have generated so much interest in maritime problems in the Parliament that, in 1876, the Merchant Shipping Act, requiring better inspection, was passed. The act was followed by others, including one known as the *Plimsoll line.* That one required that a line (a circle and a horizontal line) be placed round a merchant vessel to designate its maximum load point in salt water. The line proved valuable and resulted in fewer ships being sunk and many lives saved.

Quite naturally, Plimsoll became a hero among seamen, and they elected him president of the Sailors' and Firemen's Union. His interest in improving mercantile shipping, especially cattle ships, continued until his death.

POINSETTIA

The *poinsettia* is a genus of tropical American herbs and woody plants with inconspicuous yellow leaves and tapering bright red flowers. Especially popular around Christmas, the plants were brought from Mexico to the United States by a South Carolinian. That man, Joel Roberts Poinsett (1799–1851), had a fiery personality and style of living that matched the flamboyancy of those yuletide flowers. Poinsett brought a flower from Mexico that was renamed the poinsettia in his honor. He was the first to introduce the wild plant to floriculture.

Poinsett was born in Charleston, South Carolina, and educated in Europe, but only somewhat. He matriculated in a medical school, then in a law school, dropped out of both and devoted himself to travel for seven years in Europe and and western Asia. President Madison sent him to South America to investigate the development of independence. But

Poinsett's behavior was such that the British said, "he was the most suspicious character" representing the United States and "a scourge of the American continent, contaminating the whole population."

Poinsett served in Congress when Madison was president, and became America's first minister to Mexico. Under president Martin Van Buren, he became the secretary of war. He had a pretty good record for a man who had been declared persona non grata in South America and had been lucky to escape with his hide unscathed.

In any event, this gorgeously colored Mexican species, the *poinsettia*, takes its name from Poinsett and has become the floral symbol of Christmas, brightening, for more than a century, many Christmas hearths.

POMPADOUR

Pompadour is a style of dressing the hair in which the hair is brushed straight up from the forehead and pulled back over a pad. Whence cometh this name? Anyone familiar with French history would associate this hair style with Madame de Pompadour.

Jeanne Antoinette Poisson (1721–1764), a woman from ordinary circumstances, became probably history's most famous mistress or concubine. She married a nobleman, Charles Guillaume d'Etoiles, and soon set her cap, so to speak, for King Louis XV, whom she had met at a masked ball. The king quickly became completely enamored of her and invited her to become his mistress and to live at Versailles. She immediately divorced her husband and cheerfully accepted the offer.

This new mistress was given the title of Marquise de Pompadour and the king's *maîtresse en titre*, or official mistress. But she was better known as Madame de Pompadour. She exercised a profound influence over the king for two decades. In fact, she became politically indispensable.

When Pompadour fell out of favor with the king as a mistress (Madame du Barry, the daughter of a dressmaker, replaced her), she shrewdly maintained her political importance. But Pompadour was not in good health. She was tubercular and anemic and had suffered several miscarriages. She died at age forty-three.

Though Pompadour guided the destiny of France for two decades and had a lasting influence on French culture, she now is remembered only as the king's mistress and for the eponymous coiffure she introduced.

PRALINE

Several stories of the origin of pralines vie with one another. But all concern the chef of Marshal César du Plessis-Praslin (1598–1675), who became the French minister of state in 1652 and who concluded a successful military career upon reaching the pinnacle of military rank—field marshal in command of the entire royal army.

One story has it that Praslin's chef prepared the sugar-coated *praline* for King Louis XIV, a dinner guest of the marshal. Another, and one with more authoritative approval, is that the praline had its genesis in the marshal's stomach problems. The marshal liked to nibble almonds, but they gave him heartburn. His chef suggested that if the almonds were browned in boiling water, they would be more easily digested. The result of the chef's ingenuity was a happier marshal, with fewer heartburns, and a confection of sugar-coated almonds that has become quite popular under the name *praline*.

The American version, introduced in New Orleans, substitutes pecans for the almonds. The Creoles in Louisiana who were responsible for the preparation of these goodies chose the pecans because they were locally available. Nevertheless, they retained the name *praline*, thus immortalizing, eponymously, César du Plessis-Praslin.

Although possibly an apocryphal story, the marshal is said to have died with a silver tray of pralines at his bedside.

PRINCE ALBERT COAT, PRINCE ALBERT CHAIN

Albert Francis Charles Augustus Emmanuel, Duke of Saxe-Coburg-Gotha (1819–1861), was born near Coburg, Germany, and studied at Brussels and at Bonn. He married Queen Victoria, his first cousin, in 1840. He was much beloved by the queen, and their marriage was a happy and successful one. The prince consort was a highly cultured person who blended well with the queen's tastes and personality. The Victoria and Albert Museum, located in the Kensington section of London, houses the major collection of decorative arts in Great Britain. It stands as a monument to an enduring love and a well-mated marriage. The cornerstone for the present building was laid by the Queen in 1899, long after Albert's death.

The jewelers of Birmingham in 1849 presented to the prince consort a watch chain, which he wore from a pocket to a button in his waistcoat. The chain came to set a fashion and was known as the *Albert chain*.

The *Prince Albert*, a knee length double-breasted frockcoat, less close fitting than the usual frockcoat, was named for Albert Edward, Prince of Wales, who popularized the garment in the late nineteenth century. The Prince of Wales was the consort's eldest son, and became Edward VII, king of England, in 1901, upon the death of Queen Victoria. The Prince of Wales had traveled widely, and a number of articles were named for him, including a pipe tobacco.

PROCRUSTES'S BED

Procrustes, in Greek legend, was a brigand, a highwayman, who lived near Attica and lured travelers into his roadside home by offering them a bed for the night. Procrustes amused himself by forcing these travelers to lie on his iron bed and be fitted to it. If they were too short, he stretched them on a rack until they fit; those who were too long, he cut down to size.

The adjective *procrustean* denotes the use of violence to gain uniformity or the arbitrary imposition of conformity. Trying to make an entirely new situation fit old standards may be a *procrustean effort*. Foreordained standards that require conformity may be called a *procrustean bed*.

Procrustes, who enjoyed seeing things fit, had a fitting end. Theseus, son of the king of Athens, using Procrustes's own methods, placed Procrustes on the torture device, just as he had done to his victims so many times before. Whether he was too short or too long is unknown.

PROMETHEUS, PROMETHEAN

Prometheus stole fire from Olympus and gave it to human beings. A Titan and a son of Tapetos, he had been put to work by Zeus to make men out of clay and water. Prometheus was appalled by the misery of the creatures he was creating, and out of pity presented man with the heavenly fire. Another version is that Zeus had been tricked by Prometheus over his share of a sacrificial ox, and therefore denied mankind the use of fire. For this offense, whichever one it was, Zeus had him chained to a rock where during the daytime an eagle ate his liver, which renewed itself each night, only to be eaten again the next day. Throughout his ordeal, Prometheus was sustained by a secret known only to him: that Zeus would father a son who would first overthrow him and then someday liberate Prometheus. After thirteen generations the prophecy was fulfilled as Heracales, son of Zeus by Alcmere, set him free.

Because of this legend, a rare-group metallic element was name *promethium*. Scientists predicted the element at the beginning of the twentieth century, reported it in 1926, and definitely identified it in 1945, as a radioactive form of the element. The name *promethium* was adopted by the International Union of Chemistry in 1945.

The word *promethean* became an adjective in the English language meaning that which pertains to fire or is capable of producing fire. Anything life giving—daringly original or creative—is also said to be *promethean*. Although the early friction matches changed its name through the years, the matches were first called promethean. Darwin in his *Voyage of the Beagle* (1839) wrote: "I carried with me some promethean matches, which I ignited by biting. . . ."

PROTEUS, PROTEAN

Proteus was the herdsman for Poseiden, Greek god of the sea. He had great powers of prophecy, and he lived in a huge cave and watched over his herds of sea calves. He prophesized only if seized. But no one could catch him because he would change himself into the shape of many other things. Changing his form, like the sea, was his means of avoiding capture. The only way he could be caught was to surprise him in his sleep.

Menelaus, king of Sparta, had exceeding difficulty in returning from Troy. His trip home took eight years. When he finally ran short of provisions, he was advised by a nymph that Proteus, if forced, could tell him the way home. Menelaus found the god in deep slumber, seized him, and held on despite Proteus's successive transformations into a lion, a serpent, a leopard, a boar, water, and a tree. Proteus gave in and provided the information Menelaus wanted.

A person who can vary his attitude at will or is shifty and fickle is *protean*. In a complimentary sense, it may refer to someone blessed with versatile talents or a flexible nature.

PSYCHE, PSYCHIC, PSYCHIATRIST

Many name-words have been derived from the Greek *Psyche,* meaning "breath," hence life or the soul itself. The essence of *psyche* is one's rational and spiritual being. Its derivatives range from *psychiatrist* to *psychedelic* to *psychoanalysis* to *psychology.*

Psyche, the youngest of three daughters of a certain king, was so beautiful that people stopped worshiping Venus and turned their adoration to this young girl. Venus was so enraged that she ordered her son, Cupid, to make Psyche fall in love with the ugliest creature he could find. But when Cupid saw her, he fell in love with her himself. He then transported Psyche to a fairy palace, visiting her nightly but departing at sunrise. Cupid warned her that she must refrain from trying to find out who he was.

When Psyche became lonely, she asked that her sisters be permitted to visit her. He consented. When her jealous sisters learned that Psyche had never seen her visitor, they terrified her into believing that he would turn into a serpent and creep into her womb and devour her and her baby. Psyche's curiosity got the best of her, and so when she next went to bed, she took a lantern and a dagger with her. After Cupid had fallen asleep, Psyche lit the lamp, holding the dagger at the ready. But she beheld the beautiful features of the god of love, and was so startled that she let a drop of oil fall on his shoulder, thus awakening him. When Cupid realized that Psyche must know who he was, he rose and flew away.

Psyche wandered far and wide searching for her lover. She then became a slave of Venus, who imposed on her heartless tasks and treated her cruelly. But Cupid, despite his sudden exit, so desperately missed her that he made a clean breast of everything to Jupiter, who approved of Cupid's union with Psyche. When Psyche approached the passage leading back to the upper world, she was given a jar and told not to open it. But curiosity again got the best of her, so she ignored the warning and opened the jar. Immediately she was overpowered by a deadly sleep from its contents.

Cupid found her and brought her back to life and carried her up to Olympus. The marriage of Psyche and Cupid was celebrated by all the gods, even by Venus. Psyche bore a daughter, Voluptas, which means "pleasure," and the three of them lived together happily ever after.

PULITZER PRIZE

Joseph Pulitzer (1847–1911) was born in Hungary and immigrated to the United States in 1864 to serve in the Union Army. After his discharge, he settled in St. Louis, where he became a reporter for the *Westliche Post*, a German-language daily for which he did such an outstanding job that his popularity enabled him to be elected to the Missouri legislature. His next important move was to purchase the St. Louis *Dispatch*, which was in dire financial condition, and to merge it with the *Post*, giving it the combined name of St. Louis *Post-Dispatch*. The paper became a first-rank regional paper.

Pulitzer then changed location and papers. After moving to New York, he purchased the New York *World*, in which he introduced banner headlines and the sensational treatment of crime. The paper's style of presentation was considered intemperate, and the vulgarity of his special features intensified as he went into a circulation war with William Hearst's *Journal*. Although guilty of "yellow journalism" to involve this country in what turned out to be the Spanish-American War, the paper made a remarkable about-face and pursued such a strong anti-imperialist policy that Teddy Roosevelt became irate, and the government sued Pulitzer for libel.

Pulitzer's will provided for some notable distributions, including the establishment of the Columbia University School of Journalism, which confers the Pulitzer Prizes.

The prizes, as prescribed by Pulitzer, covered many categories. A prize was to be awarded for new writing, drama, fiction, history; for local, national, and international reporting, editorial writing, news photography, cartooning, and meritorious public service performed by an individual newspaper. Additional prizes were for biography, poetry, and music. The prizes were awarded for the first time in 1917.

Originally the prizes were for $1,000, but they are now $3,000, except for public service in journalism, which is rewarded with a gold medal. The *Pulitzer*, as it is most often called, is widely regarded as the most prestigious award in its field.

PULLMAN

The comfort of many passengers in train journeys can be credited to George Mortimer Pullman (1831–1897), an American inventor and businessman. Pullman is best remembered for improving railway sleeping cars.

Pullman was born on March 3, 1831, in Brocton, New York, where he worked as a cabinetmaker until 1855. After a failed effort to operate a general store in Colorado, he went to Chicago and persuaded the Chicago and Alton Railroad to allow him to convert two-day coaches into sleeping cars. These cars he equipped with mattresses and blankets; they had washrooms and were lit by oil lamps, all the trappings of comfort.

In 1863, Pullman built the "Pioneer," the first car that became known as a *pullman*. The Pioneer became an important vehicle when the funeral party for Abraham Lincoln traveled on it to Illinois. The car was so large that bridges along the route had to be raised and railway platforms removed. Pullman built and operated a number of these cars, and, in 1867, with Andrew Carnegie, he organized the Pullman Palace Car Company, the nearest thing to a hotel on wheels. Eventually, the Pullman Palace Car Company became the largest railroad car business in the world.

Pullman built a town called *Pullman*, south of Chicago, inhabited mostly by his employees. Eventually the twelve thousand inhabitants sued him, claiming that his charges for rent and utilities far exceeded those of the surrounding area. The court ordered the properties sold to the inhabitants.

Before long, Pullman showed an even deeper animosity toward his employees. He discharged more than half of them and then rehired them at a much lower wage. Pullman brooked no interference from his employees, saying that they were not permitted to discuss with him any problem. He fired anyone who tried to talk with him about employment conditions. "The workers have nothing to do with the amount of wages they shall receive," he declared.

The American Railway Union announced a boycott against any railway employing Pullman cars. President Cleveland apparently was unsympathetic to strikers or boycotts. He ordered federal troops into Chicago to enforce an injunction imposed by the courts. Riots ensued, and people were killed. Eugene Debs, the president of the union, was jailed. Pullman endured. He broke the strike with the aid of a cavalry escort of a trainload of meat that passed through the strike line.

In 1947, the Supreme Court upheld an antitrust suit and ordered that the company be sold to a railroad syndicate. Although all this came to pass, sleeping cars are still called *pullmans*.

PUSHKINISM

Pushkinism, in Russia, in the opinion of many critics, is the equivalent of Shakespearianism in England or Danteism in Italy. Pushkin established the techniques and provided the standards for the extraordinary development that took place in Russian arts and letters in the nineteenth century. He is generally regarded as the foremost Russian nationalistic poet. Although he was a writer from the past, the Russian communists "adopted" him for propaganda purposes.

Aleksandr Sergyevich Pushkin (1799–1837) was born in Moscow, educated at the lyceum at Tsarkoye Selo, and was employed by the foreign office at St. Petersburg. He lived a romantic life, but he was charged by the foreign office for writing subversive poetry and for affiliation with secret societies. He was punished by transfer, ultimately, to Odessa, where his love affairs with two married women (including the wife of his superior in the foreign office) occasioned some of his most passionate lyric poetry.

The secret police intercepted some of Pushkin's letters, which they considered anti-Russian. He was dismissed from his post and sent into exile. But Pushkin had a protector in the form of Nicholas I, who pardoned him and placed him under his personal protection.

Pushkin fell in love with a sixteen-year-old girl, Natalie Goncharova. As his wife, she ran into heavy debt. When an affair between her and a Frenchman, Georges d'Athnes, became the subject of widespread gossip, Pushkin challenged the Frenchman to a duel. Pushkin was wounded by a pistol shot and died two days later.

The inventory of Pushkin's writing consisted of romantic poems, dramatic poems, and narrative poems. His *Boris Godunov* was used by Mussorgsky for his opera. He worked on his masterpiece, *Eugen Onegin*, a verse novel, from 1823 to 1830. It had eight chapters, each of about fifty 14-line stanzas in iambic tetrameter. This magnificent work, which provided the story for Tchaikovsky's opera of the same name, became the linguistic and literary standard against which the Russian literary developments of the nineteenth century were measured.

PYRRHIC VICTORY

Pyrrhus (319–272 B.C.), king of Epirus, a kingdom in northern Greece, engaged the Romans in a bloody battle at Asculum in 279 B.C. Pyrrhus's troops defeated the Roman legions, but at a tragic cost. So many of his soldiers were lost—all his best officers and many men, the flower of his army—that Pyrrhus exclaimed, according to Plutarch, "One more such victory and I am undone." By the time Pyrrhus and his soldiers limped back to Epirus, the decimated Grecian army had been reduced from twenty-five thousand troops to eight thousand.

Pyrrhus was a great warrior, a second cousin of Alexander the Great, but he never succeeded in his hope of reestablishing the empire once ruled by his cousin. How Pyrrhus died is a matter of dispute among word detectives. Some say he was killed in a skirmish with the Romans at Argos; others say that he was killed by an angry mob at Argos after his attempts to capture the city failed; and still others maintain that he died a quite ignoble death from a tile that might have accidentally fallen from a roof.

A *Pyrrhic victory*, made at a staggering cost, is no joyous victory.

PYTHAGOREAN THEOREM

Pythagoras, the famous Greek philosopher and mathematician of the sixth century B.C., was born in Samos, off the coast of Asia Minor. As a mature man he immigrated to Croton, in southern Italy. Here he founded a brotherhood of religious-ethical orientation, which practiced strict self-discipline and vegetarianism. *Pythagoreanism* became politically influential in Croton, but was violently attacked throughout Italy, and the brotherhood broke into two groups. Neither branch had a long life.

Pythagoras taught transmigration of the soul and a doctrine that came to be known as the "harmony of the spheres." According to this doctrine, certain parameters characterizing the celestial bodies are related to one another "harmoniously" by a mathematical rule. *Pythagoreanism* has been a powerful force in the development of Western culture. It has creatively inspired philosophers, theologians, mathematicians, and astronomers (notably Copernicus and Kepler).

Schoolchildren are taught the *Pythagorean theorem*, that the square on the hypotenuse of a right-angled triangle is equal to the sum of the squares on the other two sides. Fewer students may remember that Pythagoras symbolized the divergent paths of virtue and vice by the twentieth Greek letter of the alphabet, Upsilon (υ).

Legend has it that Pythagoras used to write on a looking-glass in blood and place it opposite the moon, and the inscription that appeared reflected on the moon's disc; that he tamed a savage Daunian bear by "stroking it gently with his hand"; that he subdued an eagle by the same means; and that he held absolute dominion over beasts and birds by "the power of his voice" or "influence of his touch."

QUEENSBERRY RULES

John Sholto Douglas, the eighth *Marquis of Queensberry* (1844–1900), gave his name to a code of fair play for boxing. The marquis had a longstanding interest in boxing and, according to a quotation from the Duke of Manchester, was said to have "been the finest amateur boxer of his time." He was reputed to have knocked out a "gigantic cowboy" in California.

The actual rules were first formulated in 1876 by British amateur athlete John Graham Chambers under Queensberry's supervision. Because Chambers performed yeoman service in devising the rules, some believe that his is the name that should have been honored instead of Queensberry's.

The rules remained in effect from 1867 to 1929, when they were superseded by those issued by the British Boxing Board of Control. The Chambers rules included the three-minute round, the ten-second count after a knockdown, and, unquestionably the most important, the outlawing of fighting with bare knuckles. The proscribing of bare knuckles and the prescribing of boxing gloves saved the sport.

The first world championship bout in which gloves were used was staged at Cincinnati in 1885. At that time John L. Sullivan successfully defended his title against Dominick McCaffery.

The *Queensberry rules* are now a synonym for "fair play in any sport."

QUISLING

Of the many notorious traitors, Vidkun Quisling is the one whose name has entered the English vocabulary as a common word, and has continued its shameful denotation. Someone who is a traitorous puppet of the enemy, or more precisely, someone who aids and collaborates with the enemy, a renegade, is a *quisling*.

Quisling, born in 1887 in Fryesdal, Norway, became an army officer, then worked in the diplomatic service. In 1933, he formed his own Norwegian fascist party, Norway's National Unification Party, but he did not attract many followers. On April 8–9, 1940, Hitler invaded Norway, and Quisling proclaimed himself Norway's premier.

While serving as the figurehead in this puppet government set up by the Nazis, Quisling committed unspeakable atrocities. He lived in the lap of luxury on an island near Oslo, in a mansion that contained the finest Norwegian art he could steal from the museums. But Quisling was never at ease. He was so nervous for his safety that he had 150 bodyguards and an official taster of all his foods.

Finally the day of reckoning came. The war ended, and Quisling was arrested immediately, on May 9, 1945. He was charged with treason and murder, found guilty, and shot by a firing squad on October 24 of that year.

Norway's laws forbade capital punishment, but the law was changed just to execute Quisling.

QUIXOTIC, DON QUIXOTE

For the word *quixotic*, the English language is indebted to *Don Quixote*, the eponymous hero of the satire written by Miguel de Cervantes and published in Madrid in two parts, in 1605 and 1615.

Don Quixote was a visionary who, after reading books on knight errantry, believed he had to redress the wrongs of the world. This man from La Mancha was a humble, amiable character, but his wits were deranged. His baptismal name was Alonso Quijano, but in a mock ceremony of knighthood he assumed the name Don Quixote.

Quixote sallied forth on his nag, a rack of bones named Rocinante, accompanied by his squire, Sancho Panza, a short, pot-bellied rustic, untutored but shrewd. Quixote was involved in many adventures—more accurately misadventures—but his most famous was his tilting at windmills that he believed were giants. Eventually Quixote, worn out and disillusioned, returned to his home in La Mancha.

The adjective *quixotic* describes a person who is an impractical idealist with lofty visions but little common sense.

The poignant tale of the romantic cavalier *Don Quixote de La Mancha* and Richard Strauss's powerful tone poem *Don Quixote* composed in 1897 is tragicomedy; it is not a farce.

RABELAISIAN

Rabelaisian refers to a style of writing that is licentious and coarse, but also humorous and satirical. It was derived from French author François Rabelais (1490–1553).

Rabelais was a man who had a seemingly insatiable appetite for all the gutsy pleasures of life—food, drink, and love-making. He may have felt some restraint early in life because for a time he was a Franciscan monk and then a Benedictine monk. That restrictive phase of his life, however, did not last long, and his interest soon turned to medicine. As a physician, Rabelais was well-accepted and became well-known in his own country as well as in Italy for his humanism and enlightenment. But he was ever the foe of the establishment, an immutable enemy to the blindness and bigotry of the church and state. Throughout, he was a remarkably devoted scholar, and he published works on medicine and translations throughout his life.

The immortality of Rabelais rests on his ribald writing, primarily his celebrated work *Gargantua and Pantagruel*. The hero Gargantua, despite his elephantine build, had a kindly heart and was a helpful and peace-loving giant. From him English acquired the word *gargantuan*, meaning enormous or gigantic.

RAGLAN, RAGLAN SLEEVE

Raglan sleeves became well-known during the Crimean War in 1852 because of a coat worn by the commander-in-chief, Lord Raglan. The sleeve made the coat different from others, and it has continued to be stylish to this day.

Lord Raglan (1788–1855) was named Fitzroy James Henry Somerset at birth. He spent most of his life in the military as Lord Fitzroy, serving as an aide-de-camp for forty years to the Duke of Wellington, whose niece he had married. At Waterloo, Lord Fitzroy was shot in the shoulder by a sniper, and a military doctor amputated his right arm. As the amputated arm was being carted away, he yelled, "Bring back my arm. The ring my wife gave me is on one of the fingers."

In 1852 England joined forces with France against Russia, and the Crimean War began. Lord Fitzroy, now the first Baron Raglan, was appointed commander-in-chief of the British forces by Queen Victoria.

Raglan had no field experience and, according to historians, was not a military strategist. Worse, he kept confusing France with Russia and vice versa. The war had little historical significance and would probably be treated with little respect in history books were it not for the battle of Balaclava, in which confused communications between Raglan and the field commander, Lord Cardigan, led to the death of the brave Six Hundred, immortalized by Lord Alfred Tennyson in his famous poem "The Charge of the Light Brigade."

Raglan became the scapegoat for the Crimean War, a most unpopular undertaking. He was blamed for the sufferings of the British soldiers and the death of fifteen hundred of them at Sevastopol—as well as for the rout of the British army. Army medical reports said Raglan died of cholera. But attending doctors said he died of a broken heart.

RHODES SCHOLARSHIPS, RHODESIA

Cecil John Rhodes (1853–1902), for whom Rhodesia was named, was born at Bishop Stortford, Hertfordshire, England, the son of a clergyman. His family had neither wealth nor position, and Cecil suffered from poor health. In 1870, Rhodes went to South Africa, a better climate for him. There he took advantage of the rush to the Kimberley diamond fields and by 1888 had established the De Beers Consolidated Mines. This enterprising thirty-five-year-old man dominated the world market in diamonds and later the Transvaal gold fields.

Rhodes had a vision of an English-speaking empire from "Cape to Cairo." He was heavily involved in politics, becoming prime minister of Cape Colony. However, his involvement in a conspiracy to overthrow President Kruger and seize the Transvaal left an indelible scar on his political future.

Rhodes attended Oxford University several times, ultimately graduating in 1881. Three years before his death, he wrote his famous will, which set up scholarships for two years at Oxford based on high standards of scholarship, character, leadership, and athletic ability. The scholarships were to be granted annually to some two hundred students from the British colonies and dominions, the United States, and Germany. A Rhodes scholarship is not merely a tuition-paid form of education; it is a mark of scholarly distinction.

The territory called Rhodesia has since been split into Zambia and Zimbabwe.

RICHTER SCALE

Although no one knows how to prevent earthquakes, a gauge invented in 1935 by Charles Francis Richter (1900–1985) may give warnings of an impending disturbance so that measures might be taken to lessen the effect.

Richter, who gave his name to his invention, the *Richter scale*, was born in Ohio and attended the California Institute of Technology in Pasadena, where he became a professor of seismology. His colleague on his project to calculate the magnitude of an earthquake was Dr. Beno Gutenberg (1889–1960). The gauge they invented to assess the intensity of a quake is called a seismograph, an instrument that registers the amplitude of seismic waves emanating from its epicenter and the energy released by it. Ground motions are recorded and then calibrated by the scale.

The *Richter scale* operates on an indefinite scale from zero to infinity, which makes it a relative rather than an absolute scale. Waves close to zero are scarcely felt and do little damage. Damage begins to occur when the magnitude measures 3.5. Anything over 5 is considered serious. The highest reading ever recorded is 8.9, in a quake off the coast of Japan.

The moment-magnitude scale has largely replaced the Richter scale to measure earthquake energy.

RITZ, RITZY

César Ritz (1850–1918), a Swiss entrepreneur and hotelier and the thirteenth child of a peasant couple, built the Ritz Hotel on Paris's Vendôme in 1898, and it became a symbol of palatial living. Its grandeur and its food, under the master chef Georges Auguste Escoffier, were designed for ultimate luxury and splendor. It was the gathering place for the elite and the children of the rich, whose mothers trusted this magnificent meeting place so much they allowed their daughters to go there unchaperoned.

Ritz built the elegant Ritz Hotel in Piccadilly, London, in 1906, and it was also quickly identified with sumptuous living. Then came the Ritz-Carlton Hotel in New York, which, like its two siblings, was lavish and costly. It set a standard for fashion and luxury. "To dine at the Ritz" was the equivalent of the best and most elegant in dining.

Ritz's son and successor, Charles Ritz, carried on the family tradition by building a string of luxurious hotels around the world, all under the name Ritz-Carlton. *Ritz* became the most refined four-letter word in the English language.

Yet years ago, *ritzy* was defined by one lexicographer as "ostentatiously or vulgarly smart in appearance or manner."

With time *ritzy* became meliorated (a linguistic process whereby a word becomes more elevated in meaning) and came to signify the finer qualities inherent in *luxurious, fashionable*, and *chic*, a byword for sumptuous living. There has been since then nothing deprecatory about the word in the minds of many people—but not all. Some think that saying something is ritzy impugns good taste. It suggests pretentiousness and snobbery.

Many people today, and especially those who remember Irving Berlin's hit song "Puttin' on the Ritz," feel that *ritzy* connotes glittering opulence, but in a refined and acceptable genre; yet *putting on the ritz* is also a synonym for conspicious display or showing off.

ROBERT'S RULES

Most deliberative bodies, from the local parent-teacher meetings to the U.S. Senate, rely on a book on parliamentary procedure that was written a long time ago. The book, now called *Robert's Rules of Order*, was first published in 1876 with the title *Pocket Manual for Rules of Order for Deliberative Assemblies*, a large title for a small book. But its effect on deliberative bodies has not been small; it is the procedural bible that governs the orderly operation of their meetings.

The author of this useful set of guidelines wrote the book after presiding over a meeting hampered by lack of orderliness. The book is so effective that in all these years, it has been revised only twice, once in 1915 and again in 1943.

The author, Henry Martyn Robert (1837–1923), a South Carolinian, was graduated from West Point at age twenty, and was assigned to the Army Corps of Engineers, with which he spent his entire military life. He was responsible for defense constructions for Washington, Philadelphia, and the New England coast. During the Spanish-American War, he was head of the U.S. Board of Fortifications. He devoted his remaining years to improving rivers, harbors, and coasts. When he retired in 1901, he was a brigadier general and chief of the Army engineers. His orderly mind, which created his book on *Rules of Order*, was exemplified in his distinguished military career.

ROBOT

The word *robot* came from a Czech play, published in 1920 and premiered on stage in Prague in 1921, called *R.U.R.* The initials stand for *Rossum's Universal Robots*, a corporation that manufactured robots, mechanical creatures, enslaved to work for human beings. In the play the robots developed the capacity to feel and hate. Eventually, they rebelled, became monsters, turned on their human masters, and overpowered them.

The author, Karel Capek (1890–1938), a Czech playwright born in Bohemia, borrowed the word *robot* from the slavic *robota*, meaning a forced laborer. The play was extremely popular on both sides of the Atlantic, so much so that the word *robot* came to be used of any person who was dehumanized because of too much work involving nonproductive tasks or to a person who works automatically without employing initiative. The word was also applied during World War II to the German "flying bombs" or "Buzz-bombs" sent against England. In the scientific world of today, a *robot* is used as a term to describe automated apparatus that performs human functions.

ROCKEFELLER, CROESUS

The name *Rockefeller* has become synonymous with great wealth. From the original Rockefeller, the founder of the Rockefeller fortune, there have been children, grandchildren, and other Rockefellers, and the appellation *American Croesus* has attached to each one.

John Davison Rockefeller, more usually know as John D. (1839–1937), was born in Richford, Tioga County, New York. Rockefeller had a series of uneventful jobs, but in 1866 he joined his brother William and together with Samuel Andrews formed the firm of William Rockefeller and Company, an oil refining company. After a few business moves, the enterprise incorporated as the Standard Oil Company of Ohio. They placed other properties and interests in the Standard Oil company of New Jersey. In an antitrust suit in 1911, the U.S. Supreme Court ordered the New Jersey company to cease operation.

John D. retired in 1896 and devoted the rest of his life to philanthropy. He founded the Rockefeller Institute for Medical Research (now Rockefeller University) and established a host of other philanthropies. John D. lived a long, enriched, and useful life.

RÖENTGEN RAYS

Wilhelm Konrad von Roentgen (1845–1923), professor of physics at the University of Würzburg, Germany, was working late on the night of November 3, 1893, after all his assistants had left the laboratory. He noticed that a fluorescent surface near a cathode-ray tube was luminous, even though shielded from the direct light of the tube, which made him realize that invisible radiation could pass through substances that would block ordinary visible light. Röentgen named his find *X-strahl* (which in English is *X-ray*), the X representing an unknown quantity.

In 1901, Röentgen became the first Nobel Prize winner in physics. Röentgen's discovery of the electromagnetic rays of very short wavelength was invaluable in medicine, science, and the arts because they could penetrate human flesh as well as various thicknesses of many other things. The X-ray is possibly the medical profession's most important and useful tool in the diagnosis and cure of disease. Röentgen reportedly made no personal profit through his remarkable discovery.

RORSCHACH TEST

Hermann Rorschach (1884–1922) was a Swiss psychiatrist born in Zurich, the son of an art teacher. During his childhood, Rorschach was said to be fascinated by drawings. He was a 1912 graduate from the University of Zurich, where he obtained a medical degree. He became a follower of Freudian theories, and in 1919 was elected president of the Swiss Psychoanalytic Society.

Rorschach devised a diagnostic test intended to measure aspects of personality, primarily the unconscious. It consisted of ten ink blots in complex shapes. The way in which the subject described these pictures would reveal his or her unconscious attitudes. Some psychologists have discounted the validity of the *Rorschach test*, arguing that the assumption that the subject is projecting his inner fears and other emotional problems is too speculative.

ROSCIAN

Quintus Gallus Roscius (c.126–62 B.C.) was of free birth in the Sabine region of the Roman Empire. He became the greatest actor of his time. His grace was unrivaled, as were the mellifluence of his voice, depth of his conception of character, and subtlety of his delivery. He became a friend of Cicero. Cicero reportedly took lessons from him, and they often competed to see who could better express an idea or an emotion.

Roscius became wealthy enough to retire from the stage at an early age and to do as he wished. And so his acting career was relatively short-lived. But his name has had a surprising longevity: Today its adjective form, *Roscian*, is still used to express high standards. It is an eponym for perfection in acting. His name is a byword for a great actor. A *Roscian* performance is one of superlative skill.

Shakespeare acknowledges the superiority and versatility of Roscius's work in *Henry VI*, part 3: "What scene of death hath Roscius now to act."

RUBE GOLDBERG

The man who created, for the amusement of his readers, cartoons of preposterous, elaborate contraptions to illustrate a simple operation was Reuben Lucius Goldberg (1883–1970). His diagrams were logical and fun to follow.

Goldberg was born in San Francisco and worked for newspapers there before moving to New York in 1907 to draw for the *Evening Mail*. His wacky, weird diagrams were syndicated and appeared in newspapers throughout the country. People began to call any overly complex invention that does what could be performed in a simple manner a *Rube Goldberg*.

In his later years, Goldberg ceased drawing his "invention" cartoons and switched to political cartoons. Although he won two Pulitzer Prizes for these cartoons, Rube Goldberg remains in the mind of the public as the inventor of the zany contraptions that tickled everyone's fancy for many years.

S

SABIN VACCINE

Microbiologist Albert Bruce Sabin was born in 1906 in Bialystok, Russia (now Poland). He immigrated to the United States with his family in 1921 and was naturalized in 1930. He attended New York University, receiving an M.D. in 1931. He joined the staff of the Rockefeller Institute as a medical researcher. In 1939 he became a member of the college of medicine of the University of Cincinnati, later becoming professor of pediatrics. Sabin developed a live virus vaccine against poliomyelitis that can be given by mouth; it was field tested in 1959, and has largely replaced the vaccine developed by Dr. Jonas Salk, which was based on heat-killed viruses. It provides a stronger and more longlasting immunity than the earlier vaccine and protects against both paralysis and infection. In his later work, Sabin has concentrated on cancer research.

Infantile paralysis (polio), as the name suggests, was a disease that struck children particularly. However, it was no respecter of age and affected some adults with the same dire results. Franklin Delano Roosevelt, the thirty-second president of the United States, was stricken at thirty-nine.

SADISM

A *sadist* has come to be thought of as one who delights in cruelty. In psychology, however, *sadism* is the association of sexual gratification with the infliction of pain on others. The word was derived from the name of Count Donatien Alphonse François de Sade (1740–1814).

The Count de Sade (he preferred to be called Marquis) came from a prominent French family and received, beginning at age fourteen, the expected military training for a person of such standing. The marquis, however, found that such service interfered with his life of pleasure, and so he gave up the military.

His pleasure, which consisted in deviant sexual satisfaction, was expensive, and so a marriage was arranged with Renée Pelagie de Montreuil, the daughter of a wealthy man. Despite the marriage, de Sade continued to have affairs with other women, mostly prostitutes, enjoying a form of sexual perversion that he pursued for the rest of his life. His favorite romantic pastime, his great, uncontrollable urge, was to abuse sexually and even torture his partner. For such activity, de Sade was arrested and imprisoned, but once released, he would continue to seek gratification of his deep-seated desires, and would be arrested again. He was even sentenced to death in 1772 in absentia for committing "an unnatural offense." (The Marquis had fled the country to avoid further imprisonment.) After three years, he decided to return, and he was arrested and imprisoned for the next thirteen years. He escaped the guillotine during the Revolution.

While confined in the Bastille, de Sade decided to write, in novel form, about his sexual compulsion to torture his partner (*Justine, Philosophie dans le boudoir, les crimes de l'amour*, and others). He completed his writing, but with a change of scenery—in the Charenton Lunatic Asylum. De Sade was eventually discharged, but was rearrested seven years later as an incorrigible, and spent the rest of his days at Charenton, from 1803 to 1814.

The marquis realized that he was subject to mental aberrations and contended that no treatment could cure him. He wrote: "As for my vices—unrestrainable rages—an extreme tendency in everything to lose control of myself, a disordered imagination in sexual matters such as had never been known in this world, an atheist to the point of fanaticism—in two words, there I am, and so once again kill me or take me like that, because I shall never change." His last written words were, "The ground over my grave should be sprinkled with acorns so that all traces of my grave shall disappear so that, as I hope, this reminder of my existence may be wiped from the memory of mankind." So long as the name-word *sadism* exists, however, de Sade's memory will be kept alive.

SALISBURY STEAK

James H. Salisbury (1823–1905) was an English physician who promoted a diet of ground beef, which was just common hamburger, but dressed up with brown gravy to make it more appealing. The name *steak* was an elegant designation for ordinary meat, but one that looks more inviting on a menu and makes the dish more palatable.

Dr. Salisbury, a dietician specialist, maintained that his suggested diet would cure hardening of the arteries and colitis and a number of other ailments, including anemia, bronchitis, and tuberculosis. The diet had many followers. His patties, usually twice the size of a hamburger, were mixed with eggs, milk, and bread crumbs, making the dish very tasty. But whether this high-cholesterol concoction would cure you or kill you is a question for trained physicians to ponder. The *Salisbury* faddists are no longer heard from, but the "steak" is still a good seller in restaurants and cafeterias around the country.

Perhaps Dr. Salisbury's chief failing was "oversell." Not satisfied to have people eat his "steak" occasionally, even regularly, he urged everyone, with a fanatic's zeal, to eat it for breakfast, lunch, and dinner.

SALK VACCINE

For many years the scourge of human existence was a disease called *poliomyelitis*, or *polio*. It is caused by a virus that destroys the nervous tissue in the spinal cord, resulting in paralysis. Quite often children seemed to develop this virus after swimming in lakes or pools. Some parents sent their children to a remote mountain area for protection, but not always with favorable results. Children contracted this vicious malady no matter where they were. It seemed that no one could hide from it.

And that's why Dr. Jonas Edward Salk—scientist, a bacteriologist, who eventually found a vaccine for this dread disease—became a national hero. Salk was born in 1914 in New York City and received an M.D. from New York University Medical School in 1939.

In 1947, after several years teaching at the University of Michigan, Salk became head of the University of Pittsburgh's Virus Research Laboratory, where he began his work on the vaccine for polio. He first tested the vaccine on a member of his own family, and it proved effective against the disease.

His vaccine was used throughout the world until 1960, when it was largely supplanted by Albert Sabin's live-virus vaccine. In 1963 he became director of the Salk Institute for Biological Studies at the University of California, San Diego, and served until 1975. His later efforts concentrated on the search for a vaccine to prevent the nearly always terminal illness resulting from immune deficiency that can lead to AIDS.

SALMAGUNDI

Many years ago *salmagundi* was a certain concoction of various foodstuffs. Today, it means any variety of things brought together.

Salmagundi, according to Dr. Ebenezer Cobham Brewer, is a mixture of minced veal, chicken, or turkey, anchovies, or pickled herring, and onions, all chopped together and served with lemon-juice and oil. The word entered the English language in the seventeenth century, although its origin is unknown. Fable has it that *salmagundi* may have been invented by a lady of that name in the suite of Marie de Medici, wife of Henry IV. Others attribute the dish to a shawdowy eighteenth-century chef named Gondi or Gonde. Willard R. Espy says the word has even been associated with the nursery rhyme character Solomon Grundy. In 1807 Washington Irving published a humorus periodical titled *Salmagundi*. A magazine of the same name appeared in the 1960s. The name was also adopted by a club of prominent writers and artists.

William and Mary Morris contribute a chant by children jumping rope called *Salmagundy* a bastardization of "Solomon Grundy": "*Salmagundy*, born on Monday, christened on Tuesday, married on Wednesday, sick on Thursday, worse on Friday, died on Saturday, buried on Sunday, and that was the end of *Salmagundy*."

SALMONELLA, SALMONELLOSIS

A common form of food poisoning that sometimes is fatal comes from meat or vegetables contaminated by a bacterial genus, *Salmonella*, of which there are many species. The infection, known as *salmonellosis*, is characterized by nausea, vomiting, diarrhea, and abdominal pains and is caused by infected and insufficiently cooked beef, pork, or poultry, or by food, drink, or equipment contaminated by the excreta of infected animals. Many recent outbreaks of Salmonella poisoning resulted from frozen poultry that was not properly defrosted before cooking.

A veterinary surgeon, Dr. Daniel Elmer Salmon (1850–1914), identified the *Salmonella* genus and gave his name to it. Animals are subject to this infection, too. Dr. Salmon was at one time an investigator for the U.S. Department of Agriculture and became the chief of the Bureau of Animal Industry.

SAM BROWNE BELT

A *Sam Browne belt* is a sword or pistol belt for officers. The strap supports the left side from the hip, passing over the right shoulder. Originally the belt was supported by two shoulder straps that crossed each other, one for each shoulder. Later only one strap was used, and it passed over the left shoulder to keep the trouser from sagging from the weight of the sword. Still later, when the belt became primarily an ornament of dress, the belt was transferred to the right shoulder. The belt became de rigueur for dress uniforms in the British army and was widely used by armies throughout the world.

Today the belt is a standard part of the dress of drill groups, marching bands, and cadets.

Born in India, Samuel Browne (1824–1901) spent a distinguished career in that country. He was awarded the Victoria Cross for crushing a native rebellion. In 1888 he was named a general, but he was unable to don the belt he invented because he had only one arm. The other had been lost in the rebellion.

SAMSON

Samson's birth had been foretold by an angel to Manoah's wife, who had been barren for many years. The son was to be a Nazarite and thus had to take certain vows, the most important being not to cut his hair. Samson wedded a Philistine maiden. At the festivities Samson propounded a riddle based on his experience with a lion and wagered that no one could answer it. His wife begged him to tell her the answer secretly. He gave in and complied, and lost the wager when she betrayed the answer to the Philistines. To pay for his lost wager, Samson went to Ashkelon, slew thirty Philistines, and took their spoils. He returned and found that his bride had been given to another, making him so incensed that he slew a thousand Philistines with the jawbone of an ass.

Samson then went to Hebron, where he became enamored of another Philistine maiden, Delilah. Delilah, at the instigation of the Philistines, used her charms to elicit the secret of Samson's strength. He fended her off for a while, but at last fell victim to her wiles. Learning that his strength lay in his long hair, she cut off the hair while Samson was asleep. He was then overpowered by the Philistine enemy, and his eyes were put out. He was taken to Gaza, where he was forced to turn the mill in prison. However, as his hair grew back, so did his strength return.

One day Samson, still confined in prison, was dragged to a temple to grace a victory orgy of the god Dagon. At the orgy the Philistines, led by Delilah, heaped scorn on Samson. While they were mocking him, Samson invoked the true God Jehovah, praying for a brief return of his strength. As Samson was standing between the two largest pillars supporting the temple, his prayer was answered. He grasped the pillars, pulling them down upon the drunken Philistines, Delilah, and Samson himself.

A *Samson* is a man of unusual physical strength.

SANDWICH

Today's gamblers around the world have their hunger and thirst quenched by waitresses who serve them at the gaming table so that they will not have to leave their seats. But such service was not available in the eighteenth century when John Montagu, the fourth Earl of Sandwich (1718–1792), an inveterate gambler, spent days on end at the casino. On one occasion, the story goes, the earl, loath to leave the gaming table, even to eat, ordered his servants to bring him two pieces of bread with a filling of meat to eat while he played. The earl did not know then that this gastronomic quickie would become the most ubiquitous and popular term on the menus of American restaurants—the *sandwich*—and that his name would be immortalized.

As First Lord of the Admiralty, Sandwich was responsible for preparing the British fleet for action at all times. But because his mind was on gambling and not on the ships at sea, he neglected his naval duties. Indirectly he helped the cause of the American Revolutionaries because his fleet was no longer a commanding force.

Captain James Cook, wishing to honor the earl when he was the First Lord of the Admiralty, named a group of islands in the Pacific Ocean after him, the Sandwich Islands. These are now known as the Hawaiian Islands.

In addition to serving as a noun, the word *sandwich* is used in other ways. It is an adjective in the phrase *sandwich man*, a man who parades along streets to advertise something written on the signs he's wearing. Charles Dickens first dubbed this man, in his *Sketches by Boz*, calling him an "animated sandwich." The word is also a verb, as in "I thought I was getting *sandwiched* between those two cars."

SARDONIC, SARDONIC LAUGHTER

A poisonous plant called *Herba Sardonia* gave the English language the word *sardonic* and gave the Italian island of Sardinia its name. The island in turn gave English the word *sardine*, the name for a small fish of the herring family.

The dictionary defines *sardonic* as bitter, cynical, scornful. That which is *sardonic* has come to mean disdainfully or sneeringly derisive. A *sardonic smile* is contemptuous. *Sardonic laughter*, as used by Homer, is bitter, mocking laughter.

Unfavorable connotations come naturally from the namesake herb, "which renders men insane, so that the sick person seems to laugh." The acrid plant was reputed to be so very bitter as to cause convulsions that distort the face of one who eats it into a grin. But actually the twisted face reflected the throes of death.

SAXOPHONE

Antoine Joseph Sax (1814–1894), better known as Adolphe, was born in Dinant, Belgium. His father was a distinguished instrument maker and cabinetmaker. Of the eleven children in the family, Adolphe showed the greatest aptitude while training in his father's shop. At an early age he evinced a talent for inventing brass instruments.

That Adolphe lived long enough to invent the saxophone is a miracle. In *O Thou Improper, Thou Uncommon Noun*, Willard Espy reports: "Adolphe Sax . . . grew up accident prone: He was struck on the head by a brick, swallowed a needle, fell down a flight of stairs, toppled onto a burning stove, and accidentally drank sulphuric acid. None of this prevented him from perfecting, in 1835, the wind instrument named after him, which contained the reed mouthpiece of a clarinet with a conical tube of metal, equipped with finger keys." His instrument was patented in 1846.

Through his association with the composer Hector Berlioz, Adolphe decided to try his luck in Paris. Sax had many influential men sounding their horn for him, but he was unable to market his instrument because suppliers of musical instruments took a dim view of this Belgian upstart. Even musicians expressed no enthusiasm; they preferred to continue with the instruments with which they were familiar. In 1844, at a show featuring musical instruments, Sax performed on his saxophone, playing a piece Berlioz had written for him. The saxophone he used had not been completely finished. Sax was so apprehensive that the instrument would fall apart that he lost his place in the music and held onto one note until he could find his place. The French were delighted with the long sound—they had never heard anything quite like that before—and they kept applauding.

In the light of that good fortune, a band using Sax's instruments competed against a band using the common instruments of the day. Sax's group won handily, setting the stage for Sax to become the musical supplier to the French military band. He was on his way to financial success, but although he knew how to handle musical instruments, he had no head for business. At the age of eighty, Sax became bankrupt and slipped into oblivion, just before the *sax* became an important instrument in modern bands.

SERENDIPITY, SERENDIPITOUS

Horace Walpole (1717–1797) coined the word *serendipity*, which he used in a letter addressed to a friend dated January 28, 1754, and formed from the title of a Persian fairy story, *The Three Princes of Serendip*. This was a happy coinage, for in their travels the princes of Serendip repeatedly discovered, by chance, rewards they were not seeking. Walpole said it just a little differently. The princes "were always making discoveries, by accident and sagacity, of things they were not in quest of."

Serendipitous describe something obtained or characterized by lucky and unexpected "finds." The classic example, from the Bible, is the story of Saul, "who set out to find his father's asses but instead found a kingdom."

A person who goes to Sri Lanka in search of *serendipity* goes to the right place. Sri Lanka was formerly called Ceylon, and before that—long before that—Serendip.

SEQUOIA

A *sequoia* is a giant conifer. Of its several varieties, the redwood tree is especially well-known. These trees are the tallest living things on earth. The term *sequoia* was taken from the name of the Cherokee Indian who devised the Cherokee syllabic alphabet.

Sequoyah (known in English as *Sequoia*) lived with the Cherokee tribe in Tennessee. He was the son of a white trader named Nathaniel Gist and a Cherokee woman related to a legendary warrior, King Oconostota. Sequoyah's English name from his father was George Guess, a slight change from Gist. The word *sequoyah* means "guessed it." Sequoyah became a silversmith and enjoyed singing and athletics. One day while hunting, he had an accident that crippled him for life. Restricted from many of his usual activities, Sequoyah looked into something that had bothered him for a long while, the "talking leaf." Sequoyah and other Indians could not understand how white people could look at paper and read. He decided that the secret of writing, this "talking leaf," was in sounds. After twelve years of work (1809–1821), and carefully noting the sounds uttered by the Cherokees, he came up with eighty-six characters representing all the sounds spoken. This alphabet—really a syllabary—enabled the Cherokees to publish in their own language.

The Indian chiefs were not easily convinced that the alphabet had merit and were reluctant to adopt it. The turning point came when the chiefs devised a test by having Sequoyah write a secret message on a piece of paper. They then handed the paper to Sequoyah's little daughter, who proceeded to read aloud what had been written. The chiefs were amazed, and the Cherokee written language was born.

When Sequoyah was in his seventies, he learned that some Cherokees lived in New Mexico. He set out with a small group to find the legendary lost band of Cherokees. Whether he located his tribal Indians is not known. He died in Mexico shortly after he began his search in 1843. Sequoyah was immortalized in 1847 by having a giant conifer named for him, the *sequoia*, by the Hungarian botanist Stephen Endlicher (1804–1891).

SEWARD'S FOLLY

William Henry Seward (1801–1872) was born in Florida, Orange County, New York. He graduated from Union College in 1820, was admitted to the bar in 1822, and practiced law in Auburn, New York. After two terms as governor (1838–1842), he took the advanced antislavery position, which helped his election to the U.S. Senate. He declared that the struggle over slavery was "an irrepressible conflict."

Seward served as secretary of state in Lincoln's administration, but it was under President Johnson's administration that he became convinced of the value of the Pacific Coast to the United States. The purchase of Alaska from Russia in 1867, which came about solely through Seward's determination, was decried by many and mocked as "Seward's Folly." Some even called it "Seward's Icebox." Few had the forethought to realize the bargain that was struck. The purchase of $7.2 million amounted to 2 cents an acre.

Of course, many minds changed after gold was discovered there. And consider the $900 million bid for Alaskan oil leases in 1969.

SHAKESPEAREAN

The greatest of all English writers, William Shakespeare, is the most difficult to write about because one can describe him only with superlatives. Or one can take the easy road and say he was the most renowned dramatist and poet that the world has ever known. No other writer's plays have been performed so many times in so many countries. Nor is it easy to use the adjective *Shakespearean*, which correctly means "pertaining to Shakespeare" or "concerning or like the works of Shakespeare," because comparisons are heady and useless. Other than the Bible, his works have been translated into more languages than that of any book in the world.

Not very much has been documented about Shakespeare's life. He was born in Stratford-on-Avon in the year 1564. Shakespeare's father, John, was a fairly prosperous glove maker and dealer in wools and hides. He was mayor of the town when William was four years old. John and Mary Arden Shakespeare, had eight children, William being the third. He attended the local grammar school, but very little else is known about his childhood. After his marriage to Anne Hathaway, a woman eight years his senior, he went to London and became an actor, meanwhile writing some plays to keep the wolf from the door. His plays were immediately popular, and he became prosperous. He bought a share of the Blackfriars Theater and the Globe Theater. The few fragmentary records extant give no real picture of Shakespeare's activities in London. He withdrew more and more from acting and devoted much of his time to writing. During his last illness, he was at Stratford-on-Avon and revised his will with his lawyer, Francis Collins, on March 25, 1616. He made many generous provisions for friends, but kept the property together for his descendants, the children of his two daughters. Shakespeare died at age fifty-two.

SHAW, SHAVIAN

George Bernard Shaw (1856–1950) was born in Dublin, Ireland, attended school there, but left for England to earn a living. Intensely interested in socialism, Shaw was an early member of the Socialist Fabian society. He was appointed reviewer for the *Pall Mall Gazette*, which enabled him to see many plays. Shaw became disgusted with what he saw and decided to write plays of better quality. He wrote five unsuccessful novels before his first play, *Widower's Houses*, produced in 1892.

Despite Shaw's inauspicious beginnings he rose to be the greatest literary figure of his time. He wrote *Arms and the Man* (1894), *Man and Superman* (1903), and *Pygmalion* (1912), for the actress Mrs. Patrick Campbell, on which the hit show *My Fair Lady* was based.

Shaw was a legend in his day. His personality, his wit, his movements—everything he said or did—received international notice.

Realizing that many adjectives would be used to describe him, Shaw decided to come up with one himself. *Shawian* didn't ring well, so he Latinized his name and came up with *Shavian*, which has been used to refer to his style of writing ever since.

SHRAPNEL

Henry Shrapnel (1761–1842), born in Bradford-on-Avon, received a commission from the British army and served as an artillery officer in Gibraltar, the West Indies, and Newfoundland. During his career he rose from the rank of lieutenant to lieutenant general.

Shrapnel began investigating hollow projectiles at age twenty-three and worked on this project for twenty-eight years, sometimes spending his own money to buy necessary materials. His first shell was used with horrendous effect in Surinam on the coast of South America to capture the Dutch possessions in Guiana in 1804. The Duke of Norfolk spoke highly of this projectile, and the Duke of Wellington used it in 1808 and later against Napoleon at Waterloo.

The shrapel shell consisted of a spherical projectile filled with a number of lead balls and a small charge of black powder set off by a time fuse so that it would explode in midair, scattering the shot with great force over a wide area. It was considered an excellent and reliable anti-personnel weapon for offense until World War II, when it gave way to more advanced weaponry. However, the word for shell fragmentation or any explosive device came to be called *shrapnel*, now a generic name applied to a variety of shell explosives, whether from artillery, bomb, or mine.

Shrapnel never understood why the British government would not compensate him for his untiring and persistent work in perfecting the invention of the explosive or even to reimburse him for the personal money he spent on it. As an old soldier, he faded away, a disappointed man.

SIAMESE TWINS
On April 15, 1811, in Mekong or possibly Bangesau, Siam, two boys were born joined at the waist by a short tubular cartilaginous band through which their circulatory systems functioned. Physicians said that it would be fatal to cut them apart because they shared the same liver tissue. The boys, Chang and Eng, had mirror organs in that what one had on the right side, the other had on the left, what is known scientifically as *situs inversus*. They could walk, even run fast, and in some ways seemed normal. They had short tempers with other people, but they were solicitous about each other's comfort.

P. T. Barnum, the great showman, discovered the boys, sons of a Chinese father and Siamese mother, and brought them to America. He named them the *Siamese Twins*, and the name became generic for twins joined at birth side by side or front to back. Barnum exhibited them until they became adults. They then exhibited on their own until they acquired enough money to become farmers. This they did in North Carolina, whose legislature gave them the surname Bunker. In 1843 they married two sisters and eventually fathered twenty-two children, all physically normal. While returning from a visit to Liverpool, Chang suffered a paralytic stroke. On January 16, 1874, at their home in Mount Airy, North Carolina, Eng awakened to find that his brother had died. Three hours later, Eng was dead.

Some such twins have been surgically separated and are able to live normal lives. The key is the site of the connection.

The name *Siamese twins* has persisted for physically attached twins. In general usage, the expression means that two persons are so friendly that if you see one, you are bound to see the other.

SILHOUETTE
Etienne de Silhouette (1709–1767), an author and politician, became French controller general of finances in the mid-eighteenth century through the influence of Madame de Pompadour. Silhouette instituted

strict reforms to help the failing economy. Everyone seemed delighted with his program, especially when he negotiated a large loan to adjust France's fiscal position. At last someone was seizing control and turning the financial structure of France around.

The people's enthusiasm turned when Silhouette ended the public funding of the king's gambling losses, proposed a land tax on the estate of the nobles and the church, and ordered a cut in state pensions. Tax collectors could no longer retain for themselves a portion of their collections, and everyone, including nobility, became liable to taxation. And then he proposed to tax bachelors and luxury items. He also ordered the elimination of trouser cuffs, which created the phrase *culottes de Silhouette*.

This minister of finance was clearly out of sync with the ruling hierarchy. An uproar erupted that could be heard from palace to palace. The king quickly put a stop to Silhouette's program, but the crafty finance minister then imposed a tax on "all articles of consumption." The euphoria that Silhouette had stirred in the populace a little while before was replaced with alarm. He became so exceedingly unpopular that he was forced to resign after having served for only eight months.

Etymologists believe that Silhouette's tight-fisted, cost-cutting economic policies reminded people of shadow cut-outs, the cheapest form of art (in an art-conscious country), which they identified with his niggardliness. These profile cut-outs were long popular because they were much less expensive than a miniature painted by hand. All one needed to make them was a pair of scissors and some paper to fold. Many artists had made these black outlines on light paper, serving as modern snapshots would after the invention of photography. Some said that Silhouette made shadow portraits as a hobby and that his château at Bry-sur-Marne was decorated with them.

SIMON-PURE

Susannah Centlivre, a prominent writer of farcical comedies, wrote a play in 1718 that has provided the English language with a new word meaning "utterly pure or real." This play, titled *A Bold Stroke for a Wife*, had as its hero a man named *Simon Pure*. The name of that man has come to mean, in everyday English, the real or genuine article. When the authenticity of a thing is unqualified and beyond dispute, it may be said to be *simon-pure*.

In the play, Simon Pure, a Quaker from Philadelphia, is a man of impeccable reputation. He has received a letter of introduction to a Miss Anne Lovely, a pretty young woman and heiress to a handsome fortune. Meanwhile, a certain Colonel Fainwell steals the letter and gains entrance into Anne Lovely's home by passing himself off as Simon Pure. Fainwell obtains the guardian's written consent to marry Anne. Simon

Pure has a difficult time proving that Fainwell is an impostor, but in the end the hero gets the girl.

The only thing about all this that is not a farce is the genuineness of the hero—he was simon-pure.

SIMONY, SIMONIAC

Simony is the crime of buying and selling ecclesiastical offices or favors. The word is seldom used today, and then only in a religious context. Simon Magus, a Samaritan sorcerer, is responsible for this eponymous term. Many stories about him have circulated. In Acts, Simon offered money to Peter and John to purchase the power of giving the Holy Ghost. Hence the crime of simony, practiced by simoniacs.

The story of Simon's conversion to Christianity is told in the Bible (Acts 8:9-24). The passage points out that Simon's conversion was made only so that he could obtain the new powers of sorcery that he thought the apostles possessed.

SIREN

The sound-producing device called a siren was invented by the French physicist Charles Cagniard de la Tour (1777–1859) in 1819. His invention determined the frequency, or number of vibrations per second, corresponding to a sound of any pitch. Sirens are now used only as signals.

In Greek mythology, Sirens (from sirenes, meaning "entanglers") lived on an island off southern Italy. They were mythical monsters, half woman and half bird, who, by their sweet singing, lured mariners to destruction on the rocks surrounding their island. And if they were not shipwrecked, the sweetness of the singing was such that the listeners forgot everything and died of hunger.

Two experiences reported by the poets proved the ingenuity of man over the beguiling nymphs. In the first, Odysseus, returning from the Trojan War, skirted the island, stuffed wax into the ears of his sailors, and lashed himself to a mast. With the crew thus secured, the vessel sailed on until Odysseus could no longer hear the singing of the Sirens. In the second tale, the Argonauts, heroic sailors of the Argo (the ship Jason had built to help him fetch the Golden Fleece), sailed the ship dangerously near the beach on which the Sirens were singing. Aboard was the celebrated poet Orpheus, whose golden lyre enchanted everyone who heard his music. He played his lyre, thus preventing the crew from hearing the Sirens's deadly songs. The Argonauts sailed safely by the Sirens's habitat. Defeated, the nymphs threw themselves into the sea and became rocks.

A siren suit is a one-piece, lined, warm garment on the lines of a boiler suit, and was sometimes worn in London during the air raids of World War II. It was much favored by Winston Churchill and so named from its being slipped on over night clothes at the first wail of the siren.

SMART ALECK, SMART-ALEC

No viable theories have come forth on why *smart aleck* developed at the beginning of the last century. But it did, and the expression is still very much with us today. By *smart aleck* we mean a bumptious, conceited know-it-all. *Brewer's Dictionary of Phrase and Fable* says it is an American term that goes back to the 1860s and that it can be found in the literature of this country. The expression first appeared in print in 1862 in a Carson City, Nevada, newspaper. But no record remains of Aleck's identity. Some sources say that the term was first used in the sixteenth century to designate a questionable scholar named Alexander Ross, who possesed various tiresome qualities. (Ross was referred to by Samuel Butler in *Hudibras* [1663–1678]: "There was a very learn'd philosopher / Who had read Alexander Ross over.") But this belief has not been attested. Whoever the original Aleck, once a common nickname for Alexander, he was smart enough to cover up all leads to his identity.

SMITHSONIAN INSTITUTION

James Smithson (1765–1829), an English chemist and mineralogist, was born in France, the illegitimate son of Sir Hugh Smithson (Percy) and Elizabeth Keate Macie. He made many important analyses of minerals and discovered an important zinc ore (calamine) which he gave his name to—*smithsonite*.

This British chemist, who had no connection with the United States, left his entire estate of some $508,000 "to the United States of America to found at Washington under the name of The Smithsonian Institution an establishment for increase and diffusion of knowledge among men." There was only one catch. Smithson actually left the estate to his nephew, with the stipulation that should he die leaving no children, the estate would go to the Smithsonian Institution as just described.

The nephew died in 1835—childless. One would imagine that a half-million-dollar bequest would have been received with open arms. Not so. At the time there was much opposition to accepting this bonanza. John Forsyth, Secretary of State, told President Andrew Jackson that anyone offering such a large amount of money as a benefactor must be a lunatic. Vice President John C. Calhoun said it was beneath the dignity of the United States to receive presents of this kind from anyone. Some congressmen said the gift was an attempt by a foreigner to acquire immortality.

Smithson died in Genoa, Italy, on June 26, 1829. In 1904, the Institution had his remains removed to Washington, D.C., under the escort of Alexander Graham Bell. Smithson is buried in a chapel in the main entrance of the Smithsonian building.

An international conference at the Smithsonian Institution was responsible for the parity of major currencies, which came to be known as the *Smithsonian parity*.

SOCRATIC METHOD

Socrates (c. 469–399 B.C.) was born in Athens, the son of a sculptor. The educational facilities of that day were meager, and so Socrates walked the streets to talk with people and to learn their philosophies, especially their thoughts about morals. Later he served as a soldier. To the chagrin of the government, he kept defending people he thought unjustly accused. He spent some years as a teacher, employing a method that taught, by questions and answers, a form of cross-examination which tangled his students in a network of errors. When asking questions, Socrates feigned ignorance (which is known as *Socratic irony*), luring the students to feel free to speak their minds. Through a series of questions, the students were led to the conclusion that Socrates had reached long before the class convened (which is known as the *Socratic method*).

Socrates was sentenced to death after being convicted of impiety and the corruption of youths through his teachings. The form of execution at that time was the drinking of hemlock. Socrates had acted as his own lawyer, and in his defense offered the famous "Apology of Socrates," which explained his thinking and the motivations of his life.

Socrates spent his last day speaking with friends. At nighttime he bade them farewell by saying, according to Plato's account, "The hour of departure has arrived; and we go our separate ways—I to die, and you to live. Which is the better, God only knows." With that he lay down on his couch, drank the hemlock, and died.

Although Socrates left behind no philosophic writings, we know about him and his thought primarily through the *Dialogues* of Plato, Socrates's most distinguished student.

SOLECISM

A grammatical mistake, a blunder, or any deviation from correct idiom is, in English, termed a *solecism*. The word's history can be traced to the Greek city of Soloi in ancient Cilicia, which was in what is today southern Turkey.

Soloi was far removed from the Greek homeland. Because of the distance, the colonists developed a dialect of their own. When the snooty sophisticates back home paid a visit to Soloi, they were shocked to hear their mother tongue "debased" by corrupt dialect of Greek. The Greeks termed what they heard *soloikos*, meaning speaking incorrectly. The noun that evolved was *soloikismos*. Latin borrowed it as *soloecismus*, from which came the English word used today—*solecism*. That English word has immortalized the substandard form of Attic dialect.

SOLOMON, SOLOMONIC

King Solomon, the son of David and Bathsheba, ruled Israel from about 973 to 933, before the Common Era. He was an able administrator, and his political acuity enabled him to form alliances, primarily by marrying women from surrounding regions. His country prospered so well that he was able to construct a massive temple in Jerusalem.

Solomon may have been the most renowned lover of all times, and perhaps the greatest. In addition to his publicized affair with the Queen of Sheba, he is credited, by the Bible, with having married seven hundred women. Quite clearly, in addition to his wisdom, Solomon must have had enduring strength. The erotic *Song of Songs* is thought to have been composed by him. He is also credited with having written certain psalms and the entire Book of Ecclesiastes.

Solomon's most famous mediation concerned a dispute by two women who claimed to be the mother of a certain child. The Bible passage reads: "And the king said, Bring me a sword. And they brought a sword before the king. And the king said, Divide the living child in two, and give one half to the one, and half to the other" (I Kings 3:24-25). The woman who immediately withdrew her claim was in Solomon's judgment the real mother. This example of astuteness is known as the *Judgment of Solomon*.

The Queen of Sheba visited Solomon to "prove him with hard questions." He answered so well that she gave him, for starters, "a hundred and twenty talents of gold, and of spices a great store, and precious stones." In return she received from him "all her desire, whatsoever she asked, besides that which Solomon gave her of his real bounty."

SOLON

Solon (640–560 B.C.), known as "one of the wise men of Greece," was one of the most famous lawgivers of all times. A well-educated Athenian who supported himself by foreign trade, he was elected archon of Athens and was given authority to change the laws. He thereupon initiated many social and legal reforms, including a reformed constitution for Athens. Most of the money was in the hands of a few powerful citizens, placing the ordinary citizen in financial straits. The small farmers had to mortgage their lands, giving themselves and their family as security; many of them became slaves. Solon passed a law that canceled these debts and mortgages, and freed those who had become slaves.

His constitutional reforms divided the citizens into four classes, but any citizen could become a member of the assembly and the public law courts. He established a council of four hundred to which citizens could appeal the decisions of the officials. Although he maintained an oligarchy, he had made definite steps toward democracy.

Solon made the Athenians promise to keep the laws for ten years, during which period he left the state. Where and how he wandered for that period has never been documented. Some say that he returned to Athens and found a civil war in progress and that the tyrant Pisistratus was in control. Others say that Solon died while wandering in the East.

Solon was known for his love poems and political verse. Some word sleuths, but not all, credit him with the proverbial "Call no man happy till he is dead." In any event, everyone agrees that Solon was a great statesman and lawgiver and that his motto, "Know thyself," deserves as much consideration today as it did then.

The word *solon* today is used ironically to mean "representative," "legislator," "congressman," and "lawmaker," because *solon* is a short word that fits neatly into many headlines. And yet none may be solons in the true sense of the word.

SOUSA, SOUSAPHONE

The musical instrument that goes oom-pah-pah is generally known as a *tuba*, but it is really a helicon and is found in marching bands. In fact, it was built for use in just such a band and has been named the *sousaphone* after the great march king John Philip Sousa. This instrument is a bass tuba with a large bell, made in circular form to be worn over the player's shoulder. It has virtually replaced the tuba in military and school bands. But the name *tuba* is still common.

John Philip Sousa (1854–1932), the son of Portuguese refugees, began his career when he joined the U.S. Marine Band at age thirteen as a trombonist. At nineteen, he began conducting theater orchestras. He went all the way up to become bandmaster of the U.S. Marine Corps (1880), a band in which his father had played before him. After twelve years with the Marine Band, Sousa formed his own band in 1892 and became the brassy toast of two continents.

In addition to being a superb band leader, Sousa became the country's most renowned and prolific composer of marching songs. He composed some 140 military marches, including such classics and perennial favorites as "The Stars and Stripes Forever," "Semper Fidelis," "The Washington Post," "Hands across the Sea," "Liberty Bell," and "The High School Cadets." In addition he wrote eleven operettas, three novels, and an autobiography, *Marching Along*.

SPARTAN

The Spartans of Ancient Greece were drilled in fortitude. They were austere and tough and lived under a code of laws that stressed hardiness and devotion to the state. Sparta was a city-state that excelled in and was governed by military perfection. Weak or disabled infants were left to die of exposure; the arts, considered enfeebling, were banished; military training began at age seven. Schoolchildren have marveled at a story of a Spartan boy who, having stolen a fox and hidden it under his cloak, stood stock still while the fox gnawed out his innards.

Sparta lay in an open plain with no natural barriers to protect it, no hills for an enemy to have to climb, no rivers to be crossed, and no dense woodland to act as a natural shield for the city. As a result the Spartans were devoted to building and maintaining an army.

An ambassador from another state once asked Lycurgus why Sparta had no walls around it. "But we do have walls," replied the Spartan monarch, "and I will show them to you." He led his guest to the field where the army was marshaled in battle array. Pointing to the ranks of men, he said: "There are the walls of Sparta, and every man is a brick."

We use such terms as *Spartan courage*, the enduring of great discomfort or pain stoically, *Spartan simplicity*, living by only the necessities of life, and *Spartan fare*, a frugal diet, a subsistence on the barest essentials to survive.

SPENCER JACKET

How the *Spencer jacket* came about is a matter of dispute. The jacket was named for George John Spencer, the second Earl of Spencer (1758–1834). One belief is that the earl was thrown from his horse and tore his long-tailed riding coat on a thorn bush. Spencer conceived the idea of a short coat that would not be damaged in such circumstances. At that time, only a coat with tails was considered proper dress.

Another belief is that the earl wagered that he could set a new fashion by wearing a short overcoat without skirts, which he wore as he strolled the streets of London. Spencer won the bet. The jacket gained immediate popularity; it became quite stylish, de rigueur among the social elite.

The name came to be applied also to a close-fitting bodice for women, but there the word's lineage is clearer: It was designed by a Mr. Knight Spencer.

SPENCERIAN PENMANSHIP, SPENCERIAN SCRIPT

The typewriter, the word processor, and the computer have almost made the need for good penmanship obsolete. But written notes are sometimes very effective in business, and socially they are a decided asset. *Spencerian handwriting* is the name given to a style of ornate penmanship introduced by Platt Rogers Spencer (1800–1864), an American calligrapher. Written with a fine pen, with the down-strokes tapering from top to bottom and large loops, the writing has a forward slope and marked terminal flourishes. Spencer taught this style for many years, and it had a marked influence on American calligraphy.

Born in East Fishkill, New York, Spencer migrated to Geneva, Ohio, where he conducted unique penmanship classes in a log cabin on his farm. He then branched out with lectures and classes at business schools and academies and wrote a series of textbooks used by many schools during the pre-Civil War period. His handwriting had such a stamp of excellence that *Spencerian* became the hallmark of good handwriting. His textbooks, naturally, helped popularize his style.

Spencerian script, descriptive of his penmanship, although considered dated and old-fashioned, has become a collectors' items.

SPOONERISM

The Reverend William A. Spooner (1844–1930), an Anglican clergyman, had a habit of transposing the initial sounds of words, forming a ludicrous combination. Whether his slips of tongue were accidental or simply the result of absentmindedness has never been determined. His position in life as dean and later warden of New College, Oxford, would seem to have called for simple and direct dialogue with no tongue twisters.

Spooner's students so enjoyed hearing his transposition of the initial sounds of words that they made up some combinations themselves for their own amusement—for example, "Is the bean dizzy?" for "Is the dean busy?"—but they could never surpass those attributed to their master. When he preached, he carried with him his lapses of speech. On one occasion he said to a person who had come to pray, "Aren't you occupewing the wrong pie?" for "occupying the wrong pew." When the startled parishioner looked at him ungraspingly, he continued with, "Were you sewn into this sheet?" for "shown into this seat." Possibly the funniest mistake of his twisted tongue was at the end of a wedding ceremony when the bashful groom simply stood there. Spooner intoned, "It's kisstomary to cuss the bride."

The technical name for this form of twisting words is *metathesis*, but better known is the nontechnical name *spoonerism*.

Some of Spooner's phrases that are used as examples are "a well-boiled icicle" for "a well-oiled bicycle"; "our shoving leopard" for "our loving shepherd"; "a half-warmed fish" for "a half-formed wish." One of his most repeated transpositions is "Kinquering congs their titles take" for "Conquering kings their titles take." And he is supposed to have made a toast to the dear old queen by saying, "Let us now drink to the queer old dean."

Spooner closed his academic life in an appropriate style. When, because of age, he was forced into retirement, he remarked, "It came as a blushing crow," instead of a "crushing blow."

ST. BERNARD

For centuries people have tried to traverse the Alps through passes that were more than 8,000 feet high and always covered with snow. Many didn't succeed and simply froze to death, their corpses covered with new snow, never to be discovered.

In the year 982, high in the Alps, a French nobleman who had renounced his wealth to become a monk built two shelters for pilgrims on their way to Rome and for any other adventurous travelers who faced the rigors of uncertain weather conditions while crossing over what came to be called the Great St. Bernard Pass and the Little St. Bernard Pass. This man, who was canonized in 1691, is known throughout the world as St. Bernard de Menthon (923–1008).

The dog known as *St. Bernard* was bred by monks long after the death of St. Bernard, and the dogs are still trained at the Alpine hospice. The heaviest of breeds, they measure up to six feet in length. Their ancestor has not been established, but some believe that the Molossus hound, imported from Asia, might have been crossed with a Newfoundland breed.

This breed has generated many heart-warming stories, foremost of which may be one of Barry, whose statue adorns the St. Bernard Hospice. Barry has been credited with saving at least forty lives during a ten-year period. One story concerns Barry's finding a small child unconscious in the snow. Barry warmed the chile with its breath and licked his hands and face, rousing him from what might have been a deadly sleep. By various movements, Barry got the child to climb on its back, then carried the child safely to the hospice.

ST. VITUS'S DANCE

Although Thomas Sydenham (1624–1689), a prominent English physician, conducted studies of a nervous disease causing spasmodic movements of the face or limbs, the better-known name of "Sydenham's chorea" is *St. Vitus's dance*. *St. Vitus's dance*, a neurological disease earlier attributed to rheumatic fever, has, so to speak, waltzed itself into a permanent niche in the English language.

Saint Vitus, born in the third century, was the son of a Sicilian nobleman. Together with his nurse, Crescentia, and his tutor, Modestus, he suffered martyrdom as a child during the persecution by the Emperor Diocletian. Although St. Vitus was not known to suffer from chorea, his name was given to the nervous disease *St. Vitus's Dance* because Vitus was thought to have power over epilepsy.

For some unscientific reason, a belief arose in the seventeenth century that dancing around a statue of St. Vitus would ensure good health and protect against disease. In Germany, where the custom was particularly prevalent, the dancing sometimes reached a stage of frenzy, but there are no attested reports of beneficial results. St. Vitus's name was invoked as a protection from nervous disorders and from illness caused by bites of dogs and serpents.

Although *chorea*, a Greek word meaning "dance," is not a word easily recognized by everyone, its sister words are well known: *choreography*, the art of composing dance arrangements for the stage, and the more evocative *chorine*, a chorus girl.

STENTOR, STENTORIAN

A Grecian herald of the Trojan War, Stentor faced the enemy to dictate terms. In Homer's *Iliad*, Book V, appears a reference to Stentor that is widely quoted: "And when they were now come where the most valiant stood, thronging about mighty Diomedes tamer of horses, in the semblance of ravening lions or wild boars whose strength is nowise feeble, then stood the white-armed goddess Hera and shouted in the likeness of great-hearted Stentor with voice of bronze, whose cry was loud as the cry of fifty other men."

The eponymous *stentorian*, which means loud or strong in sound, derives directly from *Stentor*. *Stentors*, a variety of aquatic microscopic animal, have mouths shaped like trumpets.

STETSON

John Batterson Stetson (1830–1906) was a New Jerseyite who went West for his health. His observant eye noticed that the headgear worn by cowboys was not so suitable as it might be. Returning to the East, he settled in Philadelphia, where he opened a hat-making factory. His hats became exceedingly popular, and soon he was the largest manufacturer of hats in the world. Although he made hats to suit all styles of dress, what made his name famous was his Western-style hats, which were more practical for wear and use on the range than the other hats made in the East. They were felt, wide-brimmed, and high-crowned. Before long they acquired the nickname "ten-gallon hat." No cowpuncher would any more bust a bronco without wearing his ten-gallon hat than he would dare walk the streets of Dodge City without his six-shooter.

Stetson University, a college in De Land, Florida, was named after John B. Stetson because of his generosity.

STRADIVARIUS, STRAD

The *stradivarius*, a remarkable violin, is believed by many musicians to be the best ever made. They say the tone and craftsmanship of a stradivarius have never been equaled.

Antonio Stradivari (1644–1737) was born in Cremona, Italy. He was apprenticed to Niccolo Amati, who was regarded as the best maker of violins at that time. When Amati died in 1684, Stradivari began experimenting with the size and shape of violins and eventually came up with one that produced more breadth of resonance and power of tone. His violins, shorter than others, with a broadening and arching of the instrument, were of unsurpassed symmetry and beauty.

Stradivari attained worldwide recognition and received commissions from several heads of state, including James II of England and Charles III of Spain. He produced more than 1,000 violins and violoncellos, and some 600 are believed to be still extant. Those violins that were given names—Alard, Betts, Viotti, and Messiah—are particularly famous.

Stradivari died without disclosing the secrets of his craft, so no one knows why a Stradivarius sounds better than other violins. Was it the varnish he used, the way he cut the F-holes, the aging of the wood? The term *strad* is a shortened form of the word and denotes the tops in a field.

SVENGALI, TRILBY

Trilby, a novel written by George Louis du Maurier in 1894, was exceedingly popular for many years. The heroine, Trilby O'Ferrall, was so enthusiastically accepted that she became a marketing phenomenon. People bought Trilby soaps, Trilby perfumes, Trilby shoes, and a host of other Trilby articles of dress. The Trilby hat, soft felt with an indented crown, became the accepted headgear among the fashionable. After *Trilby* had a run in the theater, *Trilby* articles became worldwide favorites.

Svengali was a Hungarian musical genius who mesmerized Trilby and gained control over her. Through hypnosis, the villainous Svengali controlled Trilby's singing voice and transformed her into a great singer. When Svengali died, Trilby lost her voice, fell ill, and died, too.

A person exercising unusual or mysterious control over someone else is said to be a *svengali*.

Du Maurier (1834–1896), once a caricaturist for *Punch* and an illustrator for the works of some prominent authors, never became as well-known as his granddaughter, Daphne du Maurier, a writer of romantic novels.

SYBARITE

Around 720 B.C. a group of Greeks immigrated to Lucania, a region in southern Italy, and founded a city that they named Sybaris. Its inhabitants followed such a liberal policy of admitting people from all lands that the city flourished and was soon noted for its wealth and luxury. In fact, no other Hellenic city could compare with Sybaris in prosperity and splendor.

According to legend, a war arose between Sybaris and its neighbor, Crotona. Although the Crotonian forces were inferior, they leveled Sybaris to the ground. The Crotonians were victorious because they exploited a weakness in the opposing army: The horses of the Sybarites had been trained to dance to the pipes. The Crotonians marched in to battle playing pipes. The horses of the Sybarites began to dance, the Sybarites themselves became confused, and the Crotonians vanquished their enemy.

The Sybarites were given to such wanton luxury and sensual pleasures that they became effeminate. Seneca told a tale of a Sybarite who complained he had not rested comfortably at night. Asked why, he replied that a rose leaf had been doubled under him, and it hurt him.

The conspicuous consumption, the love of luxury and pleasure displayed by the citizens of Sybaris, led to the English word *sybarite*, a person devoted to opulence and sumptuousness; in brief, a voluptuary.

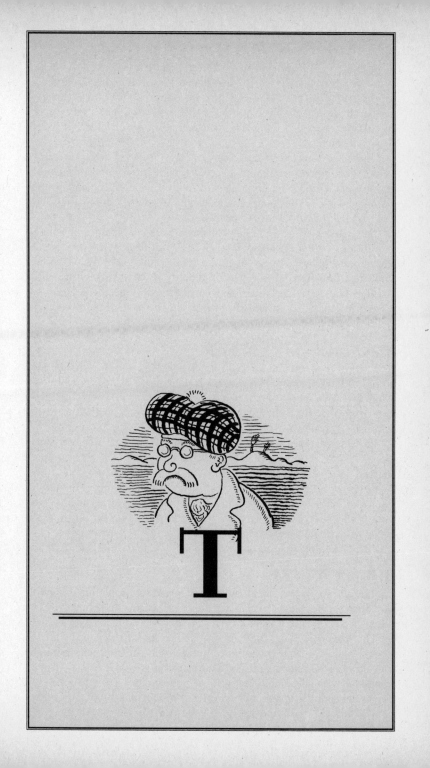

T

TAMMANY, TAMMANY HALL

Tammanend or *Tammanund*, a pre-Revolutionary Indian chief of the Delaware tribe, was supposed to have signed the document of friendly relations with William Penn. Not much is known about him except that his name meant "affable." Patriots of the Revolution borrowed his name when they organized *Tammany* societies, all of which died out except *Tammany Hall*.

This society was designated a social club for New Yorkers, but it became politically oriented and attracted prominent politicians, including Aaron Burr. During the presidency of Andrew Jackson, the organization dominated New York politics, and it continued that domination until the first half of the twentieth century.

Tammany Hall was investigated many times on charges of political corruption, including bribery. It received a great deal of unfavorable publicity from the press, especially in the 1870s when led by W. M. Tweed, known as Boss Tweed, who fleeced the city of New York of over $100 million. The continued widespread corruption and specific nefarious incidents led to the figurative use of the name *Tammany Hall* for wholesale political or municipal malpractice.

TAM-O'-SHANTER

The *tam*, the standard headgear of Scots ploughmen, was a shortened form of *tam-o'-shanter*. This cap was usually made of wool or cloth, and while fitting snugly to the head and around the brow, it was wider than the headband. Its distinctive mark was a pompom or a tassel in the center.

Its name derives from Tam O'Shanter, the hero of a Robert Burns poem (1789). The cap must have been a favorite of the poet, for in cartoons and other renderings, he is frequently seen wearing one.

Burns reportedly wrote the poem while walking along the banks of the River Nith. In the poem Tam O'Shanter had disturbed a witch revel and was pursued by the demon Cutty Sark to the bridge over the River Doon. The demon had to stop because it could not cross running water, but it plucked off the tail of Tam O'Shanter's mare, Maggie.

TANTALIZE

To *tantalize* is to tease or disappoint by promising something desirable and then withholding it or, as Dr. Johnson put it, "to torment by the show of pleasures that cannot be reached."

The legendary King Tantalus divulged to mortals the secrets of the gods, which had been entrusted to him by Zeus. In another version, he cooked his son Pelops and served him to the gods. He was thereupon condemned to an eternal and peculiar punishment. Forced to stand in the underworld in a pool of clear water, Tantalus was forbidden to drink or to eat. Every time he bent down to slake his thirst, the waters of Hades receded from him. A tree with clusters of luscious fruit hung just above his head. But every time he extended his hand, he found that the fruit was just out of reach. Tantalus suffered agony from thirst, hunger, and unfulfilled anticipation.

TARTAR

The Tatars were part of the Asiatic hordes of Genghis Khan, which, in the thirteenth century, swept into Eastern Europe by way of Tatary, in Siberia. These tribes overran Asia and much of Europe, as far west as Poland. The tribes were ruthless and massacred anyone who opposed them. They caused devastation wherever they went. Legend has it that a Tatar would bite the hand of anyone holding him and devour anyone who let him loose.

The Tatars came to be called Tartars by the Romans, after *Tartarus*, the ancient word for hell, and there was no doubt that the Tartars made life hell on earth for the Europeans. Today, a savage, irritable or excessively severe person is called a *tartar*. The expression "to catch a Tartar" is to bite off more than you can chew, or to take on more than you have bargained for, or to struggle with an opponent who is extremely hard to handle.

TAWDRY

Some words evolve in an odd way. Consider *tawdry*, which evolved from the name of St. Audrey, a person once revered in Great Britain.

The story began in the seventh century with a princess named Etheldrida (spelled several different ways) who valued chastity so much, as a personal religious vow, that she decided she should not surrender her virginity even if married. She became the wife of the Prince of Gyrwinas, who graciously and considerately died in three years without having sullied her marital bed. She then became the queen of Egfrid, the king of Northumbria, with whom she did not engage in connubial bliss either, despite his impassioned pleadings. Audrey, as she came to be called, entered a convent with her husband's consent. However, he had second thoughts and realized that he was entitled to wifely sexual companionship. Learning of his change of mind, Audrey disguised herself as an old woman and, together with two older nuns, fled to the Isle of Ely, which her first husband had left her, and ruled over it until her death in 679.

Audrey engaged in frequent prayers but infrequent baths. She bathed only four times a year, each bath preceding one of the four great feasts. A few years after arriving on Ely, she developed a tumor in her throat, which she took to be divine punishment for the youthful follies of decorating her neck with worldly ornaments. Audrey did not die of cancer, however; she became a victim of the plague.

Etheldrida, under her anglicized name Audrey, was sainted. In her memory a fair called St. Audrey's Day was held annually on October 17 until it petered out in the seventeenth century. At these festivities cheap, gaudy trinkets were sold as mementoes, and the item called "St. Audrey's lace," a showy scarf, was in great demand. These neckpieces were of poor quality to start with. They became shabbier and cheaper as time went on until finally the word to describe them, and ultimately any showy and worthless piece of finery, was *tawdry*, a shortened corrupted form of St. Audrey.

TEDDY BEAR

Theodore Roosevelt (1858–1919) was president of the United States 1901–1909. He was a soldier, an explorer, and a politician, and he was celebrated for his "Rough Riders," who fought in the Spanish-American War. As vice president of the United States, he became the twenty-sixth president upon the assassination of President William McKinley in 1901. In 1904, Roosevelt ran for the presidency and was elected.

While bear hunting around Sunflower River in 1902, Roosevelt was led to a bear cub tied to a tree by his hosts to make it easy for him to shoot. Teddy, as the president was affectionately called, refused to shoot the small bear, insisting that it be released and freed. Newspapers throughout the country carried the story, and Clifford K. Berryman, a cartoonist for the *Washington Post*, drew a cartoon titled "Drawing the Line in Mississippi," a pun on the border dispute between Mississippi and Louisiana. The incident enhanced Roosevelt's popularity with the people as well as his reputation as a conservationist.

A stuffed bear to commemorate this act of kindness was manufactured, after receiving the presidents's permission to use his name. A Brooklynite, Morris Michton, and his wife, Rose, sewed and put together many bears, and a distinctive business was born when the bears were placed on the commercial market. This business, under the name Ideal Toy Company, started in the back room of a corner candy store and grew into one of the largest toy companies in America.

Even today, *teddy bears*, more popular than ever, are in every toy store and in almost every home.

THESPIAN

Thespis was a writer of Greek choral poetry in the sixth century B.C. A chorus recited poems in unison at festivals of the gods. The festival leader would ask a question, and the entire chorus would give a poetic answer. Under Thespis's direction, one member of the cast was given the sole responsibility of answering the questions. Thus theatrical dialogue was created between the leader and the responder, and—presto— spoken drama had an auspicious start. Since Thespis is believed to have spoken these parts, this Attic poet has been considered the first actor. His name has provided the language with *thespian* both as a noun meaning "actor," and as an adjective to describe a relationship with drama.

Thespis is called the father of Greek tragedy. For his winning performance in a competition in Athens in 534 B.C., he won a prize: a goat. The source for our word *tragedy* is Greek *tragoidia*, a compound from *tragoa*, "goat," and *aeidein*, "to sing." The reason that the Greeks called this dramatic form *goat song* is obscure.

THUG

The only thing that the words *thief* and *thug* have in common, aside from their first two letters, is that they suggest the felonious taking of what is not theirs. A thief may steal secretly or slyly—a sneak thief. He might pick a pocket. A *thug* is a different breed of animal; he is a hoodlum, a ruffian, a violent criminal.

The word *thug* is said to have been derived from the Indian cult known as *Thuggee*, derived from the Sanskrit *sthag*, meaning "to conceal." But it might have come from the Hindustani word *thag*, "a cheat." Then again, the British euphemistically called *thugs* the religious fanatics who were members of an Indian sect called *Phansigars* (noose operators) from the method employed. They worshiped Kali, the Hindu goddess of destruction, and, using scarves, they strangled people, usually wealthy persons, and robbed them. Then, in a ceremony in accordance with the sect's religious belief, they buried their victims and divided the loot among the cult members.

Lord William Bentnick began the suppression of these terrorists in 1828, when the British hanged 412 of them and sentenced a few thousand to prison. It took more than fifty years to extinguish this blot on human dignity. Their brutality has given us the word *thug*, which in common parlance means any violent "tough."

THROGMORTON STREET

The English center of finance and business—*Throgmorton Street*—was named for Sir Nicholas Throgmorton (1515–1571), head of the Warwickshire family and ambassador to France and Scotland in the reign of Elizabeth I. The stock exchange is situated there, making it for England what Wall Street is to the United States.

No one knew when the street was named that it would become a hallmark of finance and that the character of the operations on Throgmorton Street would be of the highest legitimate order. If crystal balls could have predicted its legitimacy, another name might have been selected because Mr. Throgmorton was not free from criminal intrigue. He was a devious character who served two stretches in the Tower, once for alleged complicity in the Wyatt Rebellion, and the second for a spirited plot to become a matchmaker—to marry Mary, Queen of Scots, to the Duke of Norfolk.

The center of finance in the United States had no such aristocratic inheritance. Wall Street was named after an old wall built in 1653 by Peter Stuyvesant across lower Manhattan to protect the Dutch colonists. At that time the wall was the most northern boundary of the city.

TICH, TICHBORNE CASE

A dwarfish music-hall comedian has given his nickname to the English language to mean a diminutive person. Harry Ralph (1868–1928) was a pudgy infant at the time of the *Tichborne case*, in which an Australian claimed to be Roger Charles Tichborne, an heir to a baronetcy who had left England for a trip to South America some years earlier, in 1854. Tichborne had boarded the ship *Bella*, which subsequently sank with a complete loss of life.

Eleven years later, the Australian had many people believing that he was the long-lost heir. But other members of the family were not convinced, and they brought this matter to court. After a trial that lasted 188 days, the longest in English legal history, the defendant was proved to be an impostor. He was identified as Arthur Orton, a butcher from Wapping, Australia, and he was sentenced to fourteen years of penal servitude.

Harry Ralph grew into a fat adolescent. Because of his size, he was nicknamed *Tich* in allusion to the Tichborne case because the claimant was corpulent. The comedian, less than four feet tall, adopted the nickname, and thereafter used it as his professional name.

Tich had natural talent as an entertainer and was renowned for his stage pranks and satirical humor. By the turn of the century, his performances were acclaimed internationally. In due course, he hit the top of the circuit and appeared in Drury Lane. His popularity in Paris gained him the Legion of Honour.

Tich's audiences were entertained, and the English language gained a new word. A diminutive person or object may be said, affectionately, to be *tich* or *tichy*.

TIMOTHY GRASS

The spiked-head grass dried for fodder that is most widely cultivated in North America was, at one time, called *meadow cat's-tail grass*. Grown in Europe with the technical name *Phleum pratense*, the species was brought to America by New England settlers.

A farmer named John Herd reportedly discovered this grass growing wild on his New Hampshire farm in 1700. He might have called the grass by his name, but when another farmer, Timothy Hanson, moved from New York to a Southern state, he took bags of grass seed with him and introduced the grass under his first name. And *Timothy* has ever since been its name.

The Southerners were impressed by *Timothy grass* and bought the seeds, making the grass widespread throughout the South. Settlers leaving for Western land bought the seed, too, giving the grass a national presence.

TITANIC, TITANS

The adjective *titanic* is a synonym for huge, gigantic, and colossal. It is a particularly useful word to express great size; for example, the sculptures by John Gutzon de la Mothe Borglum (1867–1941) at Mount Rushmore, South Dakota, of George Washington, Thomas Jefferson, Theodore Roosevelt, and Abraham Lincoln are *titanic*. *Titanic* was the name of the White Star liner, the largest ship afloat (45,000 tons) at the time it was launched. On its maiden voyage, on April 14, 1912, the Titanic struck an iceberg and sank in less than two hours, with a loss of 1,513 lives; 711 passengers were saved.

The *Titans*, according to Greek mythology, were a race of gods begot by Uranus (sky) and Gaea (earth). The Greeks thought of them as gigantic beings who had ruled the world in a primitive age. There were twelve Titans, six male and six female. The most famous was Cronus, the father of Zeus. Cronus and Zeus engaged in a struggle for supremacy of the world in which the gods (under Zeus) and the Titans (under Cronus) were pitted against one another. The Titans lost, and the Olympian gods took control. Zeus was the ruler, and he quickly arranged to punish his enemies by dispatching them—the Titans—to Tartarus, the nethermost depths of the underworld.

The Titans were characterized by brute strength, large size, and low intelligence. M. H. Klaproth, a German scientist, who discovered *titanium* in 1795, so named the new element as an allusion to the natural strength of metal.

TITIAN

The greatest Venetian painter who ever lived, in the opinion of most distinguished critics, was Tiziano (*Titian* in English) Vecelli.

Titian was born at Pieve di Cadore in the Friulian Alps. The date of his birth is uncertain but is believed to be 1477. He died of the plague on August 27, 1576, when he was almost a hundred years of age. He reputedly started painting when only four years old and didn't stop painting until he died. He trained under the great masters Bellini and Gentile, but he surpassed them in the use of color. He often depicted his models with hair in shades of a lustrous bronze. His color was so rich, so magnificent that his name came to be the accepted name of the brownish orange color—now *titian*. What precisely is the color *titian* is hard to say. It has been called a sort of red-yellow, but some say it's a shade of reddish brown or auburn.

Color was Titian's strong point; drawing was of secondary importance. Not many of the great painters known for their drawing skills could match Titian in the use of color and design. "That man would have no equal if art had done as much for him as nature," Michelangelo said of him, adding, "It is a pity that in Venice they don't learn to draw well."

Titian executed many wonderful and magnificent paintings—portraits, religious subjects, mythological works. His paintings were so awe-inspiring and breathtakingly beautiful that selecting his most outstanding work would confound even the most sagacious art critic. His painting *Bacchus and Ariadne* in the National Gallery, London, is thought to be the best in England. In the United States his *Rape of Europa*, in the Isabella Stewart Gardner Museum, Boston, is considered his masterpiece.

TOMMY GUN

The submachine gun, which was much favored by "violin carrying gangsters" of the Capone-gang era, was invented by John Taliaferro Thompson (1860–1940), collaborating with other inventors, notably Navy Commander John N. Blish. *Tommy gun* is a nickname for the *Thompson submachine gun*, a name not generally used.

At first, the U.S. Army displayed little interest in the gun, although its use for close combat was particularly effective. But it did receive some use and favorable reactions during World War II. The gun is portable, weighing from six to twelve pounds, and its clips can hold twenty to fifty shots. It has a pistol grip and shoulder stock for firing from the shoulder, but it was more often fired from the hip. The cinemas depicting the period of warfare by Prohibition-type gangsters always showed them shooting from the hip—spraying the area, so to speak. But the gun was not easily mastered because it had a decided tendency to ride up. The gun had to be locked in place or else the shots would go over the head of the target.

Cyril Leslie Beeching reports: "The notorious 'Saint Valentine's Day Massacre' in 1919, when seven members of the Moran gang were gunned down in a Chicago garage, is believed to have been carried out by Al Capone's men (posing as policemen), using sawed-off shotguns and tommy-guns."

TONTINE

A *tontine* is a form of annuity by several subscribers, in which the shares of those who die are added to the holdings of the survivors until the last survivor inherits all. This system was devised by and named for a Neapolitan banker, Lorenzo Tonti (1635–1690), who introduced it into France in 1653. Louis XIV initiated a tontine in 1689 that attracted more than 1 million subscriptions. Thirty-seven years later, shortly before her death, the last survivor drew a dividend 2,300 percent larger than her original investment. England floated several tontines. As late as 1871 the *Daily News* announced a proposal to raise £650,000 to purchase the Alexandra Palace and 100 acres of land through a tontine.

Tontines have not been heard of recently. Perhaps they have become obsolete, especially in the light of modern gambling casinos. But they were exciting vehicles on which several mystery motion pictures were based. It is easy to imagine that when the survivors were reduced to a small number there could be an incentive to hasten the others to the Promised Land.

A bestseller written by Thomas B. Costain titled *The Tontine* was published in 1955.

TUREEN

Tureen, earlier *tereen* from French *terrine*, cognate with *terra*, "earth," traditionally was an earthen pot or pan. Its modified spelling may be due to some fanciful connection with the city of Turin. Current dictionaries define it as a huge serving bowl with a lid, specifically for soup. But in restaurant jargon, any large dish with a lid is a tureen, especially if designed for warm food.

The story that made the rounds, but may be apocryphal, is that the Vicomte de Turenne (1611–1675) sat down for dinner with his staff. They were informed that there were no soup bowls, whereupon the Vicomte, a daring and imaginative fellow, pulled off his helmet, turned it upside down, and voilà, a soup bowl. If the story is true, the forebear of all the elegant tureens made of silver or fine china was a helmet made of unpolished iron.

Tureens have been used for centuries, and some, especially those designed for royalty or for the wealthy, have warranted placement in museums. The tureens styled by Meissen, Sèvres, and Spode are sumptuous and colorful. The handles, or ears, of a tureen lend themselves to decorative imagination.

The Campbell Soup Company has a tureen museum in Camden, New Jersey.

TUXEDO

A man attending a formal affair today may wear a tuxedo and a black tie or a full-dress coat and a white tie. At one time, however, only the latter style was acceptable; the tailless formal jacket was unknown until the 1800s.

The Algonquian word for wolf is *p'tukit* (pronounced with a silent *p*) and means "the animal with a round foot." From that Indian word a lake about forty miles from New York City came to be known as Tuxedo Lake, a rather good phoneticism. Much of the area surrounding the lake was purchased by Pierre Lorillard, the tobacco heir, and subsequently a fashionable and exclusive resort and residential community was developed called *Tuxedo Park*.

At one lavish affair, perhaps given by the Astors or the Harrimans, a brave aristocrat who disliked the formal "soup and fish" full evening clothes rebelled and wore a tailless jacket. The innovation was startling, but the shortened jacket became an immediate success. The new style was dubbed *tuxedo* after the name of the place where the garment was first worn. Today many men who appear before a clergyman ready to take his marital vows are dressed in that "wolf's clothing."

UNCLE SAM

The United States government was first caricatured as Jonathan, a shrewd Yankee, in Royall Tyler's play *The Contrast*. But a new personification of the United States government surfaced during the War of 1812. He was "Uncle Sam." There are several theories of his origin, but one has been accepted by most word sleuths as the most likely. It concerns a meat packer in Troy, New York, named Samuel Wilson, whose nickname was "Uncle Sam." He stamped the boxes he was sending to the Army with the initials U.S., meaning, of course, "United States." But the employees got in the habit of saying, "Be sure the box is stamped Uncle Sam, the two words rolling off the tongue more easily than the blunt "U.S." True or not, *Uncle Sam* came to be widely accepted. In September 7, 1813, the *Troy Post*, published in Troy, New York, was the first to refer to the United States government in print as *Uncle Sam*.

Uncle Sam changed his habiliments as he grew older. He became more fashionable. When he first appeared in 1830 in cartoons, he was clean-shaven and wore a robe, no trousers. During the presidency of Abraham Lincoln, *Uncle Sam* took on another attire and, possibly aping the president, became hairy at least to the extent of a goatee. He was lanky and wore a red, white, and blue top hat and swallowtails, the dress so ubiquitously shown in the Army poster in which Uncle Sam points and says, "I Want You."

In 1961 Congress passed a special resolution recognizing *Uncle Sam* as America's symbol.

URANUS, URANIUM

In Greek mythology *Ouranos* was an ancient sky god whose name stood for "heaven." The Romans called him *Uranus*. By whatever name, he was the husband of Gaea, the goddess of Earth, the father of the Titans, the Cyclops, and the Furies, and was the original ruler of the world. (He was also castrated with a sickle by his son, Cronus, at the instigation of his mother.)

Sir William Herschel (1738–1822), a British astronomer, made a remarkable discovery on March 13, 1781. He spotted a new planet, the first such discovery since ancient times. The naming of the planet was his privilege. Up to that moment humans had observed only six planets: Mercury, Venus, Mars, Jupiter, Saturn, and Earth. (The last, of course, was not only observed but also stood on.) Herschel named his discovery *Uranus* in honor of the god of the sky. He was appointed astronomer to King George III, who later made him a knight.

In 1789, Martin Henrich Klaproth (1743–1817), a German chemist who first identified the elements uranium, zirconium, cerium, and titanium, was experimenting with pitchblende when he found within it an unusual new metallic element, one that was radioactive, element 92. In honor of the new planet discovered by Herschel, Klaproth coined a name for his find: *uranium*.

His new element contains forms called isotopes, which are used as a source of atomic energy. Little did Klaproth know, and little did the world know, that his element, now defined by Webster as "a rare, heavy, white metallic element that has no important uses," would be the cog in the wheel that produced the atomic bomb.

UTOPIA, UTOPIAN

Utopia was an ideal commonwealth where perfect justice and social harmony existed, controlled solely by reason. The name implied the unattainable, a dream world in which communism (in its purest apolitical form) was the cure for the predominating evils in public and private life. Gold was valueless (that was what the chamberpots were made of), and gems (diamonds and rubies) were used by children as toys. (Perhaps that is why Lord Macaulay once said, "An acre in Middlesex is better than a principality in Utopia.")

This beautiful dream was the gem of Sir Thomas More (1478–1535), an English statesman and author whose title for his two-volume book, written in 1516, was a coinage, *Utopia*. The term, a composite of Greek *ou* ("no") and *topos*, ("place"), means nowhere, an apt title because the subject of the book is a nonexistent island.

More, whose head was placed on the chopping block because he refused to take the Oath of Supremacy in favor of King Henry VIII, was supposedly as idealistic in the conduct of his own life as in the life he pictured on the imaginary island of *Utopia*. He was incorruptible. When someone tried to bribe him with a glove stuffed with gold, he returned the money, saying he preferred unlined gloves. On another occasion, when proffered a valuable goblet, his lordship immediately filled it with wine, drank to the briber's health, and then returned the empty vessel.

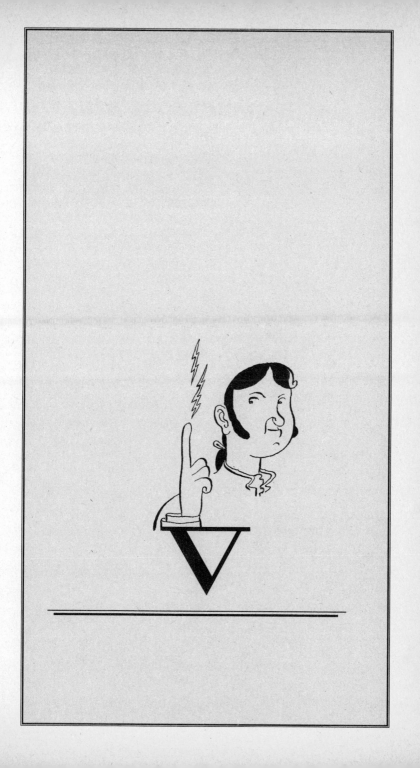

VANDALS, VANDALISM

The original Vandals (their name perhaps meant wanderers) were a savage Teutonic tribe from northeast Germany that flourished in the fifth century. According to historical records, a horde of 80,000, led by their king, Genseric, ravaged Gaul (France), Spain, and North Africa. In 455 A.D. they swooped down upon Rome and thoroughly sacked it, plundering it of its treasures of art and literature.

The word *vandalism* derives from the name of the Germanic tribe of Vandals, and it means a willful and wanton destruction of property. As in the form *vandalisme*, the word was first used by a French churchman at the end of the eighteenth century.

VANDYKE BEARD

Sir Anthony Van Dycke (or Van Dyck) sported a well-trimmed beard all his adult life. Vandyke (1599–1641), as the English spelled it, was a Flemish painter born in Antwerp, the seventh of twelve children of a silk merchant. When a youth, he was a pupil of the renowned Rubens, and at twenty-one left the continent and went to England in 1632, to become a court painter to Charles I. He married a Scot, was knighted by the king and, during his short life, became an important portraitist. Vandyke acquired so many mistresses and led such a life of luxury that he had to work long hours just to meet his expenses, but he never allowed more than an hour at a time to a sitter.

Aristocrats were proud to have their portraits painted by Vandyke because he had painted the portraits of Charles I (including the famous *Charles I on Horseback*) and his queen, Henrietta Maria. The subjects of the paintings were made similarly distinctive because they were painted with white collars with v-shaped points. The men were distinguished by a trimmed, V-shaped beard, the same style worn by the painter. The scalloped border is said to be *vandyked* and the beards, *vandykes*.

Always frail, Vandyke lived for only forty-two years. He died after a brief visit to the Netherlands and France.

VENEREAL

Venus, the Roman goddess of love (identified with the Greek Aphrodite), loaned her name to two words of dissimilar meanings: *venerable*, with its sense of respect because of old age or associated dignity, and *venereal*, pertaining to sexual love. When the word *disease* follows *venereal*, it transforms *venereal* into a fearful word. Its dictionary definition is "arising from sexual intercourse with an infected person."

A very virulent venereal disease is *syphilis*, which comes by its name through a Latin poem titled *Syphilis, sive Morbus Gallicus* ("Syphilis, or the French Disease"), written in 1530 by Girolamo Fracastoro (1483–1553), a Veronese physician and poet who was the first known victim of the disease. The poem's hero, a blasphemous shepherd named *Syphilus*, so enraged the Sun God that he struck him with a new disease as a punishment: "He first wore buboes dreadful to the sight,/First felt pains and sleepless past the night;/From him the malady received its name." Perhaps the poet was thinking of the Greek *suphilos*, which means "a lover of pigs."

The most prevalent form of venereal disease is *gonorrhea* (from the Greek *gonos*, "that which begets," "a seed," plus *rhoia*, "a flowing"). This medical term was coined by an Italian physician in 1530, but it first appeared in print in 1547 in Boorde's *Breviary of Healthe*: "The 166 Chaptaires doth shew of a Gomary passion." *Gomary* was an early name for *gonorrhea*.

Venereal disease made no distinction among the classes. Some of its distinguished sufferers were Herod, Julius Caesar, three popes, Henry VIII, Ivan the Terrible, Keats, Schubert, Goya, and Goethe.

The goddess Aphrodite also loaned her name to matters pertaining to sexual activity. An *aphrodisiac*, a drug or food that arouses or increases sexual desire, honors her.

VERNIER SCALE

In 1631 French mathematician Pierre Vernier (1580–1637) published a mathematical treatise showing that a small, movable auxiliary scale could be attached to a larger, graduated scale to obtain finer adjustments. From that beginning developed the *vernier scale*, a short, graduated scale, or ruler, that slides along a larger scale. The subdivisions on the short rule are nine tenths as long as the subdivisions on the long scale, and the scale can measure both lengths and angles.

Engineers often use calipers with a *vernier attachment*. Some of them read to one thousandth of an inch without a magnifier. The vernier scale which divides each unit of the larger scale into smaller fractions is used with such instruments as the transit, sextant, quadrant, barometer, and compass, as well as the caliper.

To grasp the fineness of the measurements made possible by the vernier, consider this: The beam of a caliper is divided into inches and tenths, and each tenth into fourths. The vernier is divided into twenty-five parts. Sometimes the beam is divided into fiftieths of an inch, and the vernier has twenty divisions to each nineteen divisions on the beam.

VICTORIA, VICTORIAN

Queen Victoria's (1819–1901) reign was the longest of any other king or queen of Great Britain. She ascended the throne in 1837 and remained on it sixty-four years, until her death. Her reign was distinguished by achievements in the arts and sciences, and the continuance of the Industrial Revolution, which added to the great prosperity that England enjoyed. During much of this time, Britain's empire expanded to such an extent that it was rightly said that the sun never set on it.

The premier British award for conspicuous bravery in the presence of the enemy was instituted by Queen Victoria. It is a bronze Maltese cross with the royal crown surmounted by a lion in its center under which is a scroll bearing the words "For Valour." It is called the Victorian Cross.

Queen Victoria gave her name to many landmarks and geographical sites, numerous towns, and a river. Victoria is the capital of both British Columbia and Hong Kong. A low carriage for two with a folding top, low hung so that the queen did not need to walk steps to enter, was named the *Victoria* in her honor. And so on.

When the queen's name is converted to its adjectival form—*Victorian*—its connotation is one of moral rectitude and conservative outlooks, but more aptly stated as prudery and stuffiness. Writers of that period are known as *Victorian* authors, although many of them don't fit that description, such as Oscar Wilde. A certain type of furniture, formal in style, popular during her reign, has been aptly named *Victorian*.

VOLCANO, VULCANIZATION

The English language is indebted to *Vulcan*, the Roman god of fire, for some important words. One is *vulcanization*, the name of a process invented by Charles Goodyear to make rubber stronger, more elastic, resistant to solvents, and unaffected by normal heat and cold. So important is this invention that almost all rubber today is *vulcanized*. Another is *volcano*, a vent in the earth's crust through which lava, steam, and ashes are thrown up.

Vulcanus, or *Vulcan* as he is known in English, lived a most unusual life. He was thrown into the sea by his mother because he was born lame. According to another version, Vulcan sided with Juno, his mother, against Jupiter, his father. Jupiter thereupon hurled him from heaven. He was nine days in falling and was saved by the people of Lemnos from crashing to earth, but one leg was broken, hence his lameness.

Vulcan, as the god of fire, became the armorer of the gods. His workshops were under Mount Etna in Sicily and in the bowels of volcanoes; the Cyclops assisted him in forging thunderbolts for Jupiter.

Vulcan was consumed by amatory desires, not only his own but also his wife's. He was married to Venus, the goddess of love and beauty. One day Vulcan learned that she was disporting herself with Mars. He schemed to embarrass them by constructing an invisible net that descended around their bed during their lovemaking. While they were still embracing, Vulcan summoned the other gods to look and laugh at the guilty pair.

A *vulcanist* subscribes to the theory that fire has changed the earth's surface. At one time the earth was in a state of igneous fusion, and its crust has gradually cooled down to its present temperature.

The planet *Vulcan*, a creation of writers of *Star Trek*, was the former home of its most distinguished character, the unflappable Mr. Spock.

VOLT, VOLTAIC PILE

Alessandro Guisseppe Antonio Anastasio Volta (1745–1827), after whom the words *volt* and *voltage* were named, was born in Como, Italy, one of nine children of a Jesuit priest who had left the order to marry.

By the time Alessandro was sixteen, he had mastered many languages and then went on to invent several electrostatic devices. He was invited, in 1778, to become a professor of physics at the University of Pavia.

Volta became internationally famous because of his controversy with Luigi Galvani over the source of electricity. After repeating Galvani's experiment, Volta disagreed with Galvani's theory and became a rallying point for those opposed to it. His prominence was such that he was elected to England's Royal Society and was the first foreigner to receive the Royal Society's Copley Medal.

Volta invented or improved a number of electrical devices, such as the electrophorus, which transfers electric charges to other objects. He discovered the electric decomposition of water and developed a theory of current electricity in physics. His inventions include the electrical condenser and the *voltaic pile*, which became the prototype of the dry-cell battery.

Volta received many honors during his long life. Statues were made of him, and kings and the heads of state requested his presence. The prestigious National Institute of France invited him to lecture there, at which time he was additionally honored by the presence of Napoleon, who bestowed on Volta the title of count. Legend has it that when Napoleon was leaving the hall, he noticed a sign reading "Au Grand Voltaire" and proceeded to cross out the last three letters.

WASSERMANN TEST

August von Wassermann (1866–1925), born in Romberg, Bavaria, received his medical degree and then joined the research community of the Robert Koch Institute of Infectious Diseases in Berlin. In 1913, he joined the staff of Kaiser Wilhelm Institute at Dahlen, near Berlin, as its director. He wrote many scientific papers and conducted research on many diseases. But his outstanding work, together with Albert Neisser and Carl Bruck—certainly the one that made him famous—was a blood test for the diagnosis of syphilis, known professionally as the *cardiolipin test*. This test is made by examining the blood of the patient. If the patient has syphilis, the sample submitted for the test will prove positive. Even though present-day methods of diagnosing syphilis have supplanted the method introduced by the *Wassermann test*, the test for syphilis still honors the name of the great physician.

WATT, KILOWATT

Although the company supplying electricity to a house charges by the *kilowatt* hour, and electric bulbs have a W on them to indicate power output, the greatest contribution of James Watt was not in the field of electricity but rather in the improvement of the engine that has given the world the practical power of steam.

Watt (1736–1819) was born in Greenock, Scotland. In grammar school he learned Latin, Greek, and mathematics. Watt had a natural curiosity for things mechanical. Repairing any kind of machinery gave him pleasure, and he became a maker of mathematical instruments such as quadrants, scales, and compasses. Through a stroke of good fortune, in 1757 he was named mathematical instrument maker to the College of Glasgow, a prestigious title for a man who had barely reached twenty years of age.

The decisive event that set the course of Watt's life came when he was asked to repair a model of Newcomen's steam engine the best-known engine at that time for pumping water from coal mines. This engine used an enormous amount of steam and therefore large amounts of fuel. Watt separated the condenser and the cylinder, keeping the cylinder hot at all times and saving three fourths of the fuel. By reducing the cost of operating this engine, Watt made it practical for other uses.

The story that made the rounds is that Watt got his idea while watching a kettle boiling on the fire at his home. His aunt rebuked him for fiddling with the kettle—holding a spoon over the spout, releasing it, and then holding it again. She suggested that he spend his time doing something more useful.

After Watt left the college, he became a partner with an engineer from Birmingham, Matthew Boulton. The company was successful, enabling Watt to devote time to other inventions—a throttle value, a governor to regulate the speed of steam engines, a smoke-consuming furnace, a machine to reproduce sculpture, and a copying press, among other devices. Watt and Boulton coined the word *horsepower*.

In 1885, the International Electrical Congress honored Watt by naming the *watt* as a unit of electrical power—736 watts being equal to about one horsepower. The honor was not bestowed for his contribution to the modern science of electricity but for his contributions to applied science. He was considered the greatest single impetus behind the Industrial Revolution.

WEDGWOOD

Josiah Wedgwood was the source of many eponymous words, but foremost is "Wedgwood blue." Much of his pottery was graced with classical figures in white cameo relief on an unglazed background. Born in Burslem, Staffordshire, England, Wedgwood (1730–1795) was poor and uneducated. His family had a small pottery shop, but pottery was not much in demand. Most pottery was imported from Delft, in Holland, and the higher-quality pottery came directly from China. Wedgwood's experiments led to a particularly refined green glaze. In 1759, he set up a factory at Ivy House in Burslem that was so successful that he soon needed larger quarters.

In 1769, Wedgwood, together with Thomas Bentley, built a factory called Etruria, where his experiments with ceramic glazes made him famous. Many of his designs on newly patented pottery were executed by a young sculptor named John Flaxman, who ultimately became the first professor of sculpture at the Royal Academy of Art. Wedgwood's china became identified with the fine cream-colored porcelainlike household ware with which Wedgwood built his reputation. He invented *jasperware* and *Queen's ware*, a household pottery named after Queen Charlotte. He also made advances in black basalt stoneware. The queen became enamored of his white stoneware, and her patronage attracted the attention of the rich, the famous, and the royal. Wedgwood's fortune was assured.

Wedgwood's children also did well. His son is credited with having discovered the basic principles of photography, long before the daguerreotype was even dreamed of. His daughter, Susannah, was the mother of Charles Darwin.

It may be apocryphal, but some word historians insist that John Keats was confused about the identity of the urn he described in his *Ode to a Grecian Urn*. This urn was nonexistent. According to the story, Keats had seen a Wedgwood imitation of a Greek vase. Thus inspired, he wrote:

> Thou still unravished bride of quietness,
> Thou foster-child of Silence and slow Time . . .
> Beauty is truth, truth beauty,—that is all
> Ye know on earth and all ye need to know.

WELLINGTON, WELLINGTON BOOTS,

Arthur Wellesly (1769–1852) was the first Duke of Wellington and one of Britain's most renowned generals. The duke's military experience is a tale of a successful strategist, from India to Waterloo, culminating in the crushing of Napoleon in 1815. After his military conquests, the duke became prime minister and was given the honorarium of commander-in-chief of the British forces for life.

Wellington, known as the Iron Duke, was honored in many ways. His name was given to a tree of the Sequoia family (the *Wellingtonia*), to the capital of New Zealand, and to a term in the card game NAP (a game devised in honor of Napoleon, in which a call of *Wellington* so that the caller is obliged to take all five tricks and wins or loses double).

His name was bestowed even on articles of clothing, such as the high boots worn by men of fashion, boots that had been required wear in the army. Although the boots came up above the knee, they were held down by a strap under the instep and were covered by the trousers. The boot was an elegant version of the military boot, with the top cut out at the back of the knee to allow freedom of action. "No gentleman," it was commonly said, "could wear anything but *Wellington boots* in the daytime." And then there were *half-Wellingtons*, which look somewhat like a pair of galoshes, also worn under the trousers. These boots, which came halfway up the calf of the leg, were made of patent leather and had a top of softer material.

A well-known story during that time was that Queen Victoria asked the duke for the name of the boots he was wearing. "The people call them Wellingtons," he replied, to which she remarked, "Impossible. I should like to know where you could find *two* Wellingtons."

WILDE, WILDEAN, OSCARIZING

Oscar Fingal O'Flahertie Wills Wilde (1854–1900) was an Irish poet, playwright, and intriguing personality. Wilde had such a sharp tongue that many believed he out-Shawed Shaw.

Wilde's life, however, was colored by his libel suit and imprisonment because of his altercation with the Marquis of Queensberry. Wilde was known for his homosexuality. In British slang, Wilde's first name, *Oscar*, came to mean a homosexual, and *Oscarizing* and *Oscar-Wilding* meant active homosexuality.

Wilde's lover was the son of the Marquis of Queensberry. When the Marquis accused Wilde of sodomy, Wilde brought a libel suit against him. The government then instituted criminal charges against Wilde based on "immoral conduct"; Wilde lost both suits. For the criminal act, Wilde was sentenced to prison, where he wrote *De Profundis* and *The Ballad of Reading Gaol*, works well appreciated by Wilde's army of aficionados.

Wilde's tongue was razor-edged. When a minor poet complained to Wilde that his poetry was receiving no reviews, that there was a "conspiracy of silence against him," and that he didn't know what to do, Wilde replied, "Join it." To a chamber of commerce he remarked, "Niagara Falls would be more spectacular if it flowed the other way."

James Whistler, the famous painter whose *Mother* is a classic, engaged in a lively exchange with Wilde, who mentioned a certain clever remark and said, "I wish I had said it." Whistler, not to be outdone, replied, "You will, Oscar, you will." But Wilde's incisive wit would not rest, for which we now have the word *Wildean*. "As for borrowing Mr. Whistler's ideas," he wrote, "the only thoroughly original ideas I have ever heard him express have had reference to his own superiority as a painter over painters greater than himself."

WINCHESTER RIFLE

The *Winchester rifle* was as much a part of the Wild West as the Colt, a pistol. The 73 *Winchester*, made in 1873, was the prototype of the Winchester rifles that followed, a gun used extensively in hunting.

Oliver Fisher Winchester (1810–1880) was an American industrialist for whom the gun he manufactured was named. He organized the Winchester Repeating Arms Company and improved on the Henry and Spencer repeating rifles of the Civil War. Winchester produced a breechloading repeating rifle at his plant in New Haven, Connecticut, an amalgam of patents acquired from different inventors, and his name became a generic term for a repeating rifle.

The *Winchester* was the scourge of the frontier, and one story about the Fetterman massacre in 1866 says that two civilians armed with Winchesters killed as many Indians as the eighty soldiers without them. Winchester employed B. T. Henry, the inventor of the Henry repeating rifle, and later acquired the patent for the Hotchkiss bolt-action-repeating rifle. The company went on to manufacture many kinds of guns, but all were called *Winchesters*.

Winchester was a philanthropic man whose generosity was so appreciated by the people of Connecticut that they elected him lieutenant governor.

WISTERIA, WISTARIA

The *wisteria* is a climbing woody vine clustered with drooping, pealike, purplish or white flowers. The name of this vine was given by Thomas Nuttal, curator of Harvard's Botanical Garden, who made an error in spelling the name of the man he planned to honor. That man's name was *Wistar*. But at the death of the honoree in 1818, the plant was named *wisteria*. Nuttal wrote in his *Genera North American Plants II*, "In memory of Casper Wistar, M.D., late professor of Anatomy in the University of Pennsylvania." But too late. Nuttal had already named the plant *wisteria*. Later writers followed the error, thus perpetuating it. Purists tried to rectify the mistake, but to no avail.

Dr. Casper Wistar (1761–1818), a Quaker and the son of a prominent colonial glassblower in Philadelphia, studied medicine in Edinburgh then returned home to teach at the College and Academy of Philadelphia, which was merged into the University of Pennsylvania. He wrote America's first anatomy book, and taught anatomy, midwifery, and surgery. His anatomical collection became the origin of the world-famous *Wistar Institute of Anatomy and Biology*, located in the heart of the university. He also became the president of the American Philosophical Society, succeeding Thomas Jefferson. His Sunday afternoon at-home gatherings attracted many of his friends who came to hear Wistar discourse on topics of interest.

Wistar's great-nephew, Isaac Jones Wistar (1827–1905), wealthy entrepreneur, endowed the *Wistar Institute*.

Joshua Logan (1908–1988), a prominent producer-director-playwright, named a play of his *The Wistaria Trees* (1950) in a fruitless effort to have the public recognize the correct spelling of the honoree's name. *Wisteria* is ingrained, however, in the spelling psyche of Americans and dictionaries perpetuate the misspelling.

YANKEE

Who a *yankee* is has been answered differently throughout the years by different people. To most people of the world, a Yankee is an American. To most Americans, he is a descendant of old New England stock. But to Southerners, a Yankee is a Northerner—someone from north of the Mason-Dixon line. But during a period of national crisis, such as World War I, Americans are all Yankees.

The origin of the term *yankee* has been a matter of dispute among etymologists since the days of the Founding Fathers. Although no provable conclusion is available, some notions sound authoritative.

Yankee appears to have started life as a disparaging nickname for a Dutchman, and it is thought that it may represent *Janke*, a diminutive form of "John," perhaps used originally of the Dutch of New Amsterdam. The idea that enjoyed the largest following was that "Yankee" came from the epithet *Jan Kees*—a dialectal variant of *John Kaas*, which literally meant "John Cheese," an ethnic insult for a Hollander. *Jan* pronounced *Yahn* was "John," and *cheese* was the national product of Holland.

Another notion espoused by some word historians is that the Dutch living in New York applied the terms to the English—who had moved into Connecticut—viewing them as country bumpkins, and mockingly calling them *Yankees*. But the English during the Revolutionary War extended the meaning further. They attached what was construed as a belittling tag to all residents in the northern territory; *Yankees* became the British nickname for the colonists.

According to James Fenimore Cooper, Indians sounded the word *English* as *Yengees*: whence *Yankee*. In 1841 he appended a note in *The Deerslayer*: "It is singular there should be any question concerning the origin of the well-known sobriquet of 'Yankee.' Nearly all the old writers who speak of the Indians first known to the colonists make them pronounce '*English*' as 'Yengees.'" But this corrupted pronunciation has not been otherwise substantiated. Other ideas abound—for example, that the word was derived from the Scottish *yankie*, "a gigantic falsehood," or from the Dutch *vrijbuiten*, meaning "freebooter" or "plunderer."

The War between the States gave the word *Yankee* a derisive twist. The Confederate soldiers didn't call the federal troops Northerners or Unionists but *Yankees*, and, to underscore the lowest meaning of this term, they prefixed it with "damn." The federal soldiers were not just *Yankees*; they were "damn Yankees."

During World War II *Yankees* became known as *Yanks* in Europe. Today both terms persist.

YARBOROUGH

Charles Anderson Worsley (1809–1897), second Earl of Yarborough, was a knowledgeable card player and was quite successful at the game, especially at bridge. He would wager a bet with his card-playing companions of 1,000 to 1 against receiving a hand in which no card was higher than nine. He did very well with the wagers because the actual mathematical odds are 1,827 to 1 against, giving him a healthy percentage in his favor. In 1900, according to the *Oxford English Dictionary*, the word *yarborough* was admitted into respectable dictionaries.

The opposite of a yarborough is a hand in which all the cards are pictures. This hand is called a *fairbanks*, the name coming from the prominent actor Douglas Fairbanks Jr., whose greatest pleasure was to associate with members of the royalty, even if they were only faces on playing cards.

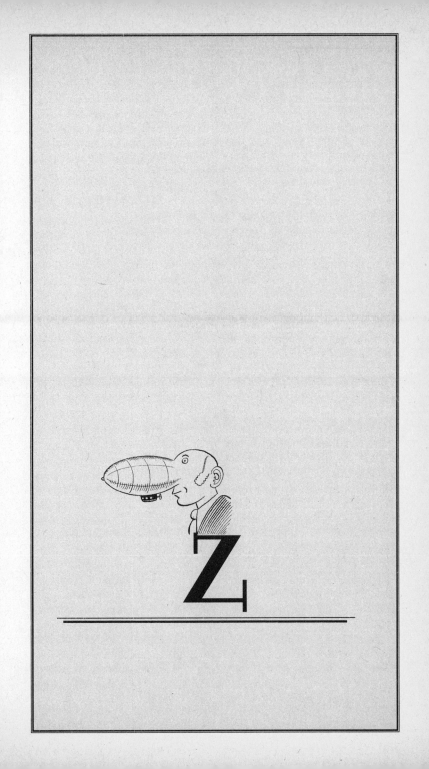

ZEAL, ZEALOT

If *zeal* is defined as earnest enthusiasm, especially for a cause, why is a *zealot* considered a fanatic? Because the original *Zealots* were dedicated to protecting a piece of ground, even at the expense of their lives.

The *Zealots*, first-century fundamentalists, were a Jewish sect founded by Judas of Gamala, who fiercely fought for God's law against the Romans, who opposed it. After the Romans razed Jerusalem—despite the fanatic defense of the Zealots in A.D. 70—a thousand of them bravely held out on the great rock on the edge of the Judean desert. It was the site of Herod the Great's palace, now known as *Masada*.

When the heroic stand by the Zealots appeared doomed, and only 960 Zealots remained to face the 6,000-man Tenth Roman Legion, their leader, Eleazar ben Ya'ir, persuaded them to draw lots to select ten men to kill the remaining defenders. Each of these ten finally slew nine fellows and then punched his sword through his own body. The Zealots preferred to die as free men than to live as slaves.

ZEPPELIN

The zeppelin, long and cylindrical, was a majestic sight in the air, but a catastrophic sight when it fell and burned with a great loss of life.

The zeppelin's creator was Count Ferdinand von Zeppelin (1838–1917), a German army officer who visited the United States during the Civil War to see the balloon operation of the Union forces. He carried a letter of introduction to Abraham Lincoln in his right pocket and a letter to Robert E. Lee in his left pocket, just in case he should be caught by the Confederates. Some say that he served a stint in the Union Army.

Zeppelin made balloon ascents in St. Paul, Minnesota, inspiring him to devote himself to balloons that could be steered and driven by power. In 1900, after thirty years of experimentation, he was able to fly a *zeppelin* (now so called) for twenty minutes. He thereupon founded the Zeppelin Company, which produced during its lifetime about a hundred aircraft. His goal was to convince the German government of the practicality of these balloon-type airplanes during wartime. His persuasive powers and his demonstration of zepplins were effective; the German government agreed that these airships had military value. During World War I, Zeppelin built many zeppelins, some used to bomb Paris and London. But these dirigibles, as they came to be called, were slow-moving and poorly maneuverable. They were not an important factor in the German military.

In 1891, Zeppelin retired from the German army with the rank of general. Thereafter, he devoted himself to his primary interest—the making of dirigible airships of rigid construction. Zeppelin died in 1917, twenty years before his zeppelin the *Hindenburg* went up in flames on

May 6, 1937, at the Naval Air Station, at Lakehurst, New Jersey, killing 36 of the 97 persons aboard. It was a grave moment for the zeppelin, which shortly thereafter became obsolete.

ZINNIA

The *zinnia* is named for Johann Gottfried Zinn (1727–1759), a German botanist and physician who was a professor of medicine at Göttingen University. Zinn accomplished much during his short life, including completion of an influential text on the anatomy of the eye, published in 1753.

Zinn's name was immortalized by the Swedish botanist Carolus Linnaeus, who named the *zinnia* genus after him. Zinn's life was reminiscent of the life of the *Zinnia* species *elegans*, which grows profusely and blooms but quickly succumbs to the first frost. Dr. Zinn died at age thirty-two, but his brief career had been productive as a botanist and a physician.

There are fifteen species of *zinnias*. The tall forms, with showy, variously colored flowers called *zinnia elegans*, native to Mexico and the Southwest, are particularly widely cultivated.

Bibliography

Books, pamphlets, magazines, newspaper articles, and other writings that fail to come to mind immediately, are all sources for eponymous coinages. But the primary sources of materials for this book, and perhaps any book on the subject of eponyms, are basically the encylopedias, with their complete reports on almost any subject. Foremost, however, is the incomparable *Oxford English Dictionary*, the research's bible. Beyond that, a good and reliable avenue for my research was any dictionary devoted to a particular field, whether it be slang, music, science, mythology, sports, the classics, or what have you.

Authors of books on eponyms are primarily compilers of information gleaned from all the foregoing sources. Styles of writing differ, naturally, and the selection of entries too are personal. What one might select, another might not. There is, of course, an almost unlimited possibility for eponymous words. Some books avoid eponyms from the Bible, some from mythology, some from fictional characters, whereas others make no such distinctions. Here again, it's a matter of personal taste.

The following books will provide a wealth of material from which can be combed whatever might be of interest to an investigator of eponymic words.

American Heritage Dictionary of the English Language. New York: American Heritage Publishing Co., 1969.

Asimov, Isaac. *Biographical Technology*. New York: Doubleday & Company, 1964.

Beeching, Cyril Leslie. *A Dictionary of Eponyms*. New York: Oxford University Press, 1983.

Boycott, Rosie. *Batty, Bloomers and Boycott*. New York: Peter Bedrick Books, 1983.

Brewer, E. Cobham. *Dictionary of Phrase and Fable*. New York: Harper & Row, 1964.

Ciardi, John. *A Browser's Dictionary*. New York: Harper & Row, 1980.

Douglas, Auriel. *Dictionary of Eponyms*. New York: Simon & Schuster, Inc., 1990.

Espy, Willard R. *Thou Improper, Thou Uncommon Noun*. New York: Clarkson Potter, 1978.

Evans, Bergen. *Comfortable Words*. New York: Random House, 1962.

Funk, Charles Earle. *A Hog on Ice*. New York: Harper & Row, 1948.

Funk, Wilfred. *Word Origins and Their Romantic Stories*. New York: Funk and Wagnalls, Inc., 1950.

Grant, Michael and John Hazel, *Who's Who Classical Mythology*. New York: Oxford University Press, 1993.

Hayakawa, S. I. *Language in Thought*. New York: Harcourt Brace Jovanich, 1949.

Hendrickson, Robert. *The Dictionary of Eponyms*. New York: Stein and Day, 1985

Holt, Alfred H. *Phrase and Word Origins*. New York: Dover Publications, 1961.

Hunt, Cecil. *Word Origins*. New York: Philosophical Library, 1949.

Mathews, Mitford, ed. *A Dictionary of Americanism on Historical Principles*. Chicago: University of Chicago Press, 1951.

Mencken H. L. *The American Language*. New York: Alfred A. Knopf, 1948.

Morris, William and Mary. *A Dictionary of Word Origins and Pharses*. New York: Harper & Row, 1947

Oxford English Dictionary. James A. H. Murray, ed. London: Clarendon Press, 1884.

Partridge, Eric. *Dictionary of Slang and Unconventional English*. New York: The Macmillan Company, 1961.

Pei, Mario. *All About Language*. Philadelphia: J. B. Lippincott Co., 1954.

Perl, Lila. *Blue Monday and Friday the Thirteenth*. New York: Clarion Books, 1986.

Pizer, Vernon. *Take My Word for It*. New York: Dodd, Mead & Company, 1981.

Shipley, Joseph T. A *Dictionary of Word Origins*. New York: Littlefield, Adams & Company, 1967.

Terban, Marvin. *Guppies in Tuxedos*. New York: Clarion Books, 1988.

Tuleja, Tad. *Namesakes*. New York: McGraw-Hill Book Company, 1987.

Weekley, Ernest. *The Romance of Words*. New York: Dover Publications, 1961.

Word Mysteries and Histories, The Editors of the American Heritage Dictionaries. Boston: Houghton Mifflin Company, 1986.